I0793419

IMAGES
of America

WILTON

ON THE COVER: STROUTIES, 1953. This was an open-kitchen luncheonette where the diners could see their food being prepared. Their jingle from a 1953 advertisement went, "Where you see it when it's cooked and that's the reason why the folks that lunch at Stroutie's all say 'They Satisfy.' " (Photograph by Harold Karkos.)

IMAGES
of America

WILTON

Tamara N. Hoke

ARCADIA
PUBLISHING

ISBN 978-1-4671-2244-3

Published by Arcadia Publishing
Charleston, South Carolina

Printed in the United States of America

Library of Congress Control Number: 2014935283

For all general information, please contact Arcadia Publishing:
Telephone 843-853-2070
Fax 843-853-0044
E-mail sales@arcadiapublishing.com
For customer service and orders:
Toll-Free 1-888-313-2665

Visit us on the Internet at www.arcadiapublishing.com

To Ruth Davis Sonier, my grandmother, in whose memory I dedicate this book

Contents

Acknowledgments

The author would like to acknowledge the Wilton Historical Society, particularly Pam Brown and Al Kaplan, for their support throughout this project. Both spent countless hours at the historical society while I scanned around 300 photographs during the first months of 2014. The heating sources in the historical society struggled to warm the building during a colder-than-average winter. They were kind enough to turn on the heat and even provide a space heater to make the task of scanning more enjoyable. This task required at least two hours of scanning every couple of weeks for about three months. I appreciate their patience during the hours that I spent at the historical society, as well as the numerous times that I had to reschedule either to accommodate my work schedule or the reading and homework load of the graduate course I was taking. They were beyond accommodating, and I will be forever thankful for that.

My endless gratitude goes to the members of the historical society, who have supported my efforts in the creation of this book. Unless otherwise noted, all images are courtesy of the Wilton Historical Society and are from its extensive collection.

I want to thank Joyce Orff for loaning a couple of photographs from her personal collection. They were instrumental in rounding out the story provided in both the farming and industry chapters.

Lastly, I am forever in debt to the work of others who have striven over the years to tell the story of Wilton and who provided invaluable source material. I relied on numerous sources for background information. A full list is included in the bibliography at the end of this book.

INTRODUCTION

In 1785, Tyng's Township (or Tyngstown) was created. One of the first settlers to the area, which would later be known as Wilton, was Samuel Butterfield, in 1796. The town was fully incorporated in 1803. Abraham Butterfield offered to pay all costs associated with incorporation if he could name the town after his native town of Wilton, New Hampshire.

From approximately 1800 to 1820, many necessities such as molasses, rum, grindstones, tea, hardware, and saws were brought from Hallowell by ox team. This trip typically took six days or more. Many other necessities families were able make themselves, such as clothing, shoes, and furniture.

Manufacturing has almost always been a part of the town. This was so even before Wilton was fully incorporated. Industrial success was possible in part because of Wilson Stream, which provided abundant waterpower to factories until electricity superseded it as a power source. Many of the early factories were established along the banks of Wilson Stream for this purpose.

Samuel Butterfield started the first sawmill and gristmill in 1789 in East Wilton. He also built the first dam on Wilson Stream. In 1820, Elisha Bass established a factory to manufacture silk and fur hats. Following that, in 1826, Hildreth Robbins built a mill for hulling and cleaning sweet clover seed. Dimon Furnel built a yarn mill in the 1830s, and, in the 1850s, the Bass family built a starch factory.

When the railroad came to Wilton in 1859, the town was then able to access items coming from a distance. Inhabitants no longer had to be entirely self-sufficient.

It must be noted that Wilton continued to remain a primarily agricultural town from 1860 to 1900. In 1861, a group of 138 men from the Wilton area responded to the call of duty to serve in the Union army during the Civil War. After the war, Dimon Furnel built a textile mill on the site of the yarn mill he had built years before. In 1880, this property was sold to the Walker family, and they, too, had a mill there. Later, in 1891, Flavius J. Goodspeed purchased the mill.

In 1879, G.H. Bass started his first shoe shop. Most of the work had to be done by hand. The first Bass Shoes were made in this year. The first records show eight people on the payroll. In 1887, Bass moved to another location. Here, machinery that could be run by waterpower was installed. Eventually, even bigger quarters were needed, so Bass purchased an old sawmill site near the lake and constructed what was later known as Building No. 1 in the early 1900s.

Some other industries of note early on include a shoe peg factory owned by a Mr. Sturtevant in the 1870s. C.G. Sawyer would also start a canning business in Wilton around this time, and he would later purchase the peg mill and establish a small grocery store there.

In 1875, John Legroo and a Mr. Goding owned a sawmill on Depot Street in Dryden, a village within Wilton. It was later co-owned with Rawson Fuller. They supplied wood to railroad cars for the Farmington-to-Livermore Falls train, which went through Wilton.

Another date of import was 1903, when Frank G. and George F. Goodspeed, owners of Wilton's first complete textile mill, formed a corporation with their father known as the Wilton Woolen Company.

In 1906, the first Bass Moccasin appeared. Preceding the moccasin were the leg boot and plow shoe for farmers and the famous river driver's boot and guide shoe.

The 1900s brought a great deal of growth to the town of Wilton. In 1901, the Wilton Academy was accredited; in 1902, a library was started; in 1912, a girls' camp, Camp Kineowatha, was started; and, in the 1920s, the town acquired a fire department. The 1930s was the decade in which the town acquired a community building and a golf course. The 1940s and 1950s saw continued growth in the town, as readers will see in the chapters on business and industry. Several businesses and industries ended up thriving in this small town, and many people had great accomplishments. This book strives to cover the major highlights; however, this author knows that it would be impossible to cover everything in the pages that follow.

Lastly, I would like to add a quick note on the use of source material. I have made every effort to be as accurate as possible. Where different sources contradicted one another, I tried to find a third source to compare to for accuracy. However, I am aware that any town history is dependent on work done previously. Occasionally, photographs are mislabeled or information believed to be true at the time has been superseded. I made every effort to see that this did not happen; however, I acknowledge that local history is dependent upon the stories of others and is only as accurate as the sources used.

One

Business

Wilton, from very early on, was made up of enterprising individuals. Business particularly flourished from the late 19th century until the mid-20th century. Both smaller and larger enterprises met much success. There was a large variety of businesses, including hotels, hardware stores, grocery stores, general stores, drugstores, livery stables, automobile garages, music stores, blacksmith shops, jewelry stores, gift shops, barbershops, department stores, lumber mills, canning factories, cleaners, and more. Some of the businesses of note were the Wilton House and Miller's Hotel (later known as Hotel Wilton), the H.R Dascomb Co. Store, B.F. Stanley's Store at Wilton Station, Larrabee Dry Goods, W.S. Wells & Sons, and innumerable others.

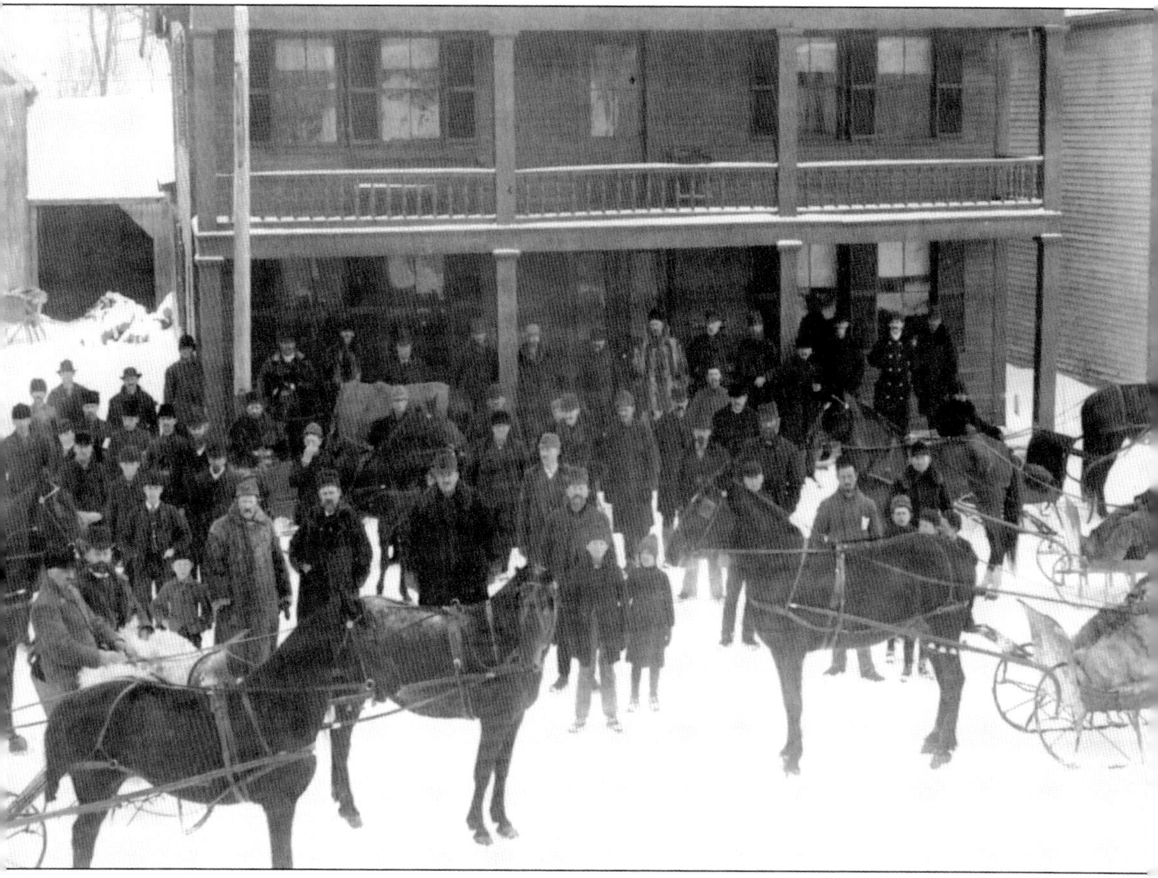

WILTON HOUSE, 1888. Also known as the Pro Bono Publico, the Wilton House was owned and operated by Norman H. and Mary W. Green from 1885 to 1888. According to one source, this is a photograph of a group of men and boys who have been racing their sleighs. Racing was done up and down Main Street and on Wilson Lake at this time.

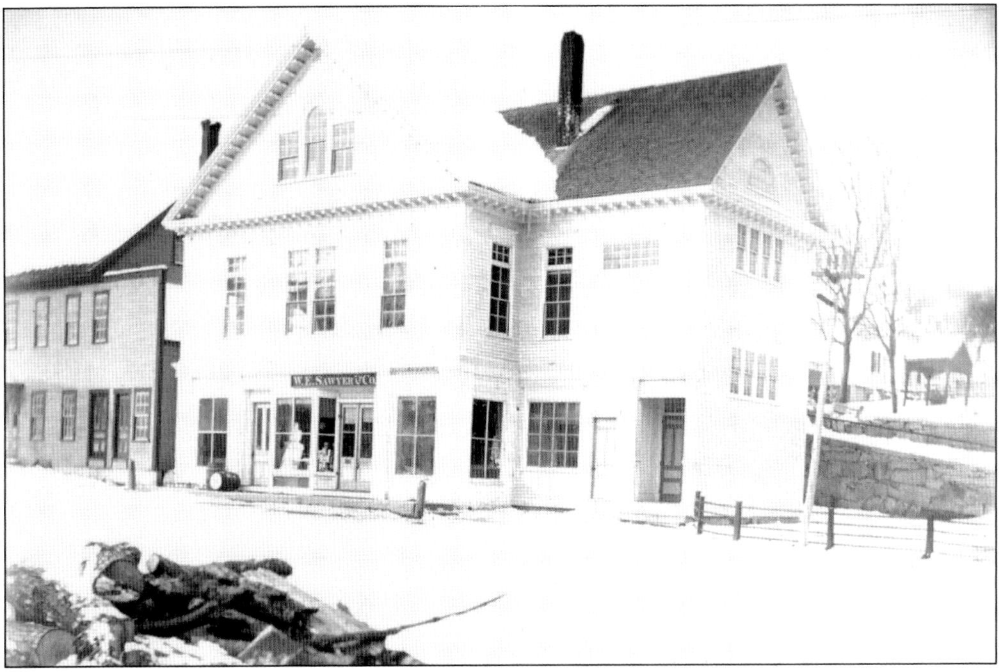

W.E. Sawyer & Co. and Post Office, 1903. The W.E. Sawyer & Co. Store had groceries, crockery, and dry goods. The business was started by C.G. Sawyer. He began a canning business in Wilton, canning corn on a small scale. Later, his business expanded, and he started a grocery store. Some years later, he built a new grocery store, seen here. It stayed in the family for three generations.

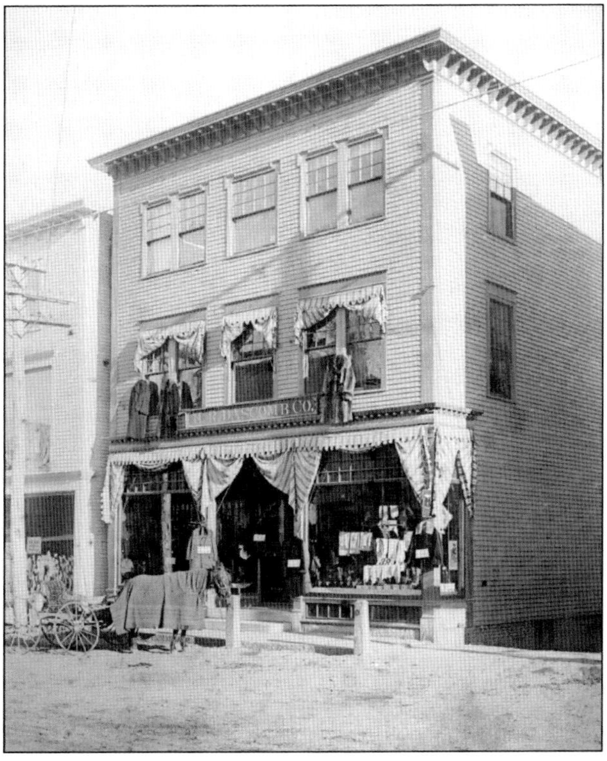

H.R. Dascomb Co. Store, Early 1900s. H.R. Dascomb was a successor to R.B. Fuller & Co., dealer in drugs and medicines. This store, on Main Street, offered a great deal more. H.R. Dascomb served as a drug and dry goods store. It also had a tailoring department on the second floor. Additionally, it served as an apothecary and had paints and oils, art supplies, books, clothing, boots and shoes, furnishing goods, hats, stationery, and paper hangings.

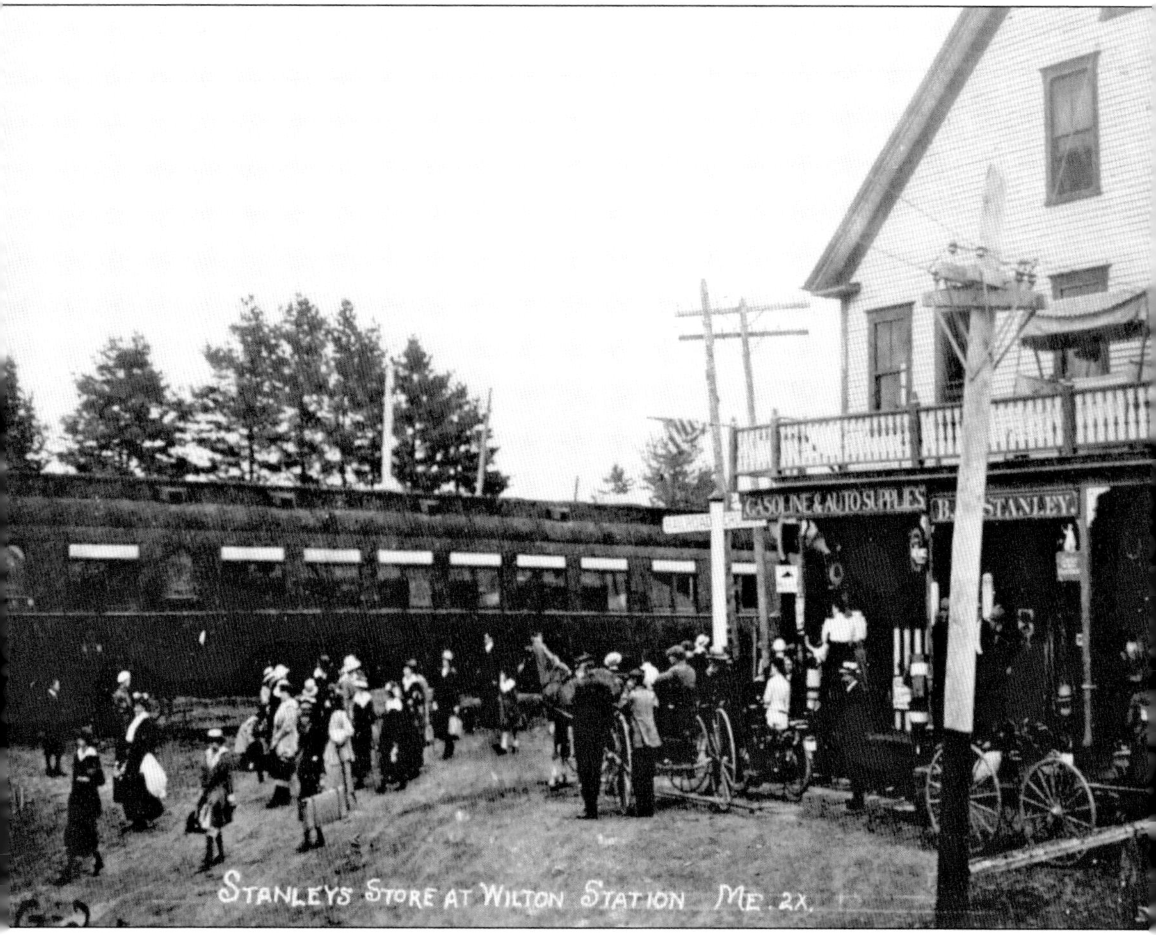

B.F. Stanley Store, c. 1910. This is the B.F. Stanley Store, at Wilton Station in Dryden. This must have been a bustling place due to its proximity to the railroad crossing. This store sold gasoline and auto supplies and was also a general store and post office. B.F Stanley served as proprietor of the store and postmaster.

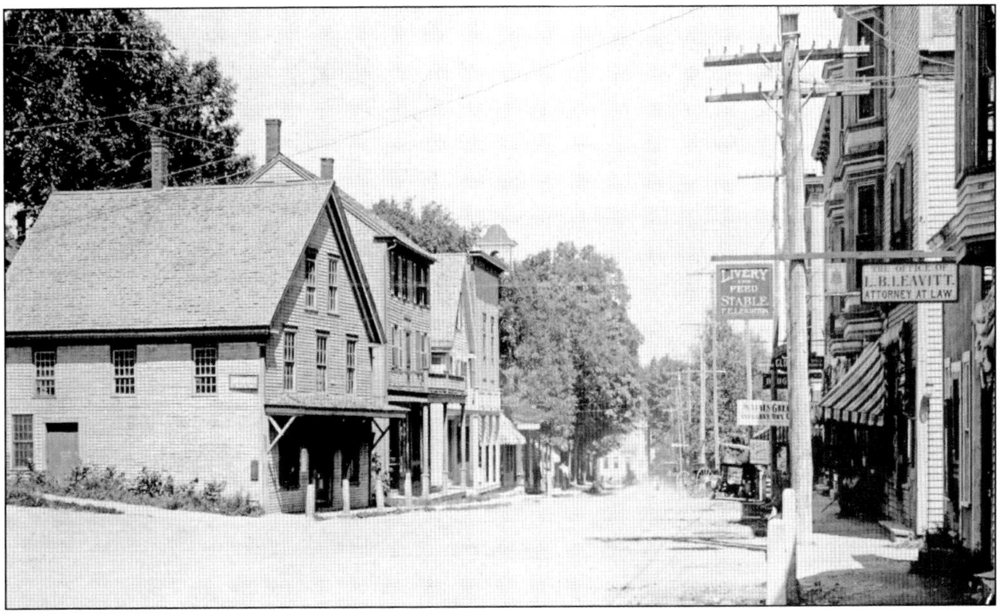

Main Street Wilton Businesses, Early 1900s. This is how Main Street looked in the early 1900s. There were posts to tie up horses while attending to business or shopping. In the foreground, there are signs for L.B. Leavitt, Attorney-at-Law, and F.E. Leighton Livery & Feed Stables. Livery and feed stables were a big business in the time before automobiles. There is also a sign for Maine's Great Larrabee Dry Goods. George W. Larrabee owned the store, which sold groceries, dry and fancy goods, hardware, and sewing machines.

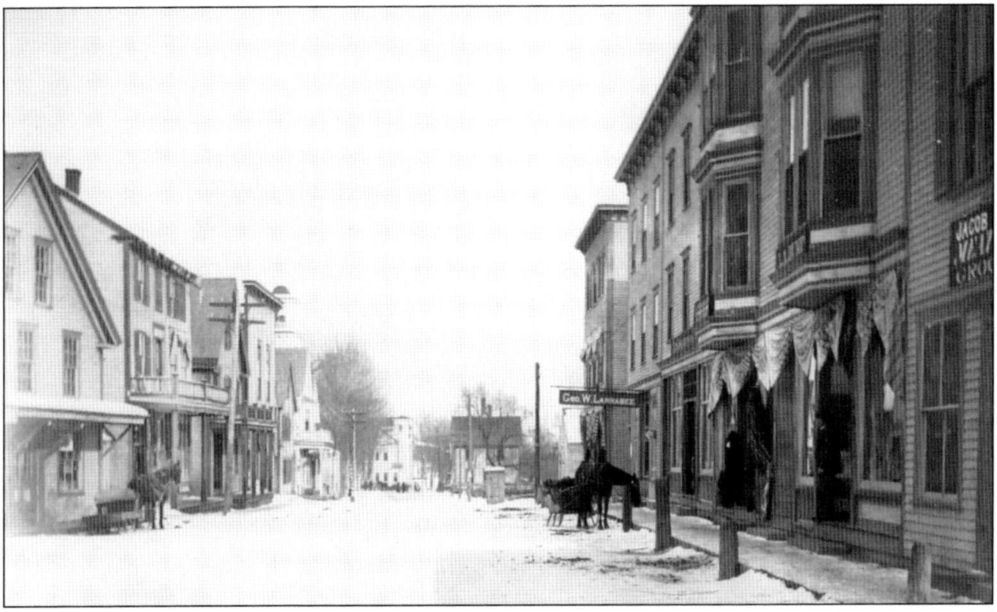

Main Street Businesses, c. 1910. This is another photograph of business in the early part of the 20th century on Main Street. This winter scene shows horses and sleighs tied up to hitching posts. Jacob B. Holmes, Meat and Grocery, can be seen in the foreground. A sign for L.A. Bump's store can also be seen. Bump was a merchant who sold books, shoes, hats, caps, and the like. A different George W. Larrabee sign from the previous photograph is seen here.

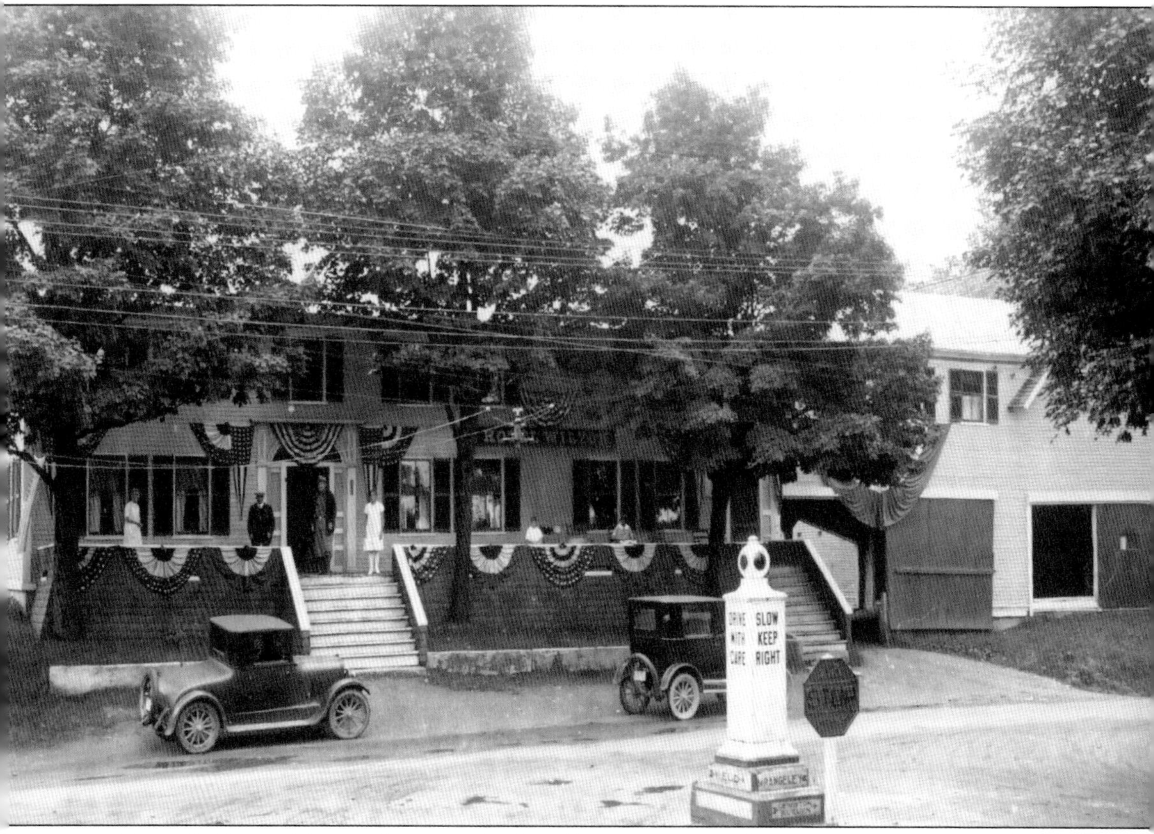

MILLER'S HOTEL/HOTEL WILTON, 1920S. This hotel existed as a tavern as early as the 1840s. Before becoming Hotel Wilton, it was called Miller's Hotel and was owned by Gilbert and Nellie Miller. Miller's Hotel played host to traveling companies of musicians and actors. There was a huge dance hall on the second floor, likely between 1876 and 1899. Gilbert Miller also ran a livery stable here. Later, the Blaisdell family owned and ran the hotel. At the time of this photograph, it was owned and operated by the Blaisdells and the name had been changed to Hotel Wilton.

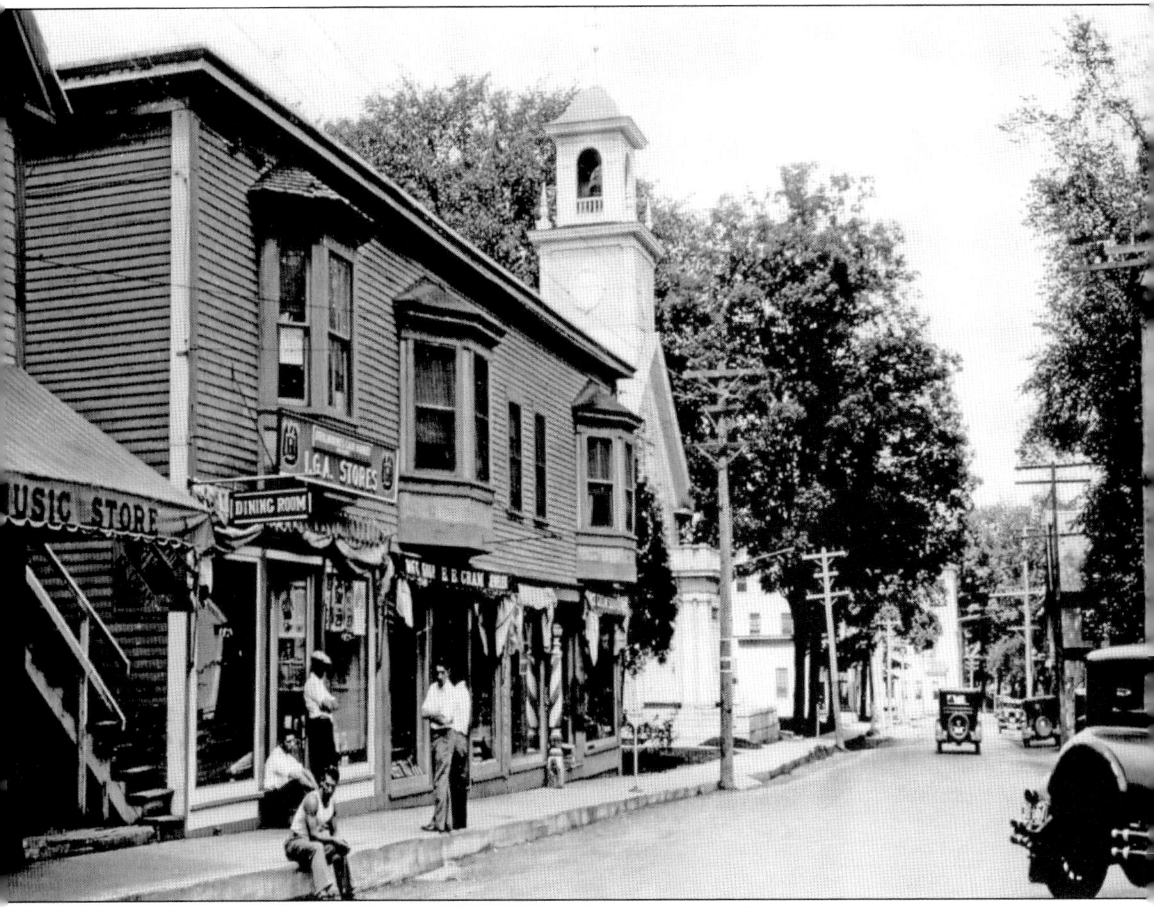

MAIN STREET BUSINESSES, C. 1930. This photograph shows vehicles now on Main Street. The businesses visible are Bailey's Music Store, which was said to have "The Most Complete Line of Musical Instruments in Franklin County," including violins, guitars, banjos, drums, cornets, clarinets, trombones, saxophones, ukuleles, music rolls, records, stands, cases, and sheet music. One can also see an IGA store and E.E. Cram Jeweler's, which sold Bulova, Elgin, and Hamilton jewelry, as well as gifts.

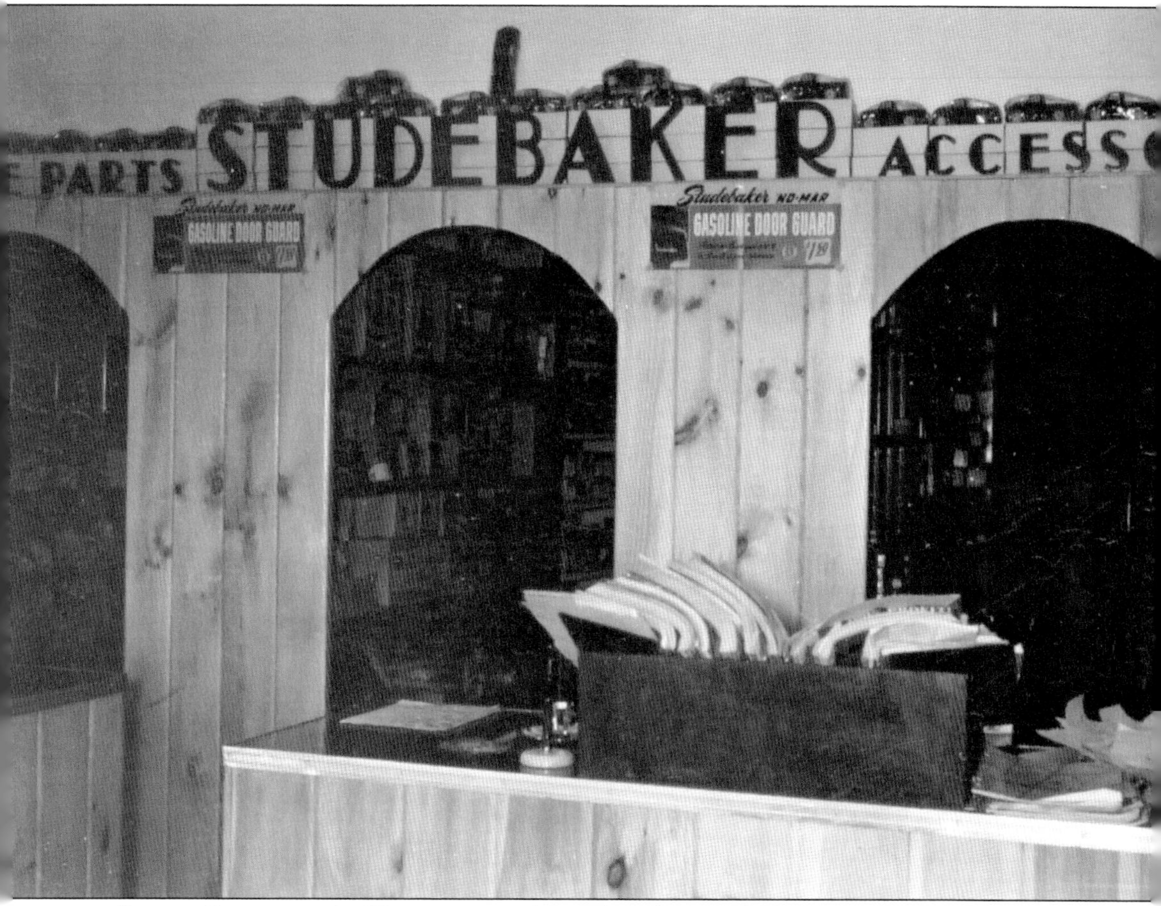

Backus Garage, 1953. This garage was located on the site of a former corn shop. Backus Garage specialized in Studebaker sales and service. It was also an Esso station. This business was established in 1946 by Wayne Backus. It would later become a Jeep dealership.

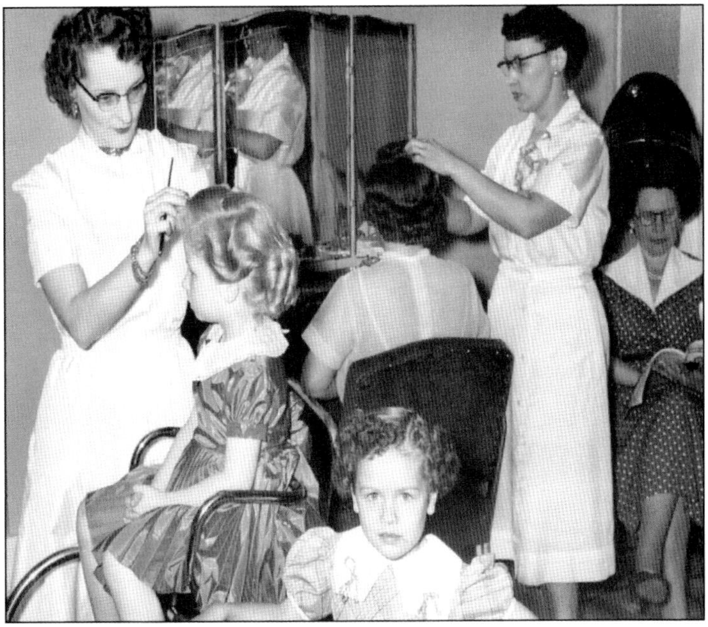

Hazel's Beauty Shop, 1953. This photograph is of the inside of Hazel's Beauty Shop, on Main Street in Wilton. Its advertisement in the Wilton Sesquicentennial booklet proclaimed, "Where Mother Nature plays second fiddle." These women are working their magic on these ladies and girls.

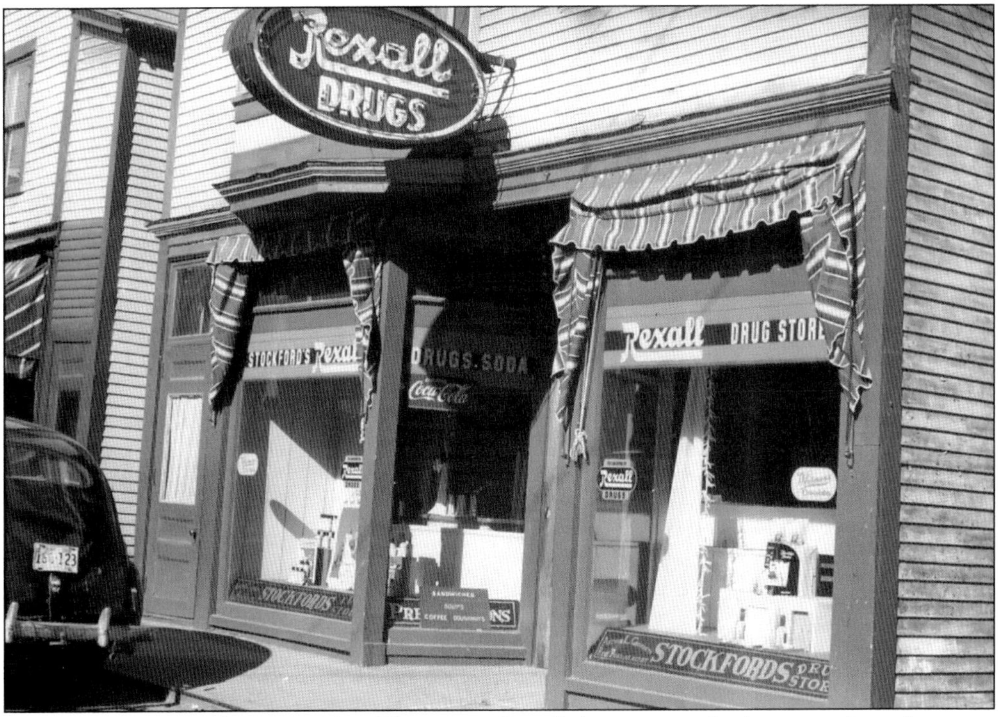

Stockford's Drug Store, 1950s. This was a Rexall drugstore and a long-standing pharmacy in the town. In a 1926 advertisement in the *Franklin County Business and Personal Directory*, it proclaimed to offer "The Best in Drug Store Goods; the Best in Drug Store Service." It offered the following: Rexall Drugs, Whitman's Chocolates, Dr. Robert's Veterinary Goods, a complete toy and gifts room, Liggett's Chocolates, sporting goods, and laundry. By the 1950s, it also had a soda fountain, sandwiches, soups, coffee, and donuts.

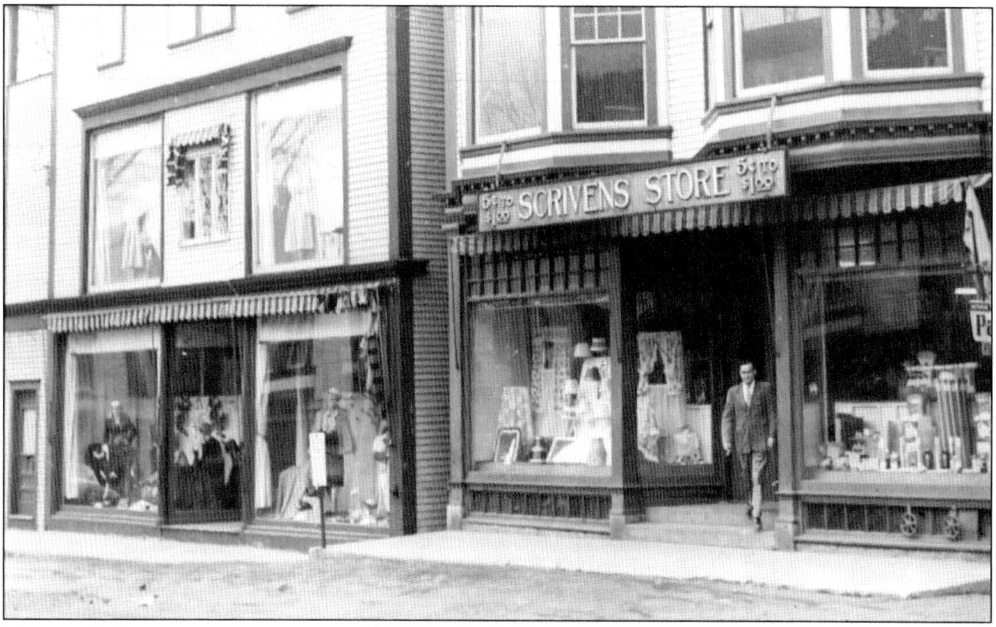

Edward's Department Store and Scrivens' Store, 1953. Edward's Department Store, on the left, offered "up to the minute apparel" for tots to teens, according to an advertisement from 1953. Scrivens' Store 5¢ to $1.00, established in 1933, was called "Wilton's Value Spot." Bob Brown can be seen leaving the store in this photograph.

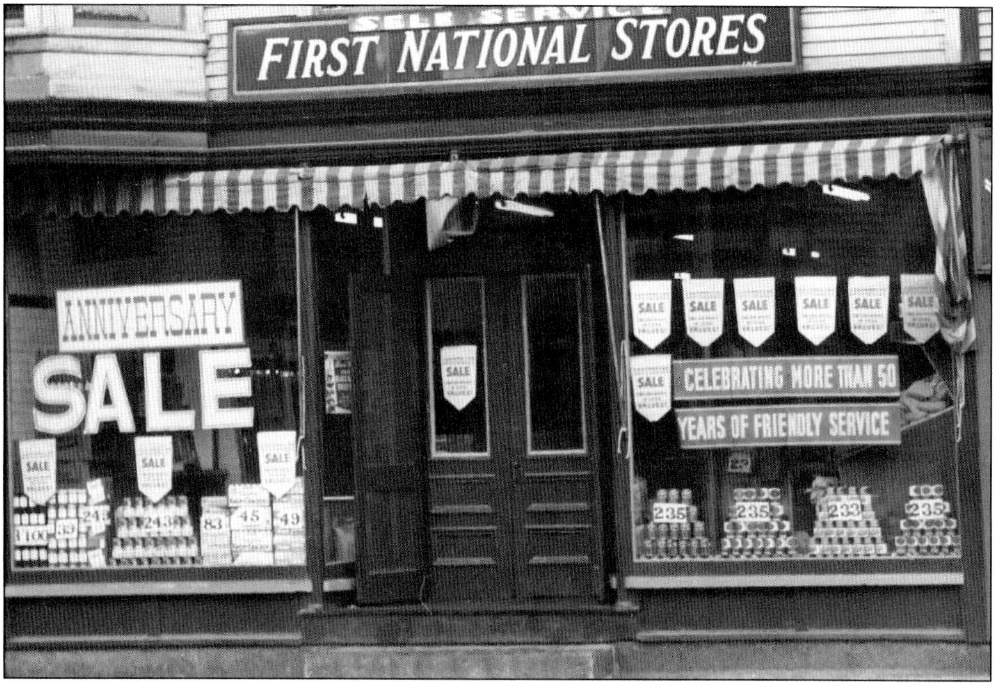

Self Service First National Stores, 1953. In 1927, this store was first opened in Wilton, but it was not until 1941 that it was operated at this location. At one time, First National was one of the largest grocery chains operating in the Northeast. When this photograph was taken, Frank Shuman was the manager.

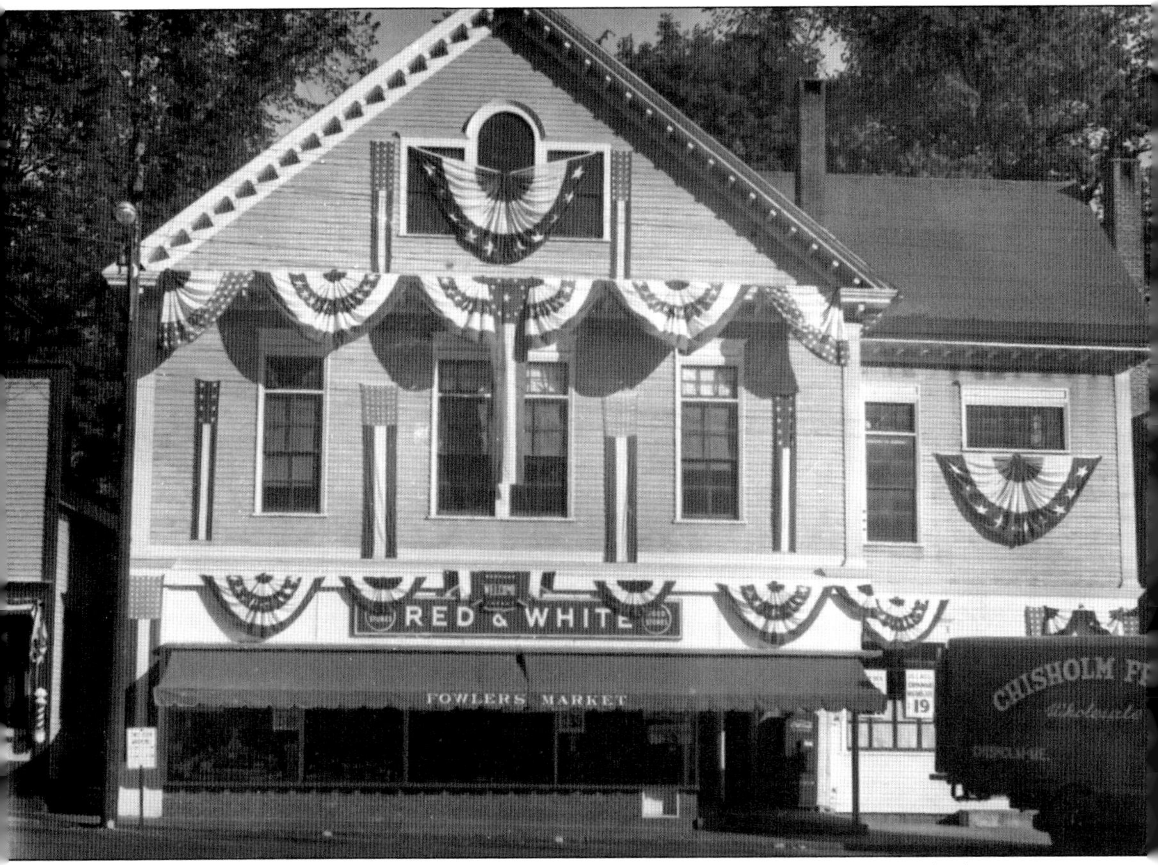

FOWLER'S MARKET, 1953. Fowler's Market was located in the building that was formerly the town hall. This was a Red & White store. Red & White Food Stores were independent food stores in small towns across the United States. This firm started in 1925 and centralized buying and distribution for small stores to allow them to compete against large chain stores, which were consolidating their power in the 1920s. All members of the group had "Red & White" on their sign and usually the name of the owner, as in the case of Fowler's Market, or the name of the town.

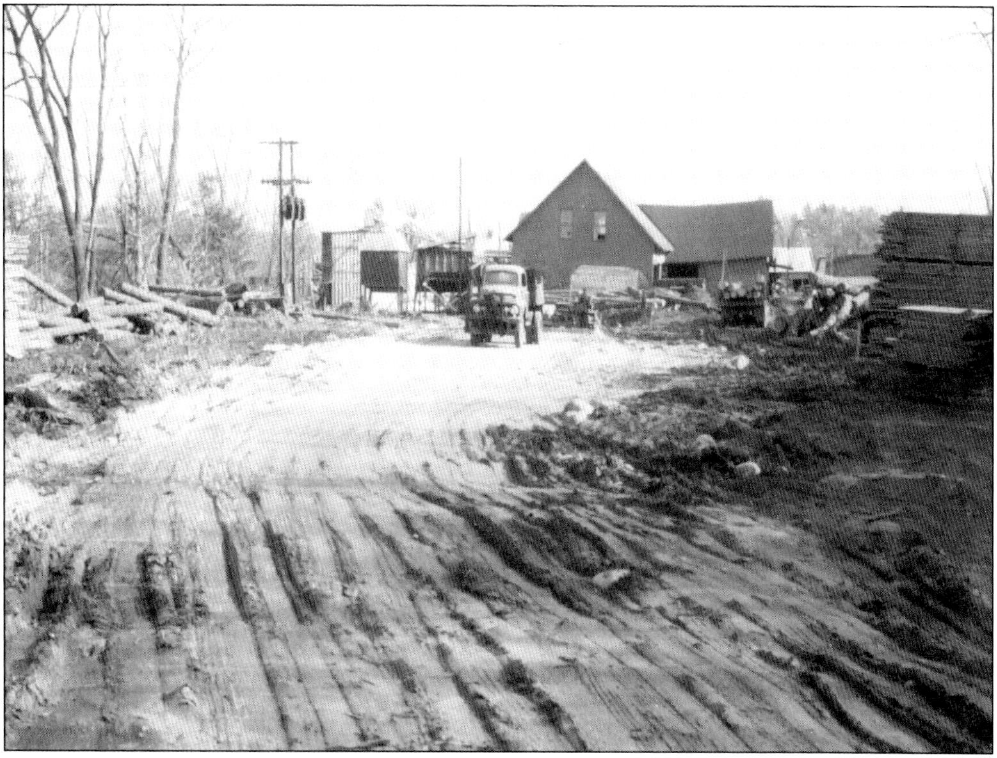

WILTON LUMBER COMPANY, 1953. The lumberyard was built in the 1890s by John Legroo and Rawson Fuller as a sawmill. It used waterpower for all of its operations. In 1939, it was purchased by Wilton Lumber Company. Eventually, all new machinery was installed, power was changed to electric, and more modern equipment was used. In 1953, it was said that this mill produced about 20 percent of the softwood manufactured in Franklin County. Conversion from water to electric power increased production by four times.

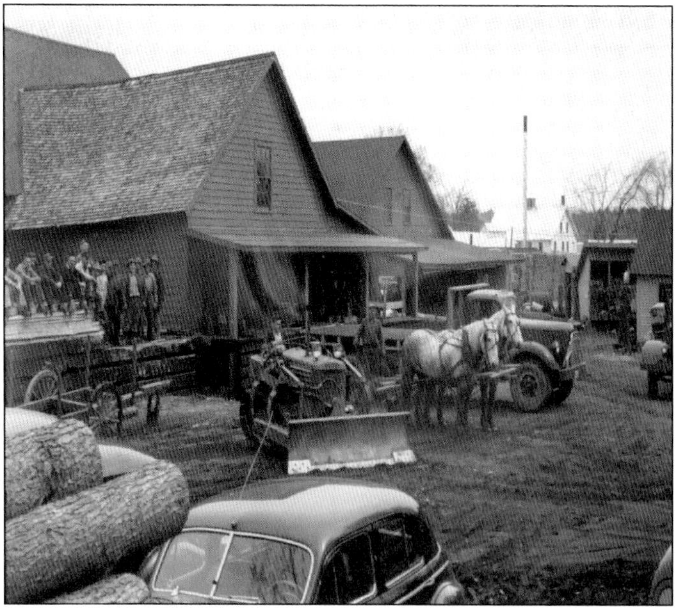

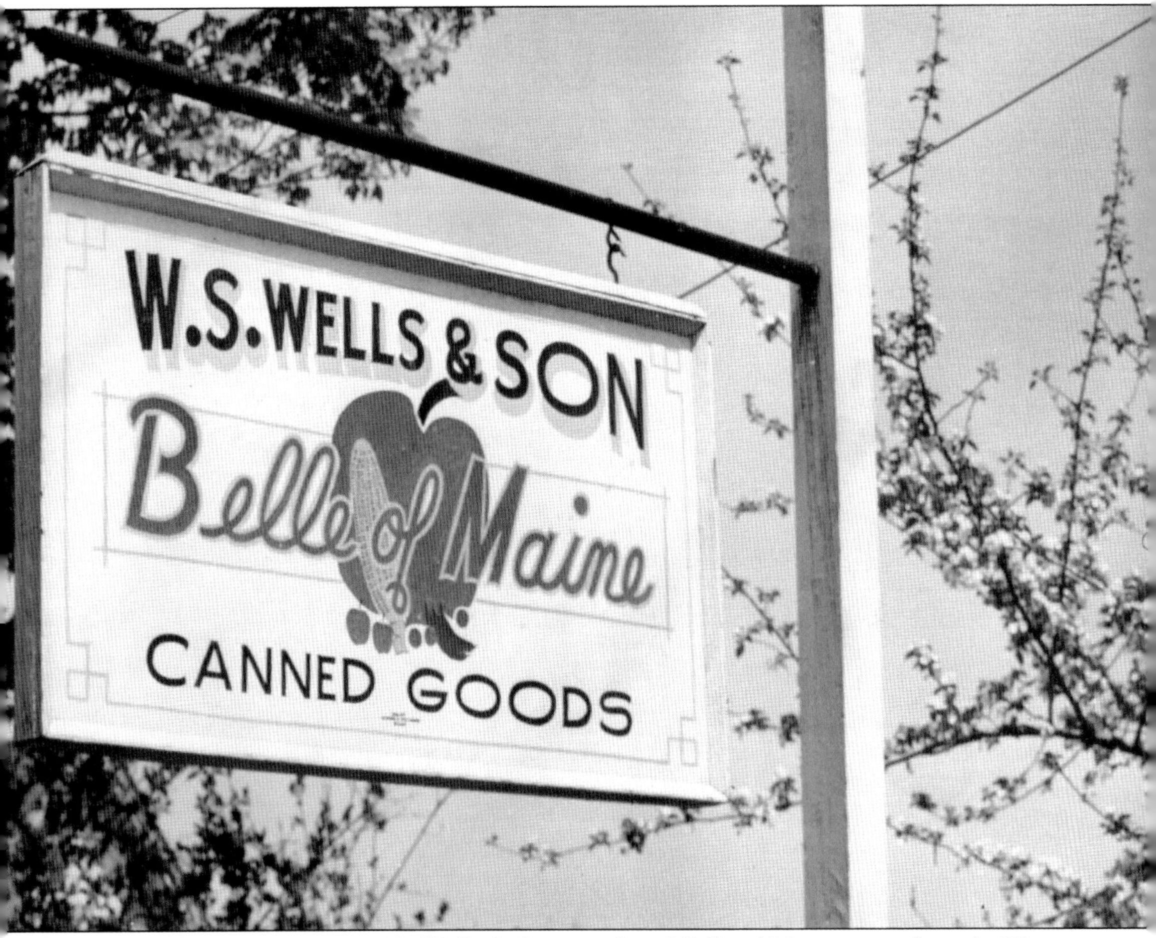

W.S. Wells & Sons, 1953. W.S. Wells & Sons produced Belle of Maine canned goods. The business started in North Anson, Maine, in 1894. A cannery was operated in Dryden for a brief time and was then moved to the property on High Street by Vance Wells Sr. At first, the business canned pie mix and sauce made from apples picked at the orchard on the site. Later, it expanded to string beans, tomatoes, and other produce grown by nearby farms. In 1967, Wells began canning fiddleheads and, later, dandelion greens.

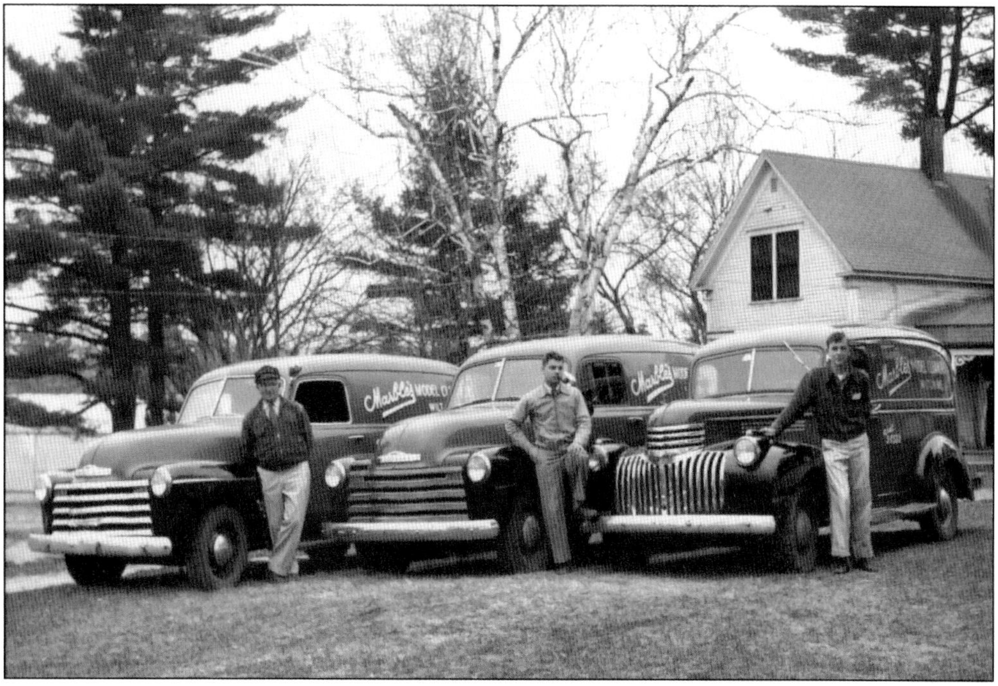

MARBLE'S MODEL CLEANERS, 1953. This cleaning business was established in 1946. It offered cleaning and pressing service and mobile delivery service. The three men in the photograph above worked and drove for the business. Marble Model Cleaners said, "We guarantee satisfaction or your money refunded."

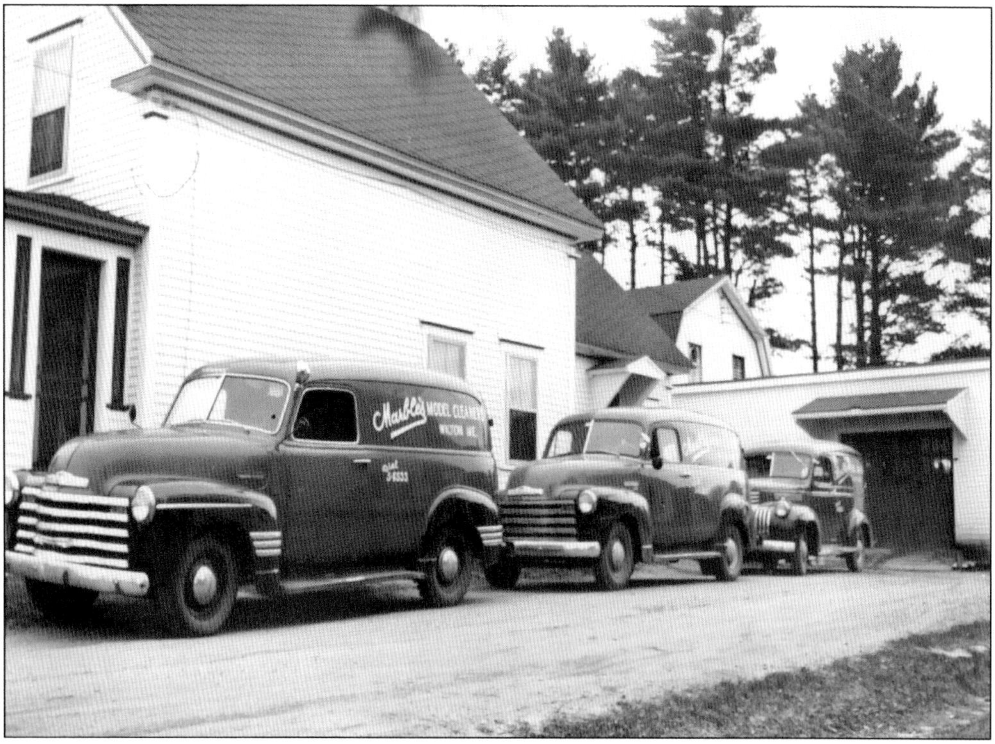

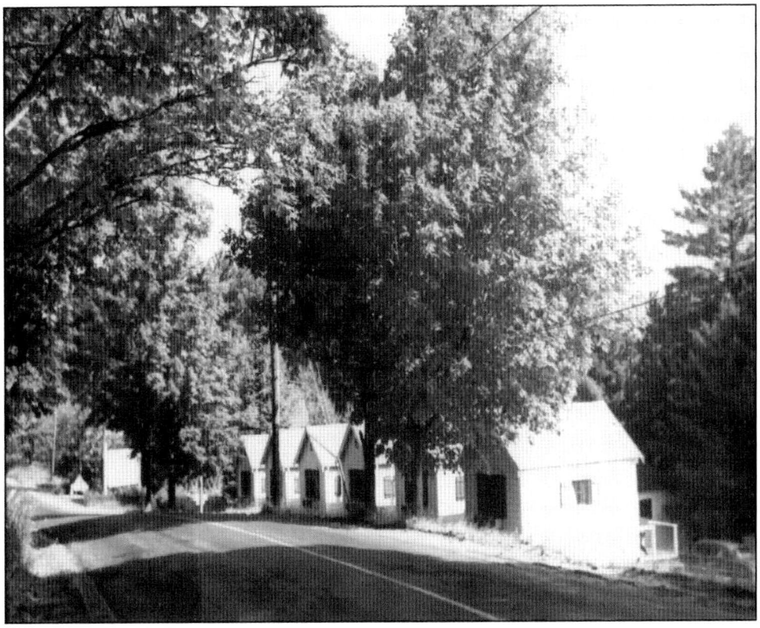

RILEY'S CABINS, 1953. This business was established in 1938 by Cecil Carter. These cabins were on Route 2, one mile west of Wilton on Wilson Lake. There were 10 single and double cooking cabins, all with hot showers and modern facilities. Activities to be enjoyed from these camps included bathing, boating, and fishing.

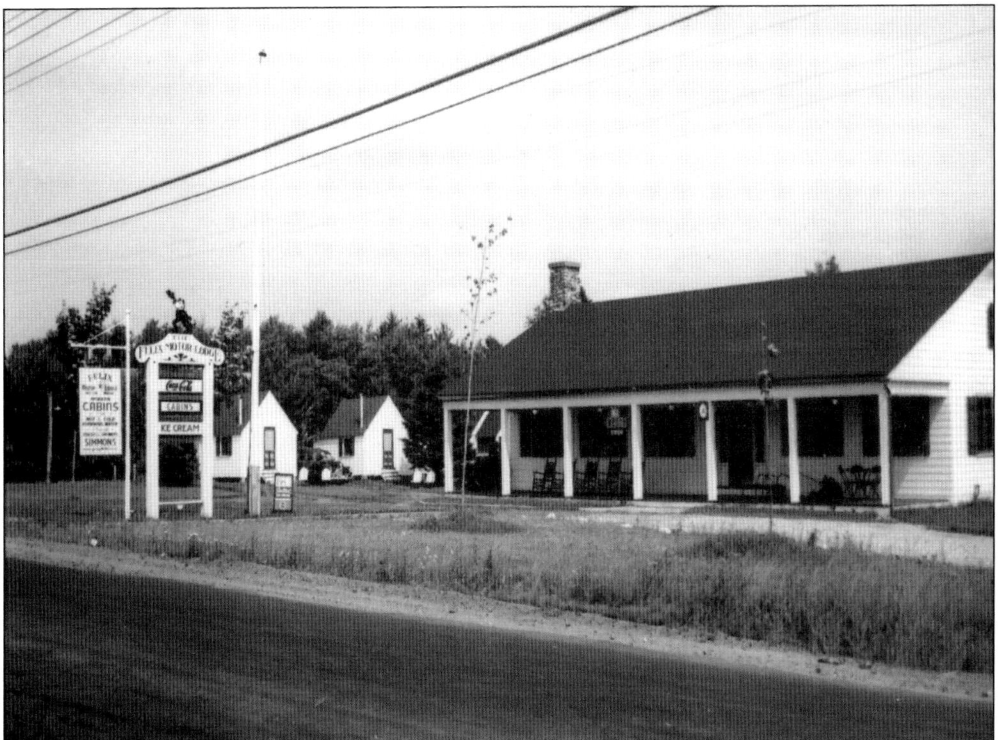

FELIX MOTOR LODGE, c. 1950. This motor lodge had a number of small cabins and featured Felix the Cat on its sign. It advertised "Modern Cabins with Every Convenience." The sign advertised the food offered there. It was owned at one time by Mrs. Frank Goodspeed.

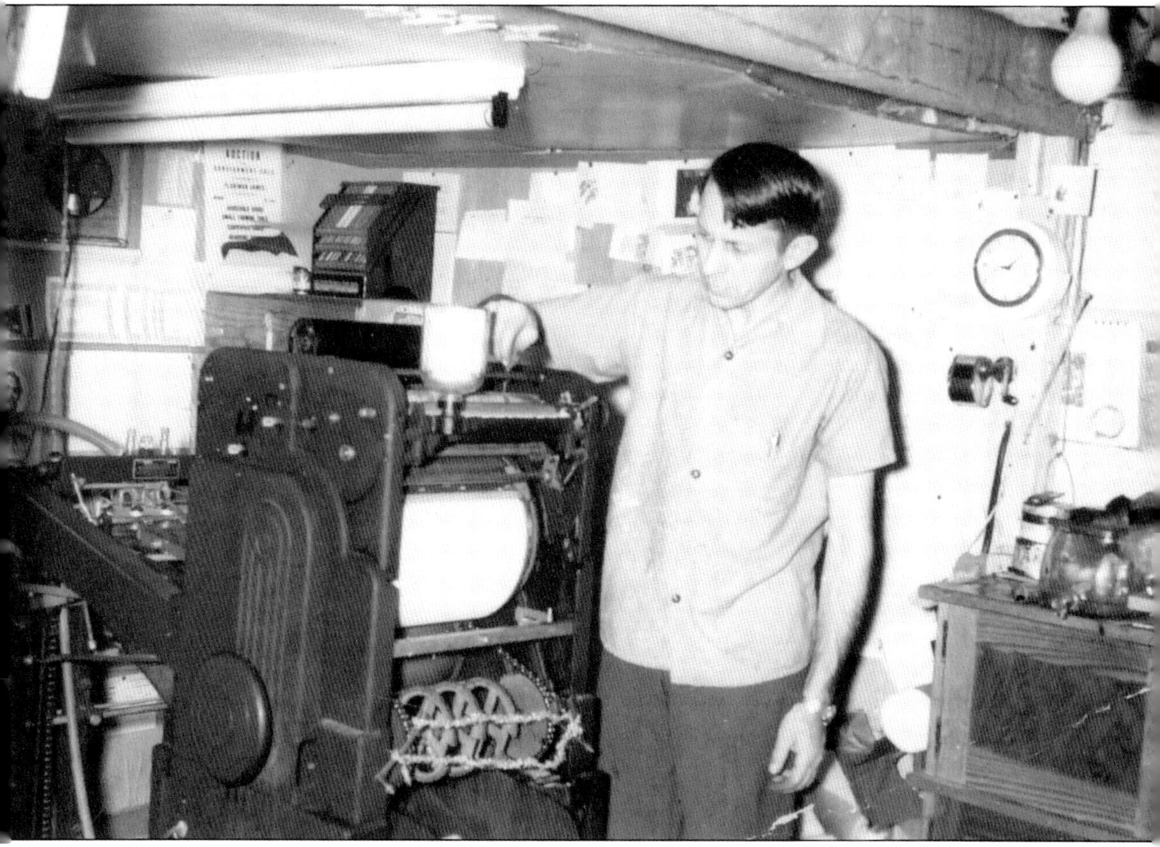

WILTON PRINTING SERVICE, 1949. This printing service was owned by Elizabeth and Harold Karkos. This photograph was taken during their first year in business. Their shop was in a basement on Allen Street. In 1954, the business changed its name to Wilton Printing Products, Inc. Harold Karkos was also a photographer.

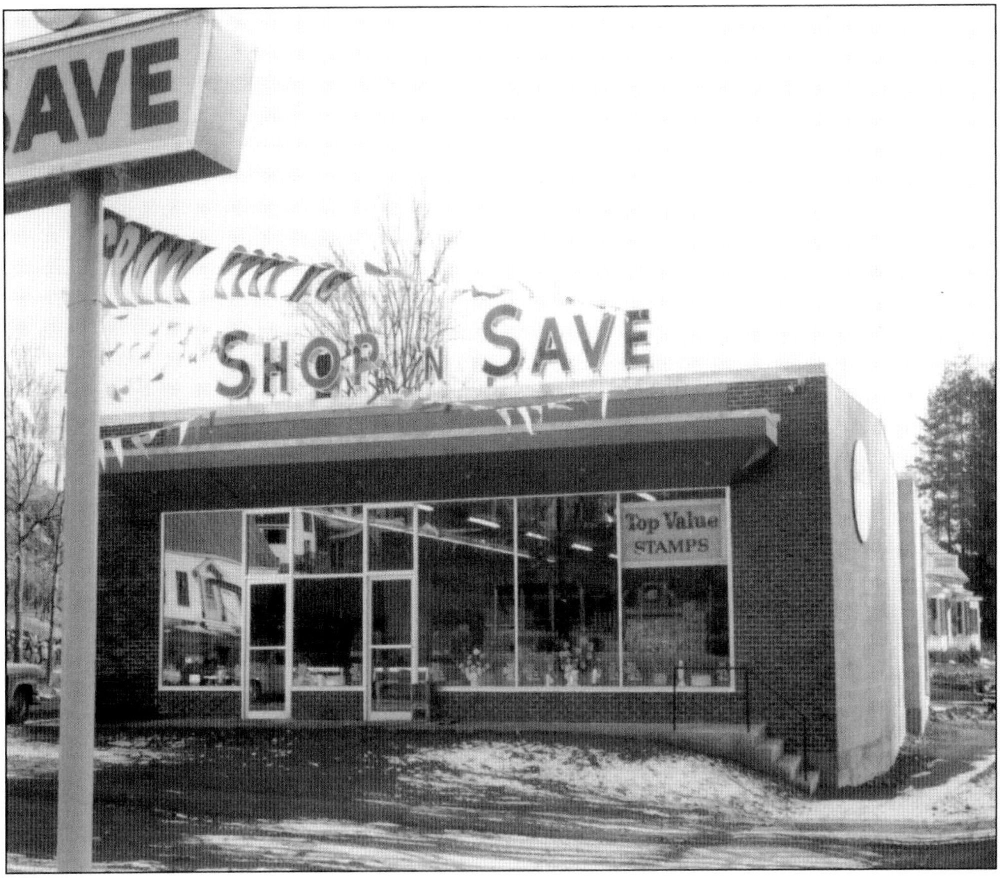

Shop n' Save Grand Opening, 1962. This is a photograph of the Shop n' Save grand opening on Main Street. In the window in the photograph above, one can see a sign for "Top Value Stamps." These were a type of trading stamp given out as incentives at grocery stores across America. One would fill up books of them and trade them in for merchandise (often housewares). The photograph below is of the inside of the new store. One can see cigarette choices within reach. There appear to be a number of people milling about the store. This Shop n' Save closed its doors in 1984.

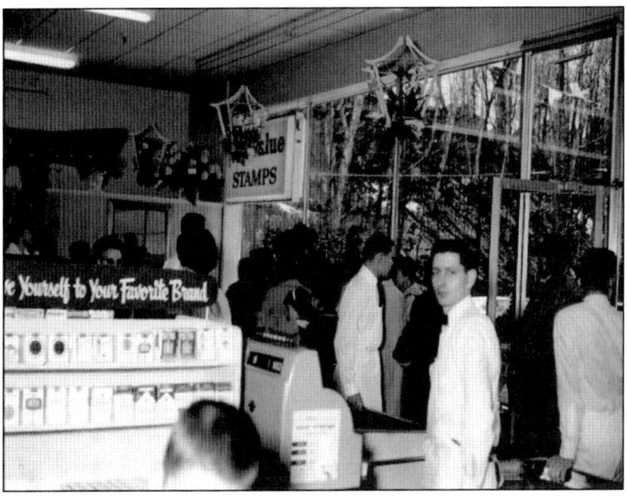

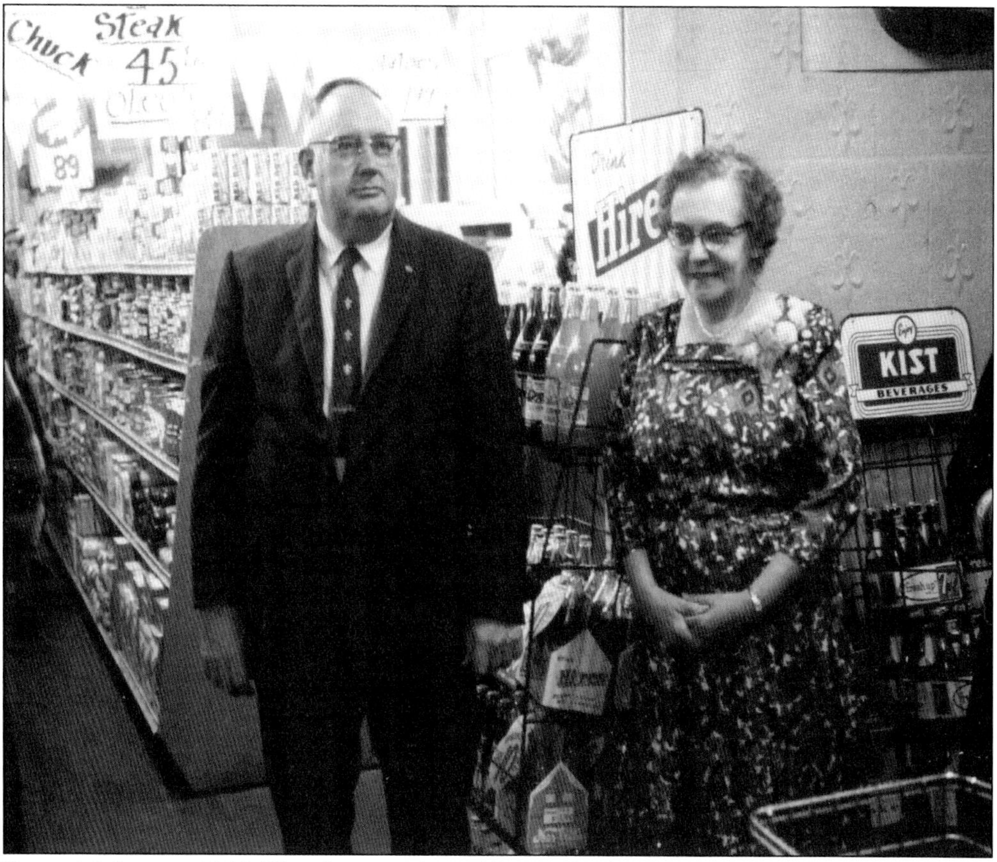

Young's Market, 1964. This photograph is of the inside of Young's Nationwide store in Dryden, including a couple of satisfied shoppers. One can see the racks of Hire and Kist soda. Both brands were very popular at that time.

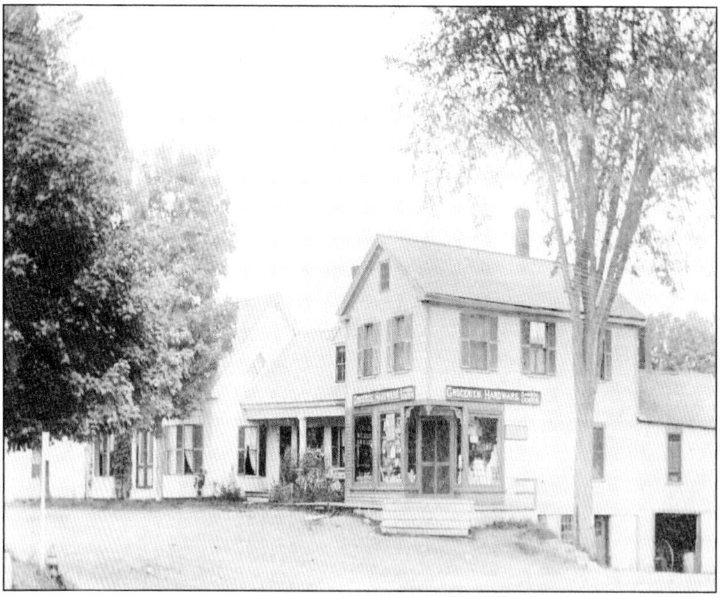

Groceries, Hardware, 5 & 10¢, c. 1900. This was a general store in Wilton that sold groceries, hardware, and other items at inexpensive prices. This business was attached to the owner's home.

Two

INDUSTRY

Industry was central to the town's growth even before the town was incorporated. There was a plethora of industry early on, including gristmills and sawmills. A gristmill of note was the G.R. Fernald & Co. Grist Mill. Hiram Holt & Co. manufactured hay knives, machetes, scythes, and other kinds of knives. It was located in East Wilton. The Walker Mills, also in East Wilton, was an early textile mill. G.H. Bass & Co. was established in the late 1800s, and, in the early 1900s, the Wilton Woolen Company was established by the Goodspeed family. These two companies would become the backbones of industry in the town of Wilton for many years to come, providing jobs for local men and, later, women.

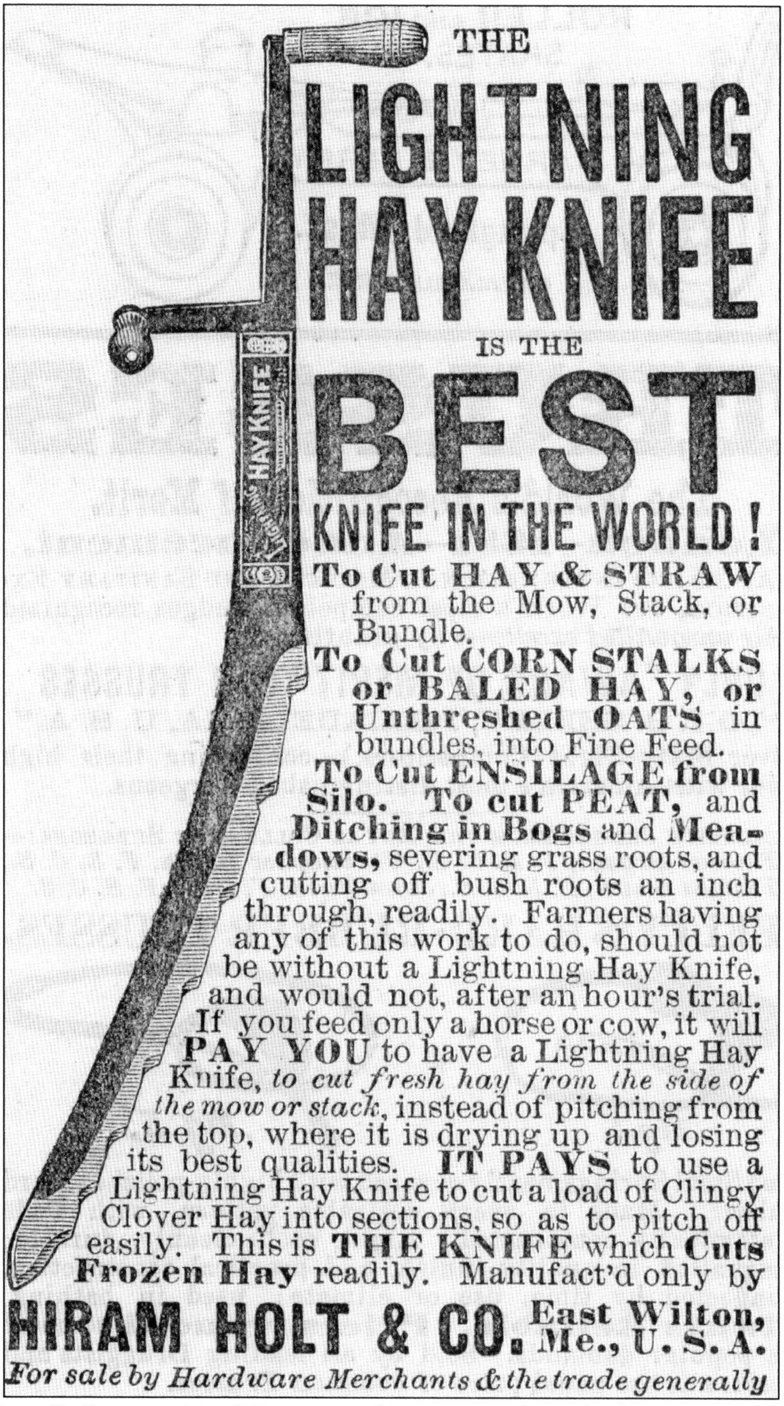

HIRAM HOLT & CO., C. 1900. This is an advertisement from the late 1800s or early 1900s advertising the Lightning Hay Knife. Hiram Holt & Co. of East Wilton manufactured hay knives, machetes, scythes, and other kinds of knives. Its hay knives were used throughout the United States. These two-handed cutters were about four feet in length and were used on many farms until hay-balers lessoned the need for large knives.

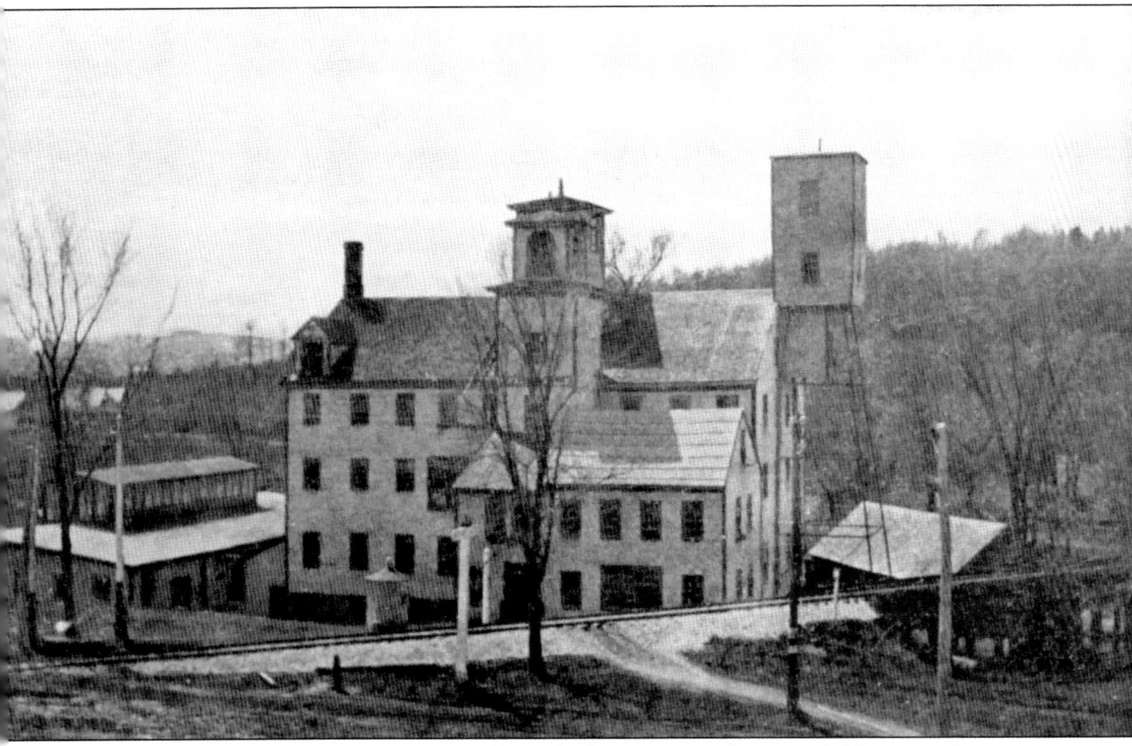

Walker Woolen Mill, c. 1900. This mill was built in 1840 and operated, like many factories of the day, by waterpower. It was located in East Wilton and was also known as the Walker Brothers Woolen Mill. James Walker was the superintendent of the mill, Thomas Walker Jr. was the president, and Edward A. Hatch was the treasurer, according to the 1899 *Franklin County Directory*. This mill specialized in woolens. It was destroyed by fire in 1931.

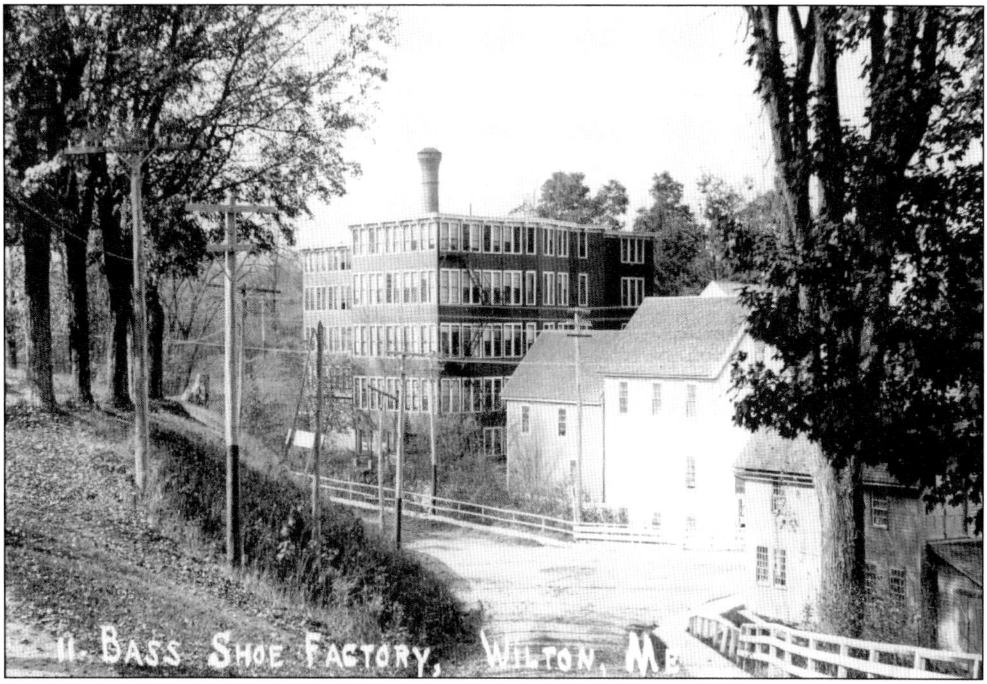

G.H. Bass & Co., Early 1900s. In this photograph, one can see the old gristmill in the foreground. The G.H. Bass factory building in this photograph was constructed in 1905, and the gristmill was torn down in 1931, so this photograph was taken some time between those two dates. Taken from Bass Hill, the photograph shows what was known as Bass Building No. 1. It was actually the third Bass Shoe Shop location, built to accommodate the needs of a rapidly growing company.

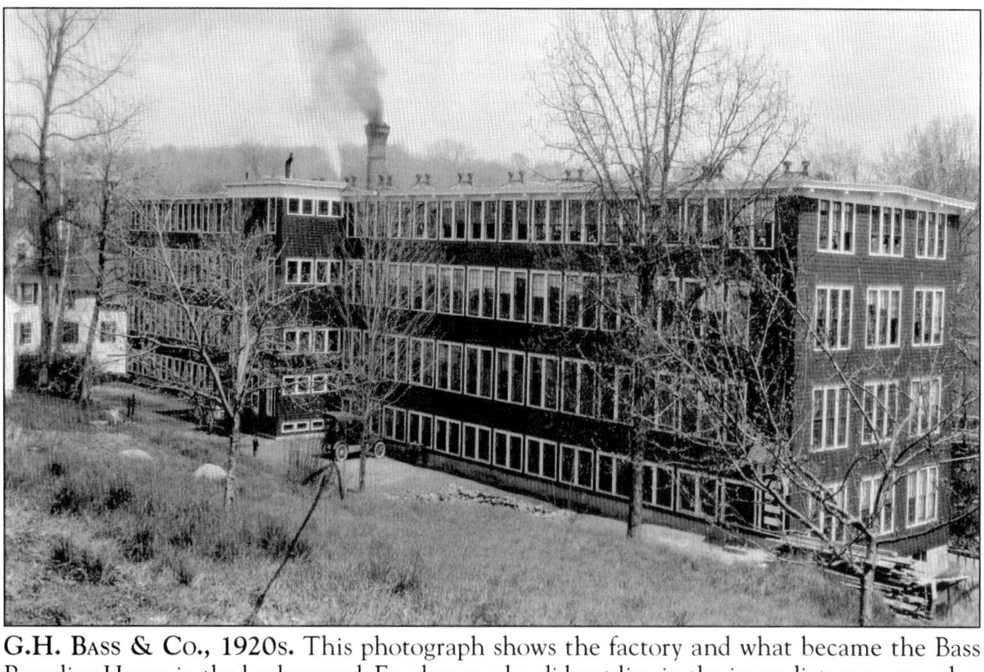

G.H. Bass & Co., 1920s. This photograph shows the factory and what became the Bass Boarding House in the background. Employees who did not live in the immediate area stayed at the boardinghouse.

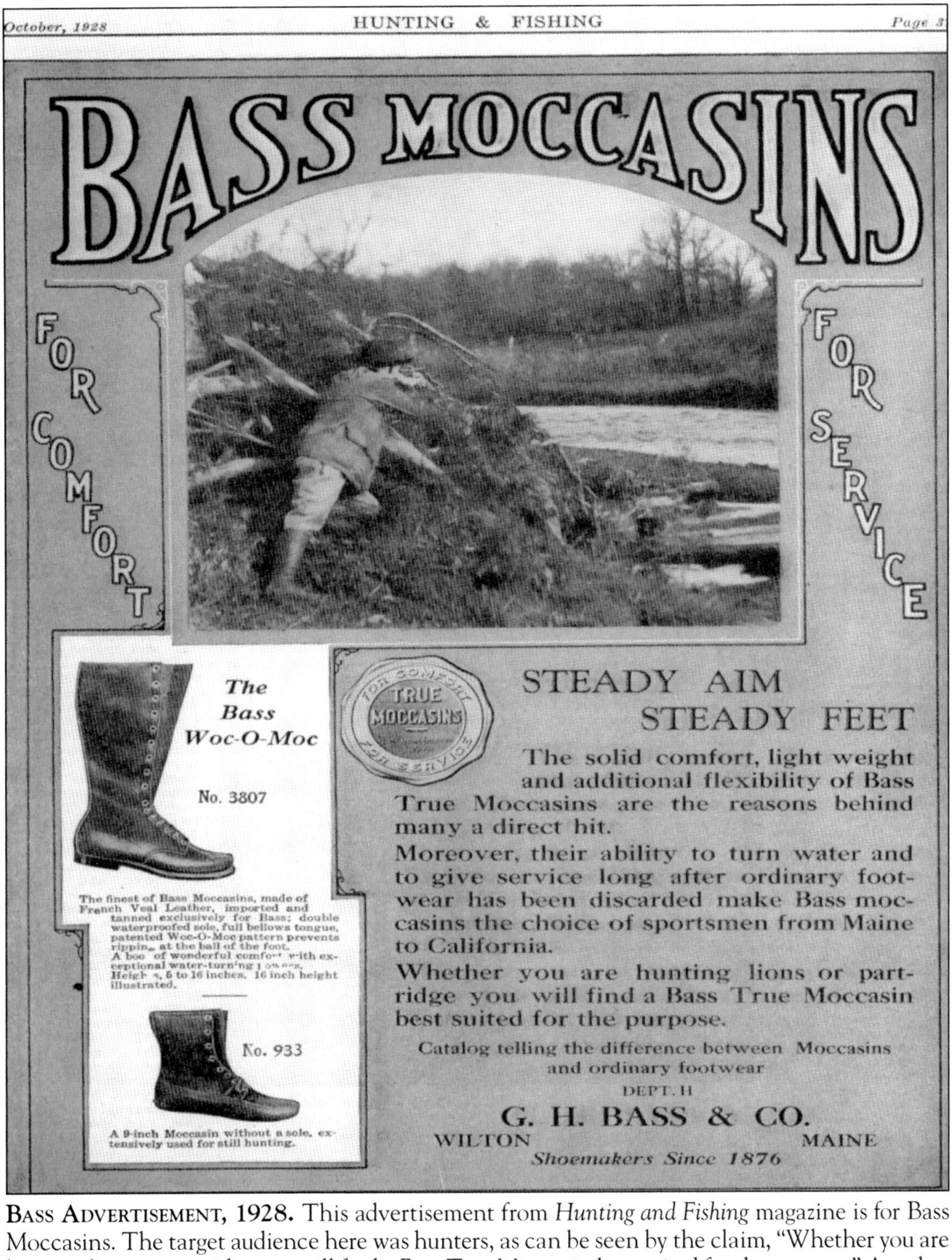

Bass Advertisement, 1928. This advertisement from *Hunting and Fishing* magazine is for Bass Moccasins. The target audience here was hunters, as can be seen by the claim, "Whether you are hunting lions or partridge you will find a Bass True Moccasin best suited for the purpose." Another advertisement (not pictured here) from *Boys' Life* in 1937 expounded on the qualities of the Bass Woc-O-Moc thusly: "Hike, hunt, camp with the foot comfort of an Indian. The Bass Woc-O-Moc is a genuine moccasin." The Bass name and the quality of its products were widely known.

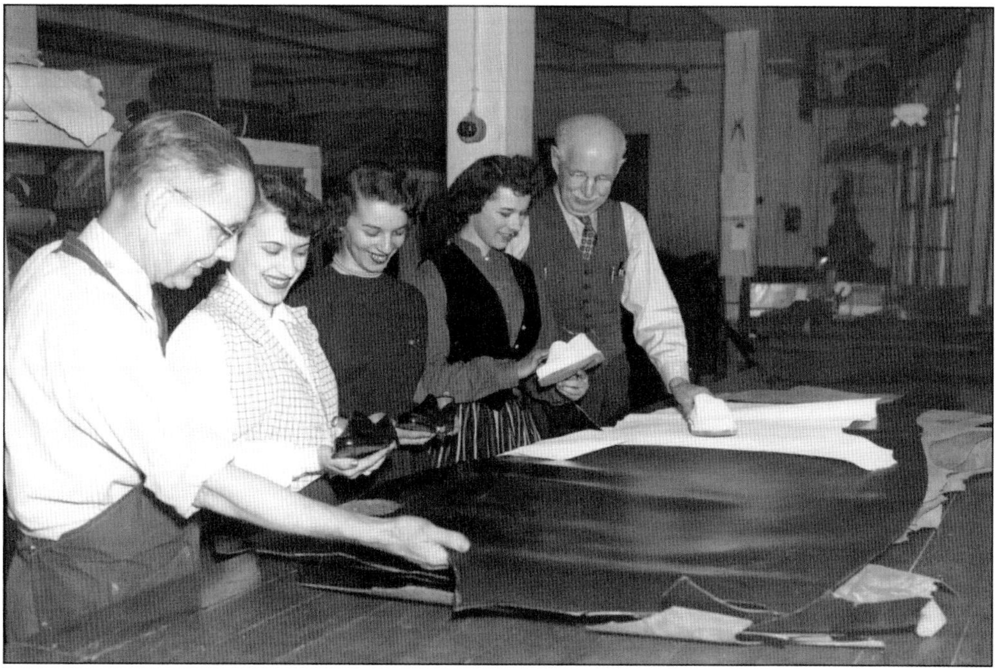

INSIDE G.H. BASS & CO., 1940S. The photograph above, taken inside Bass Shoe, shows Willard Bass on the far right, who was president of the company from 1925 to 1956. These women appear to be getting an introduction to the shoe business. The photograph below is from inside the cutting room at G.H. Bass & Co. The men working here are Lynn Miller (left) and Bill Perkins (right).

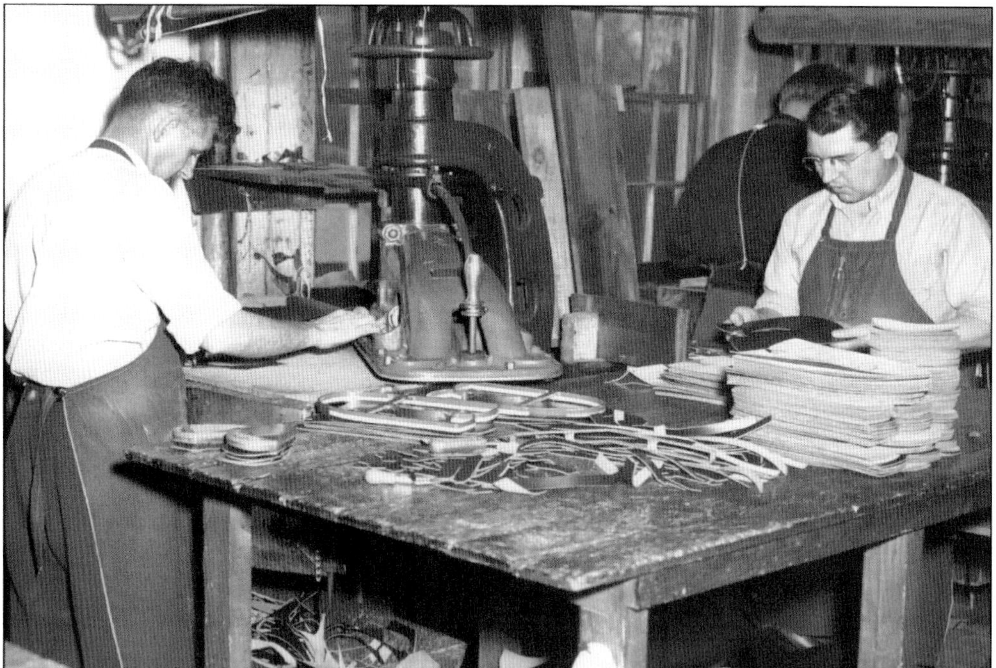

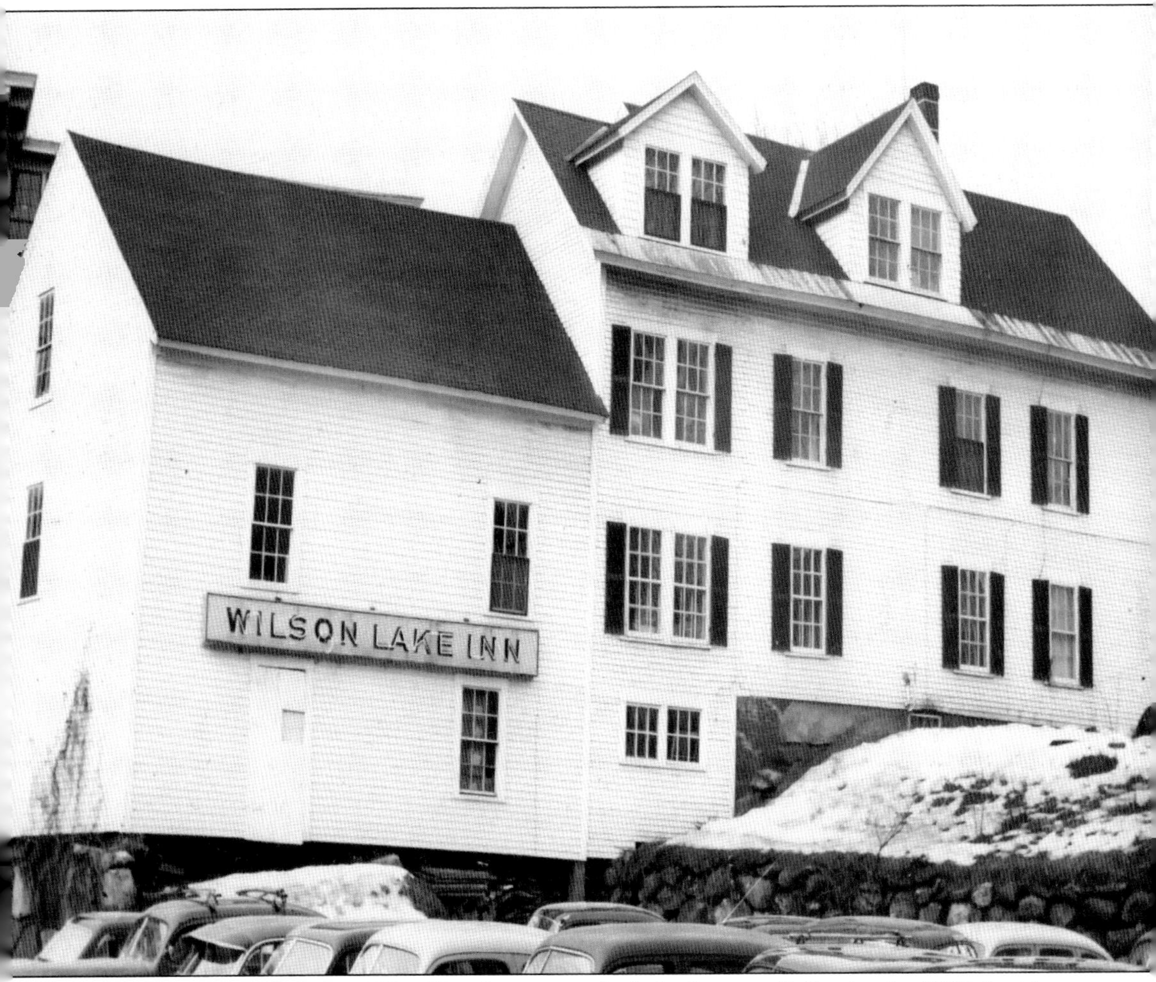

WILSON LAKE INN, EARLY 1950S. This house was built by Rawson Fuller in the 1860s beside Wilson Stream. In 1904, G.H. Bass built his third factory on Wilson Stream. At this time, G.H. Bass purchased the Fuller home to be used as a boardinghouse for his out-of-town employees. The boardinghouse ceased functioning in 1945 and was used as a facility for hand-sewers and for storage for some time. Bass eventually deeded the building to the Wilton Historical Society in 1987 to be used as the Wilton Farm and Home Museum.

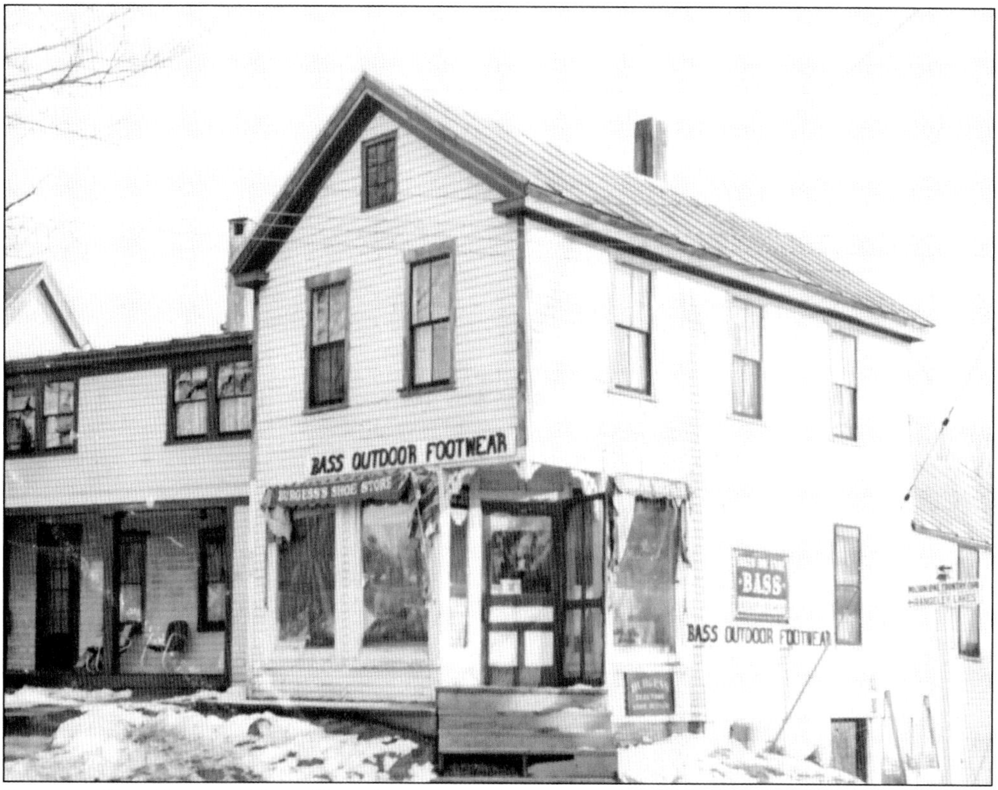

Burgess Shoe Store, 1950s. The photograph above was taken by Harold Karkos. Burgess Shoe Store was the Bass outdoor footwear outlet. It also offered Burgess Electric Shoe Repair. The outlet was later moved to a location on Allen Street.

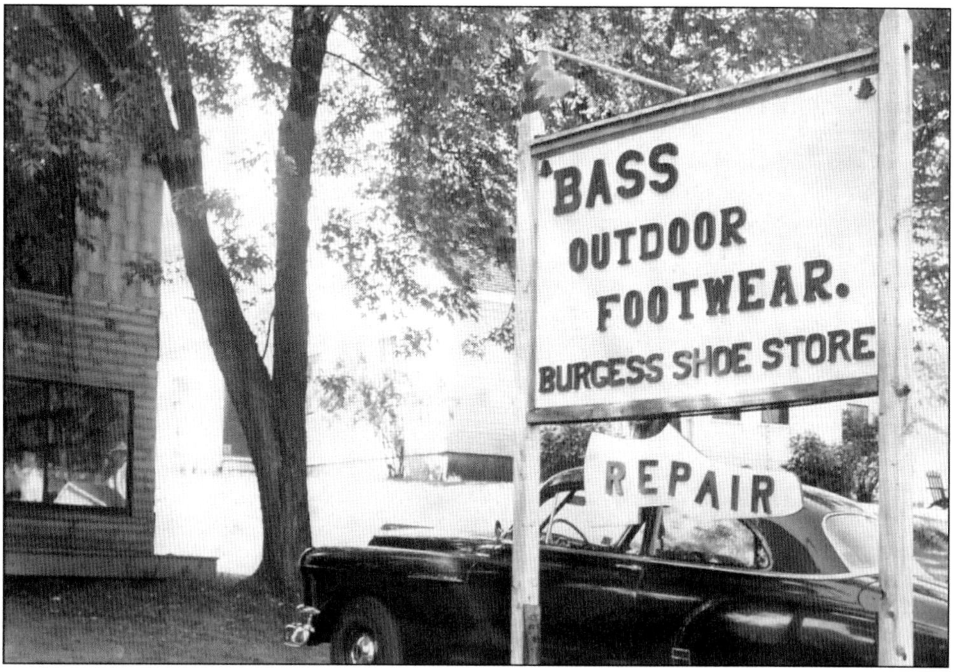

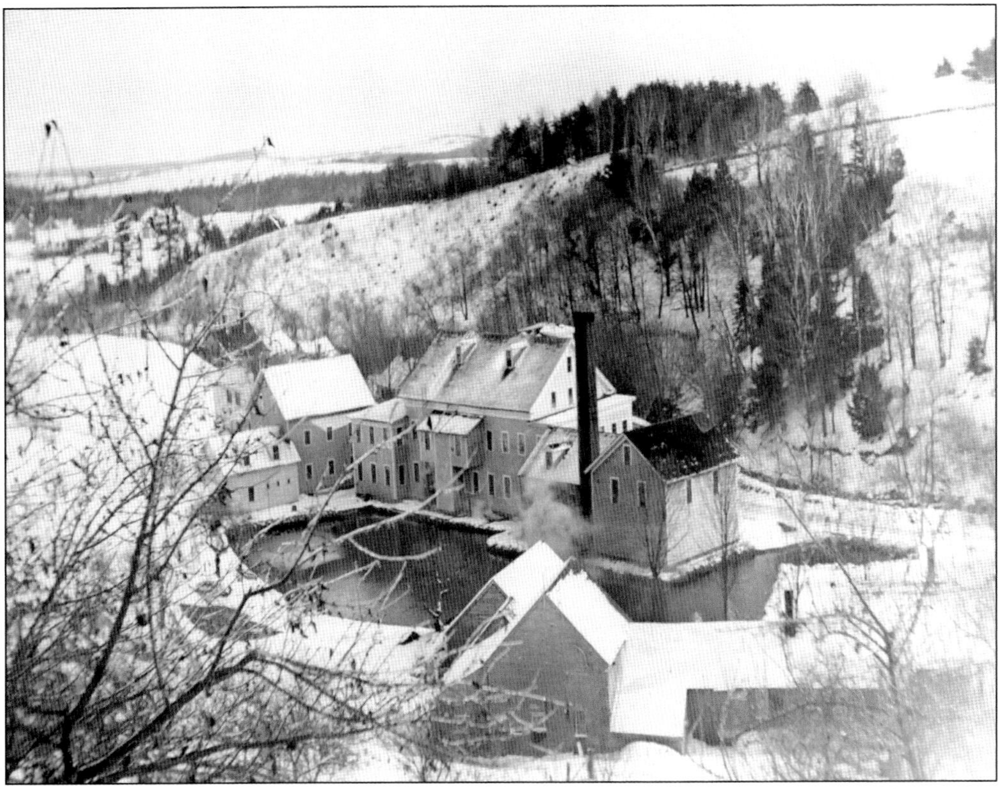

Upper Woolen Mill, c. 1900. This textile mill was built by Dimon Furnell on the former site of his yarn mill, built in the 1830s. In 1891, the mill was purchased by Flavius J. Goodspeed of the Madison Woolen Mill. Goodspeed operated the plant as a complete textile mill. The business prospered, and the building was enlarged. It continued to be operated as a woolen mill on Main Street in Wilton until 1912, beside the man-made millpond. This mill made cloth and was a branch of the Wilton Woolen Company. From 1912 to 1928, it served as a weave shed for the "Lower Mill," on Depot Street. From 1932 to 1933, the mill was used for a toy item business. In 1934, George G. Goodspeed completely renovated the building, at a cost of $32,000, into a community center. In 1935, he presented the town with a complete recreation center and community building that included a theater, a gymnasium, and other facilities.

Wilton Woolen Company, 1920s. In 1903, Frank G. and George F. Goodspeed, the sons of Flavius Goodspeed, who owned Wilton's first complete textile mill, formed a corporation with their father known as the Wilton Woolen Company. The site, on Depot Street in Dryden, where this photograph was taken, was purchased in 1903. Further additions were made in 1909, 1916, and 1928. This photograph shows the factory fairly early on in its existence. The site became the nucleus of what evolved into the largest individually owned woolen mill in New England.

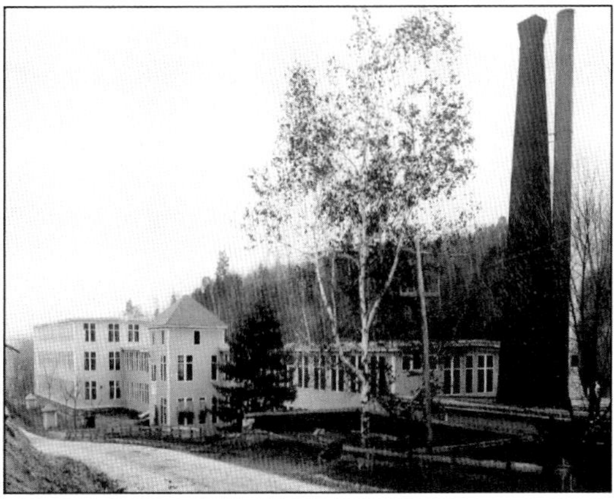

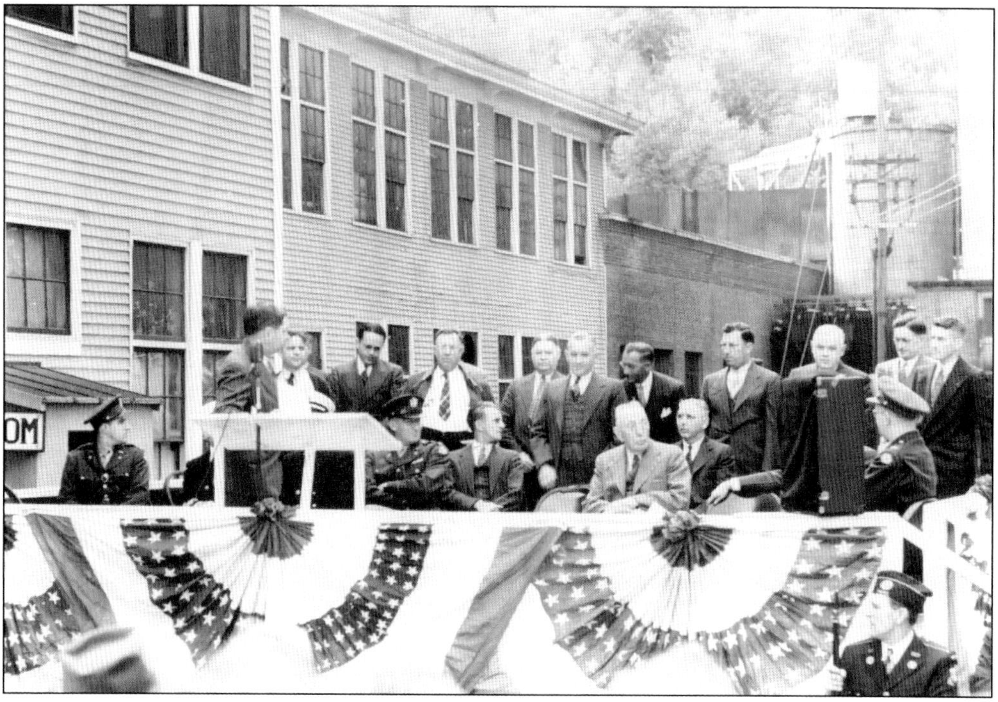

Wilton Woolen Mill, 1943. In 1943, Wilton Woolen Company was purchased by a group of prominent local men headed by Roy P. Gifford and Earl B. Foss from the estate of George F. Goodspeed. They operated it until 1955. During World War II, the mill facilities were placed at the disposal of the federal government for the manufacturing of cloth for the Army and Navy. Approximately 10 million yards of cloth was produced for the government during the war years. This photograph is of the "E" Awards from the Army and Navy for the production of cloth for the military. In this photograph are, from left to right, (first row) an unidentified soldier, Roy Gifford, Cyrus Blanchard, and Lester North; (second row) an unidentified soldier, Howard Kyes, Eddie Brougham, Rex Lake, Oscar Chandler, Dave Jones, Monroe Woodman, Parker Abbott, Carl Swett, Francis Egan, John Smiley, and Ruel Orff Sr. (Courtesy of Joyce Orff.)

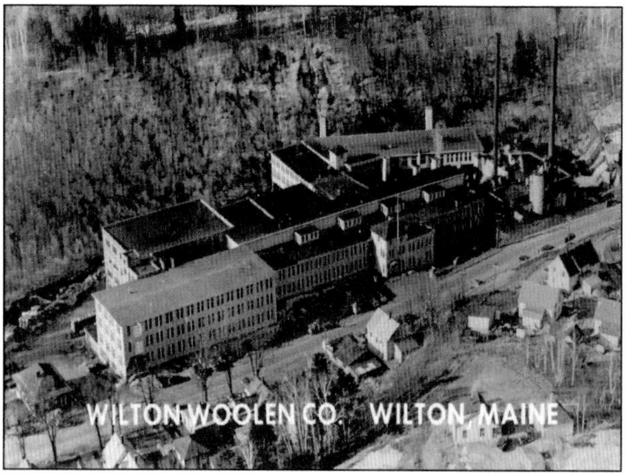

Wilton Woolen Company, c. 1950. One can see in this photograph that the factory underwent a great deal of expansion over the years. The mill was closed in the 1950s. It was owned by Roy P. Gifford and Earl B. Foss at the time. It was operated under their ownership for a period of time before it was purchased by Forster Manufacturing Company in 1960. Forster manufactured croquet sets and custom turnings and assembled snap clothespins, folding cartons, and toothpicks.

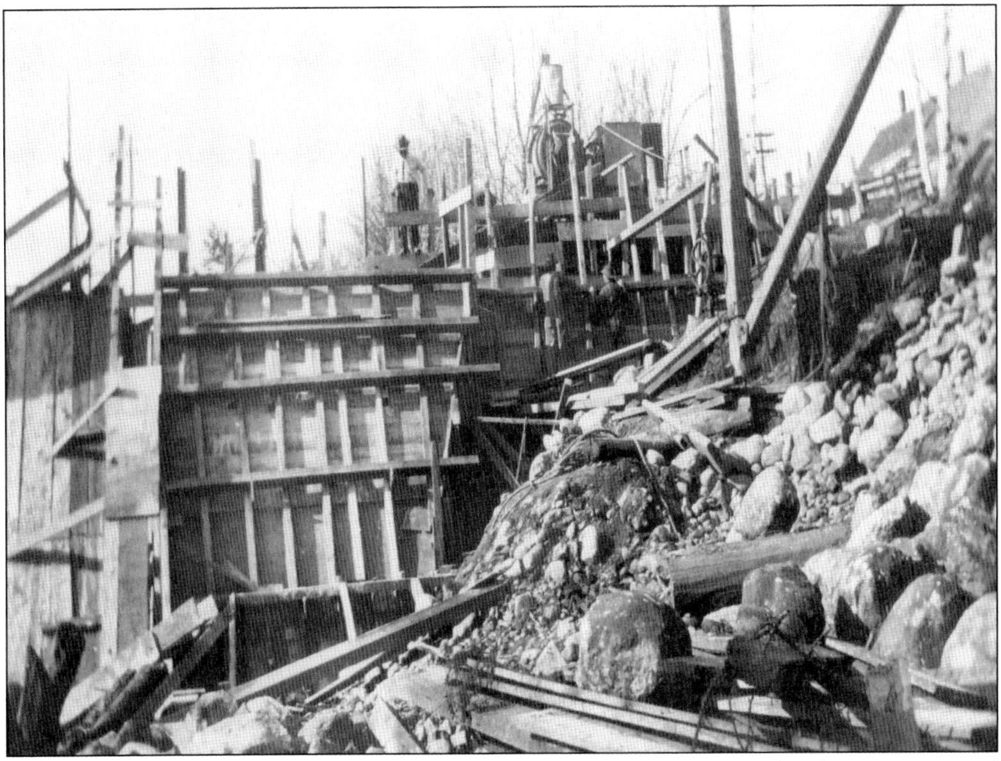

WATERPOWER, 1921. These photographs are of the new Wilton Woolen Mill dam being constructed at the Goodspeeds' woolen mill in Dryden. The machinery in their textile mill was run by waterpower at one time.

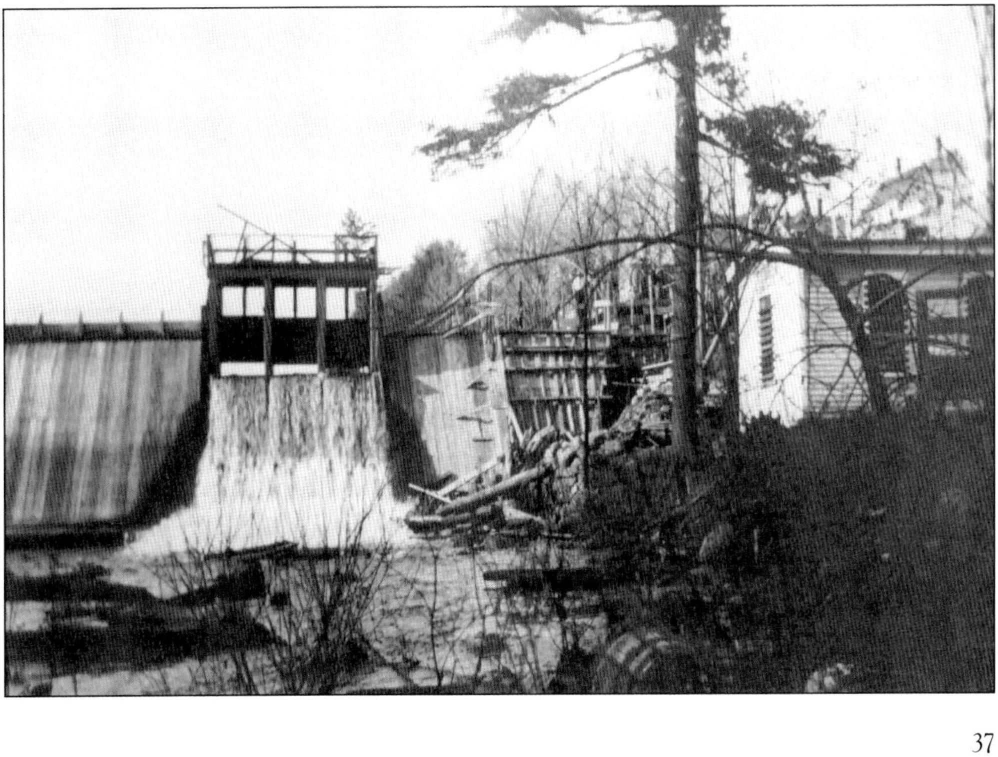

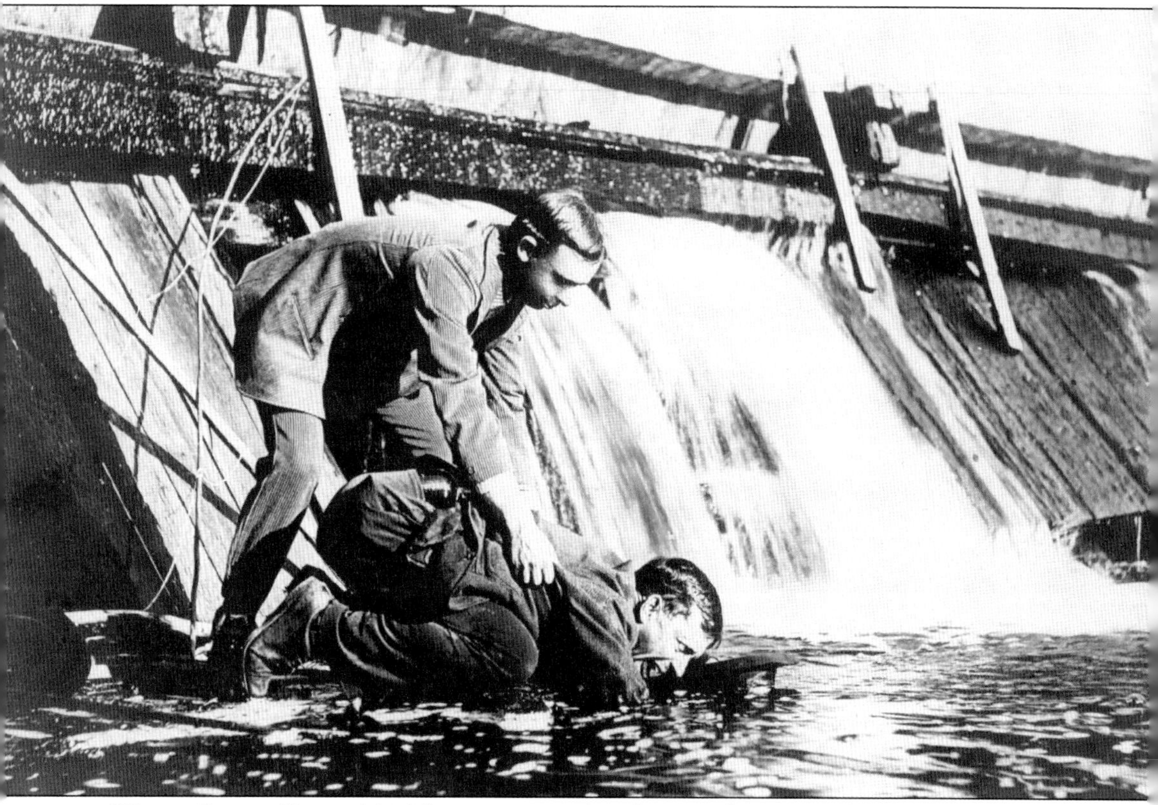

Wilson Stream Dam, 1900. The two men in this photograph appear to be brothers. It seems they are trying to retrieve something that fell in the water at the dam, which was used for waterpower for one of the industries along Wilson Stream.

Three

Hunting, Farming, and Fishing

When the town was still quite young, it was necessary for people to be more self-sufficient. This was particularly true before there were a lot of grocery stores. The inhabitants had to grow and hunt their food. The land was fertile, and fish and game were plentiful. The town of Wilton had a bounty of offerings from nature. Agriculture was very prevalent despite the harsh winters wrought upon the region. Farmers raised livestock and slaughtered it as a food source. They also grew hardy crops that required a fairly short growing season. There were also abundant orchards, lakes and streams teeming with fish, and forests with plentiful game. The 1800s and early 1900s were certainly a time of abundance.

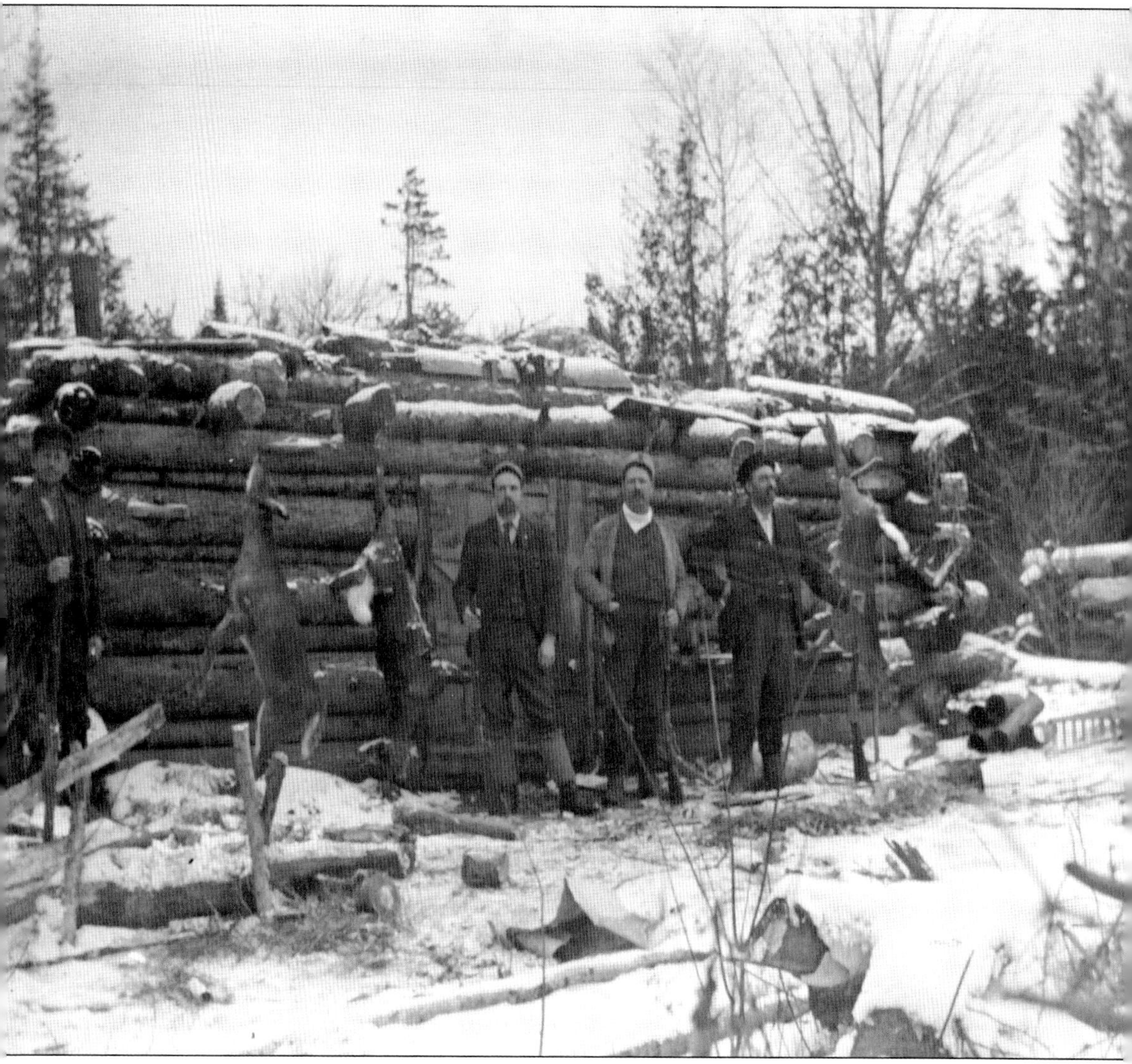

HUNTING, C. 1900. Game was extremely plentiful at this time in Wilton, as it was in many areas of Maine then. This photograph is of a primitive dear camp made of logs, perhaps cut from the surrounding forest.

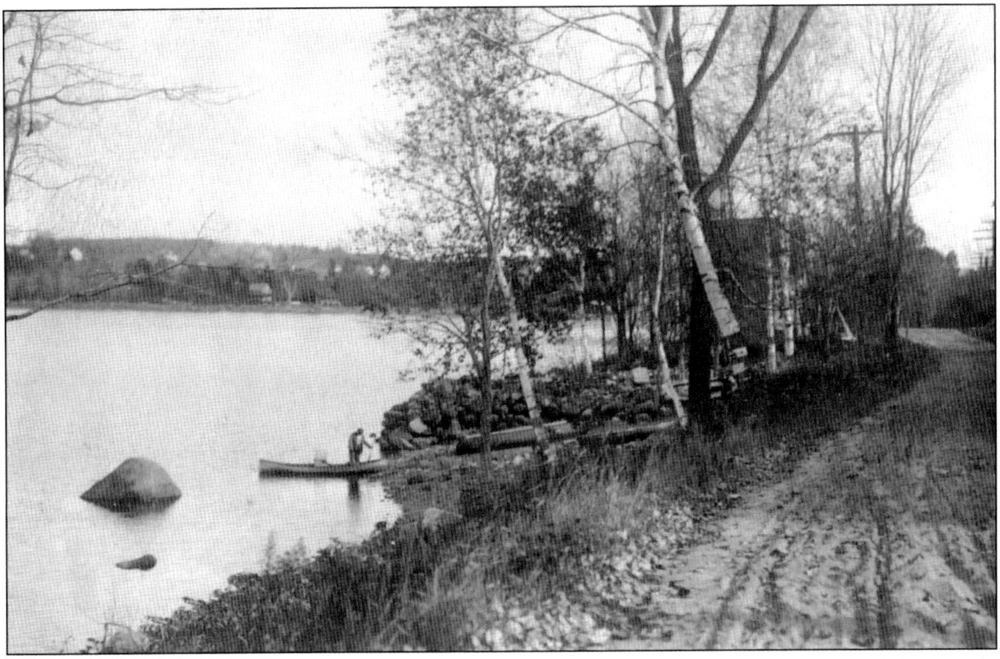

Fishing on Wilson Lake, c. 1900. This photograph shows a man in his canoe, fishing pole in hand, perhaps after a day of fishing out on Wilson Lake. In early spring, excellent fishing of salmon and togue was to be had here, followed by bass in summer and early fall. White and yellow perch, hornpout, and pickerel were also plentiful.

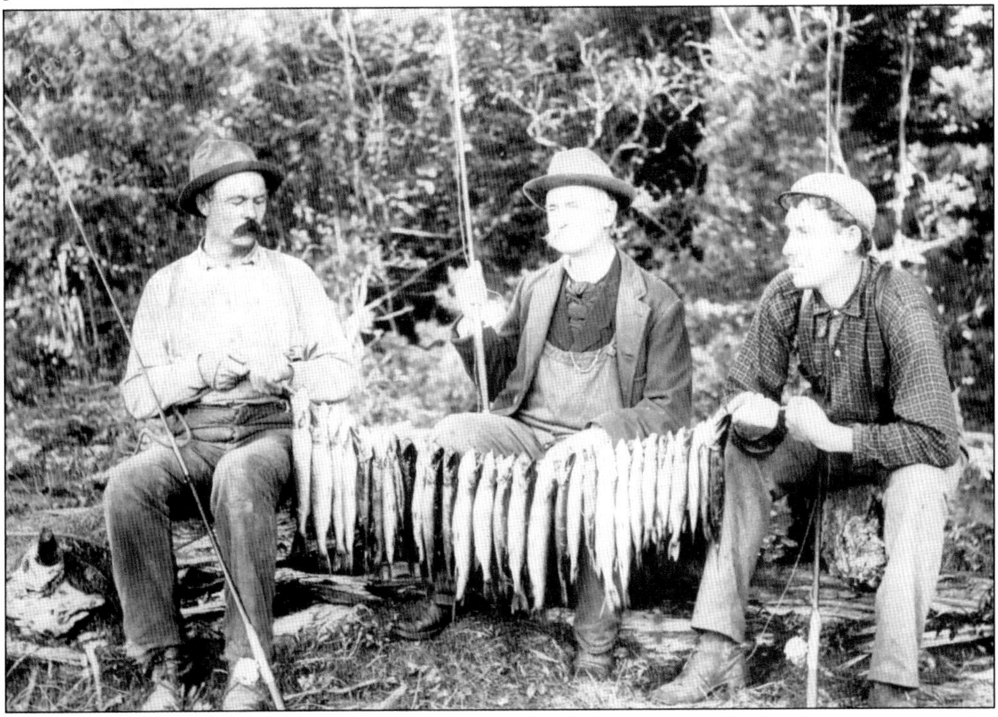

Fishing, c. 1900. The fish were abundant here, and a day's catch would often be quite impressive on Wilson Lake or Wilson Stream. These men hit the jackpot.

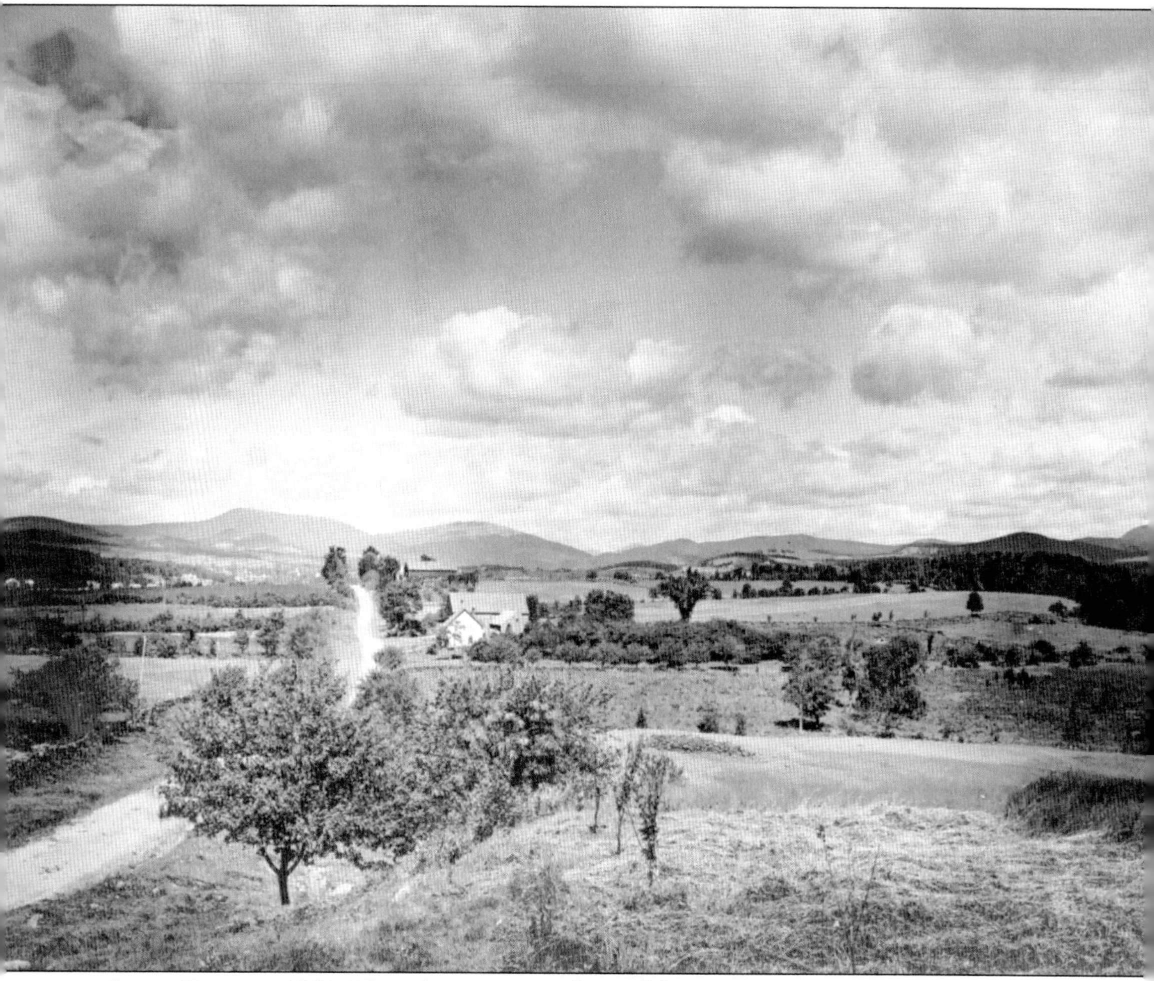

Local Farms, c. 1900. These farms were on the road from Bean's Corner in Dryden. Seen are the Packard and Farrington farms, open pastures and orchards, and mountains in the background.

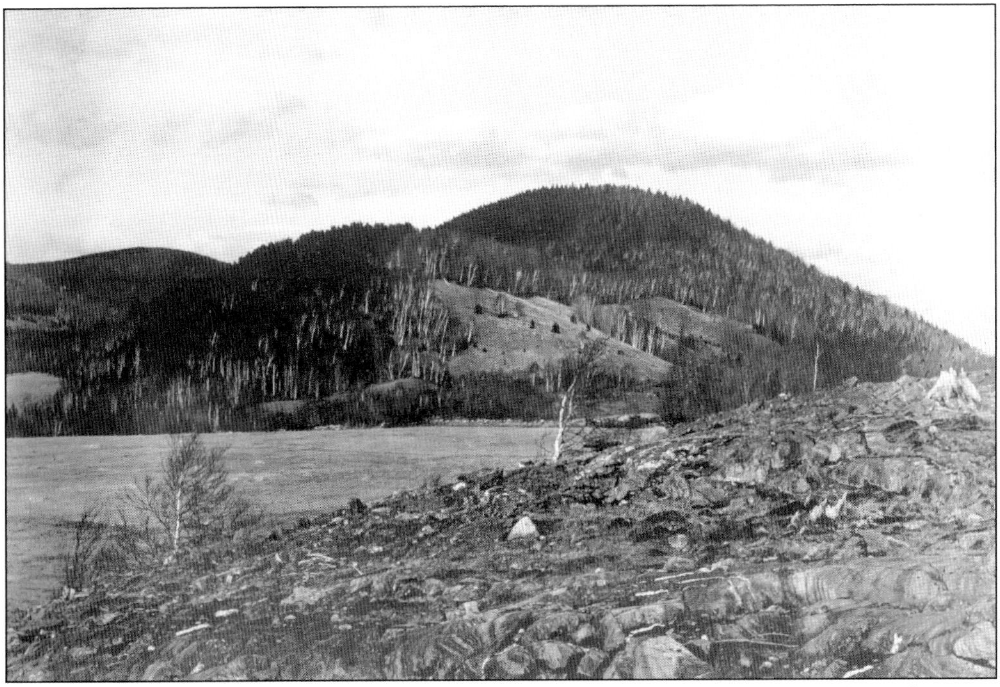

Agriculture, Early 1900s. Wilton remained a primarily agricultural town into the early 1900s. Oftentimes, hillsides were cleared of forest so that farmers could grow crops and farm animals could be pastured. In addition, many farms were built on hillsides because frost left the upper portions of land earlier in the spring and a killing frost would hit later in the fall.

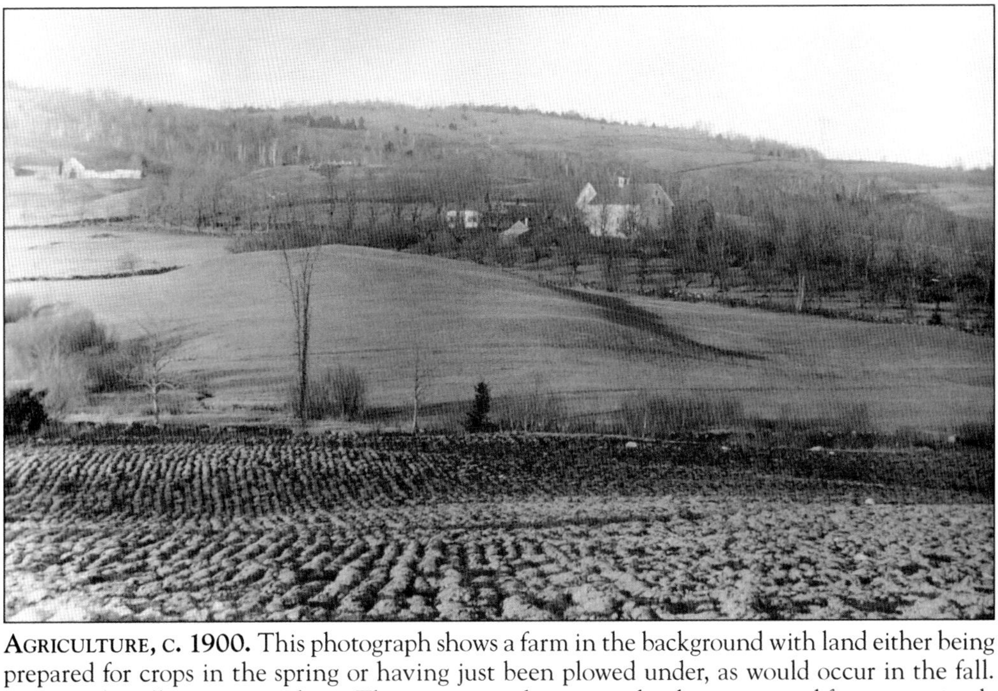

Agriculture, c. 1900. This photograph shows a farm in the background with land either being prepared for crops in the spring or having just been plowed under, as would occur in the fall. Many rock walls are present here. This was a popular way to divide pasture and fence in animals at the time. One can see orchard trees in the background as well.

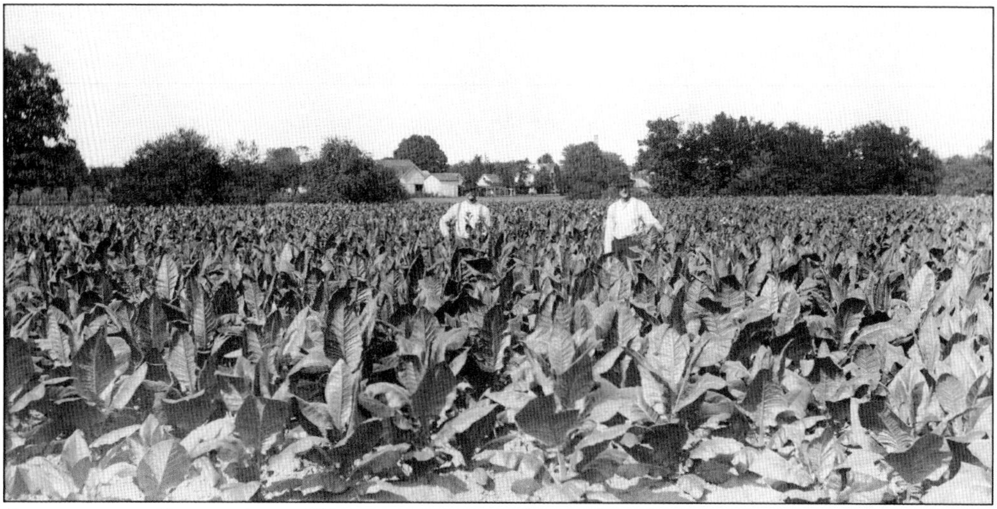

AGRICULTURE, EARLY 1900S. These men appear to be tending their crop. A great deal of land was still being cultivated at this time, with broad bands of interval land available. As of the census done in 1903, there were around 250 persons in Wilton, East Wilton, East Dixfield, and Wilton Notch who listed farming as their primary livelihood.

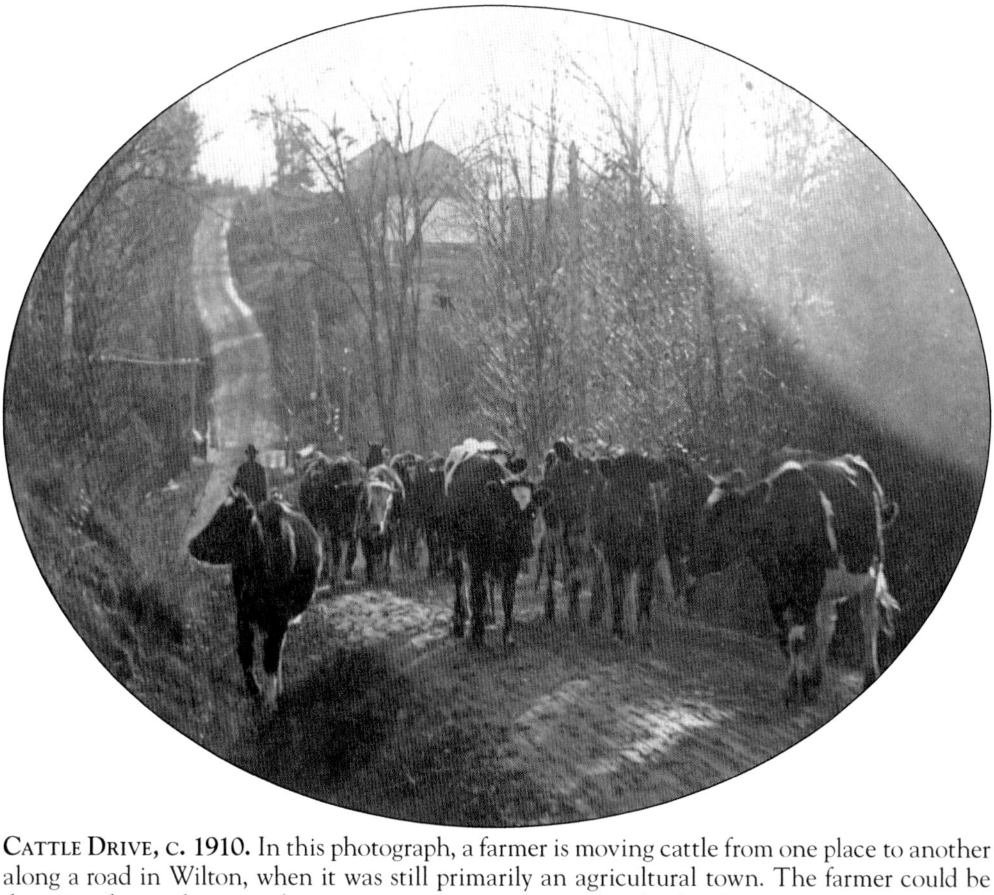

CATTLE DRIVE, C. 1910. In this photograph, a farmer is moving cattle from one place to another along a road in Wilton, when it was still primarily an agricultural town. The farmer could be directing the cattle to another pasture or even to the market for slaughter.

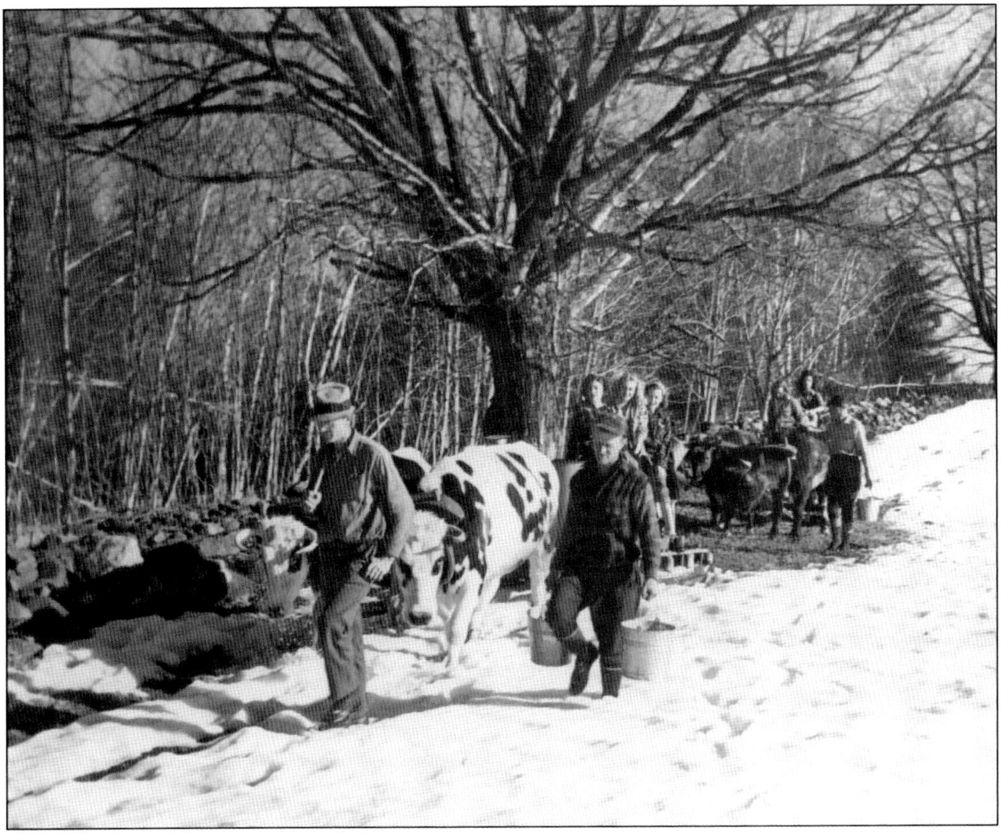

Freedom Rand Farm, 1940s. In the photograph, taken in late winter or early spring, sap is being gathered from the maple trees and very likely being carried to the sap house, where it will be boiled down and made into maple syrup. In this photograph are, from left to right, Freedom Rand, Hazen Mayo, Jean Trask, Peggy Watson, Joyce Rand, Omer Mace, Roberta Melendy, and Jane Franchetti. To the right is a label that would go on the maple syrup containers that were sold. (Both, courtesy of Joyce Orff.)

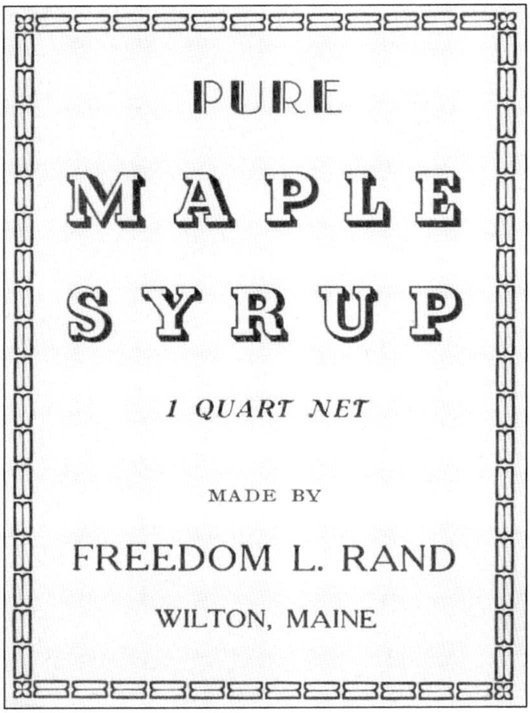

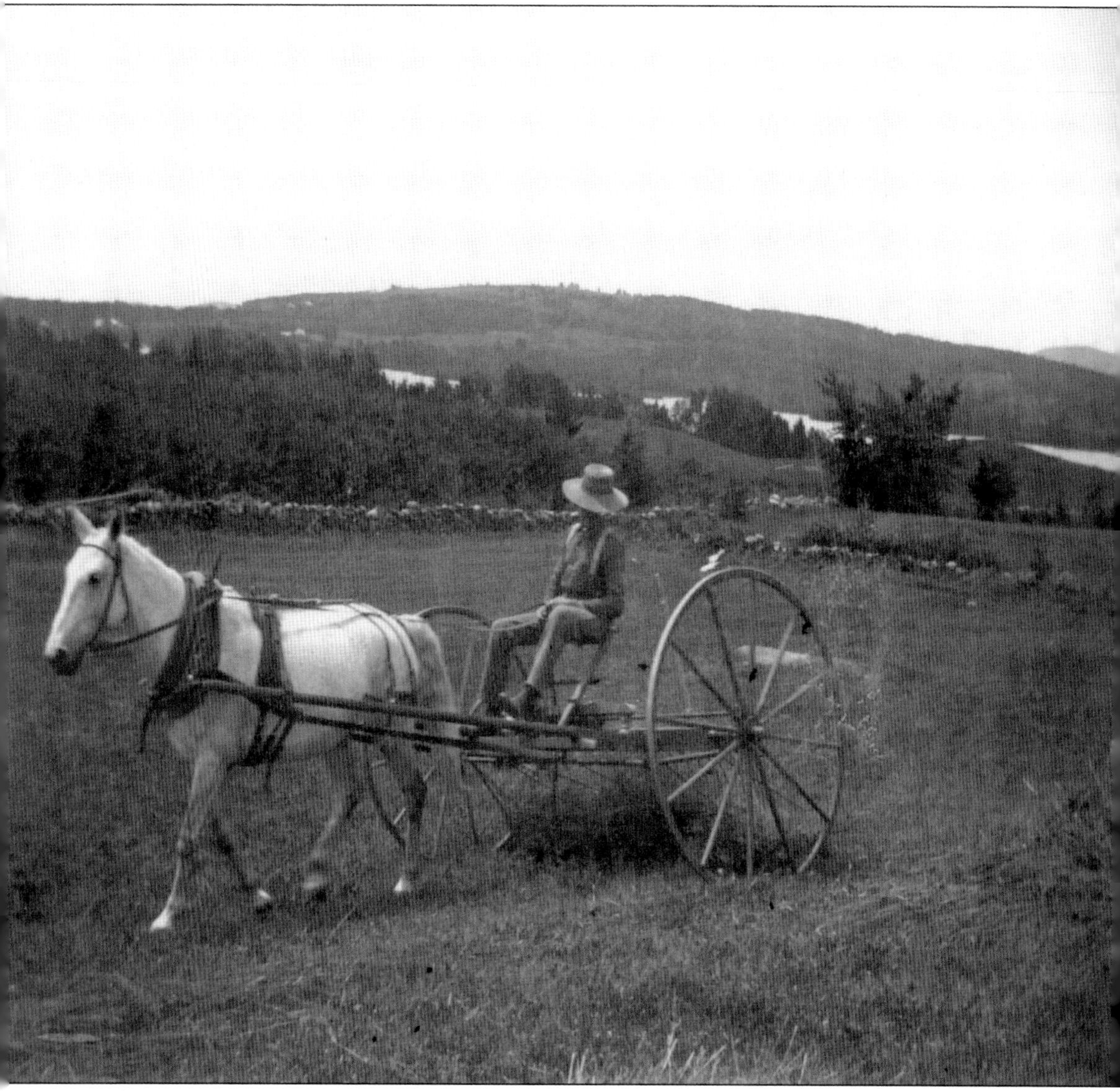

HORSE AND CART, LATE 1800S. This photograph was taken on the farmland that would later become the Wilson Lake Country Club. Here, the rock walls, horse, cart, and farmer assist in creating a bucolic image. This is a pastoral vista with Wilson Lake in the background.

Four

CELEBRATIONS

Over the years, the town of Wilton has had many things to celebrate. Whether it is for the dedication of a new flagpole, parades, holidays, centennial celebrations, or sesquicentennial celebrations, this town has known how to mark important occasions in its history. The events focused on in this chapter are a flagpole dedication and Memorial Day celebration by a group of schoolchildren in 1914, the Wilton centennial celebration in 1903, which was a five-day gala event, the Fourth of July celebration in 1919, and the equally extravagant sesquicentennial celebration held in 1953.

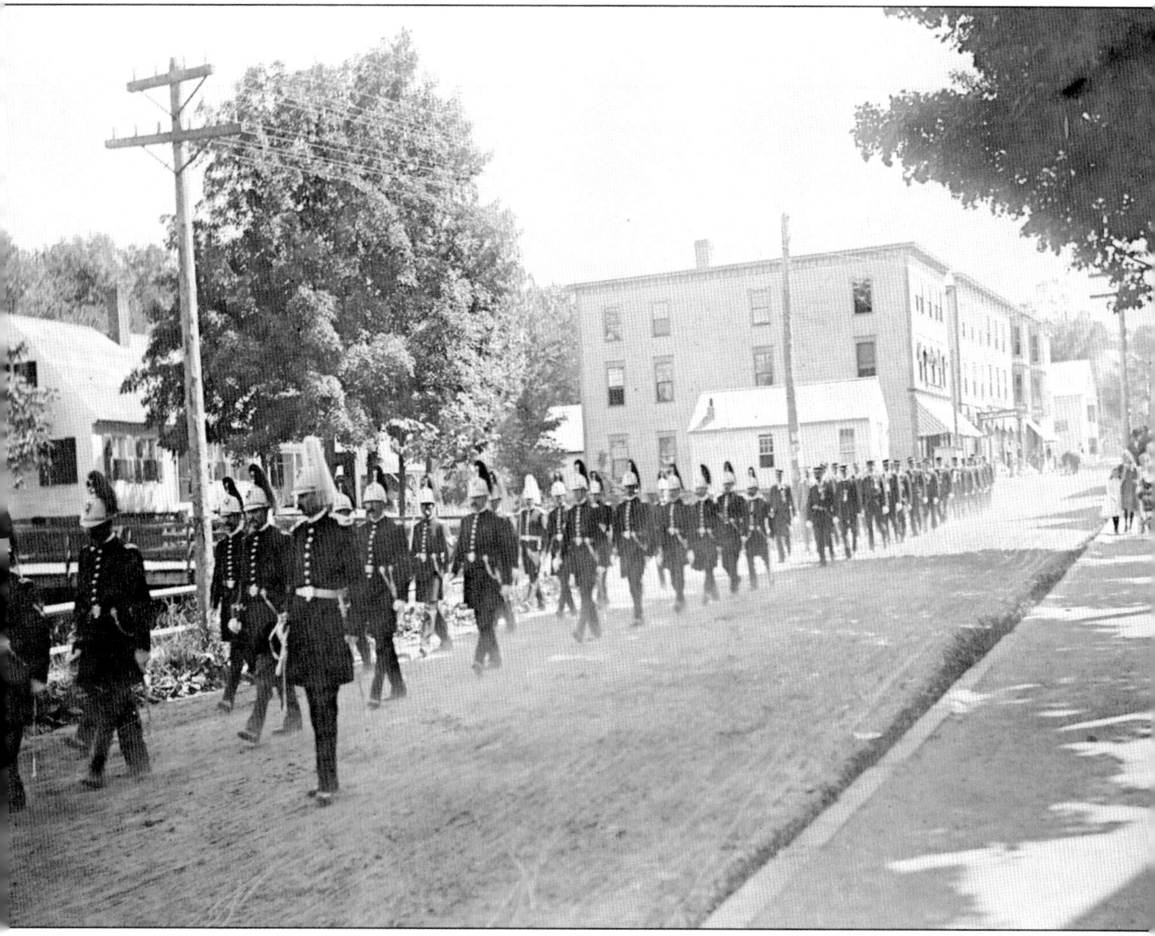

Parade, 1900–1910. This photograph is of a parade on Main Street prior to 1910. The occasion is unknown, but the men appear to be in military regalia. This may have been part of the centennial celebration.

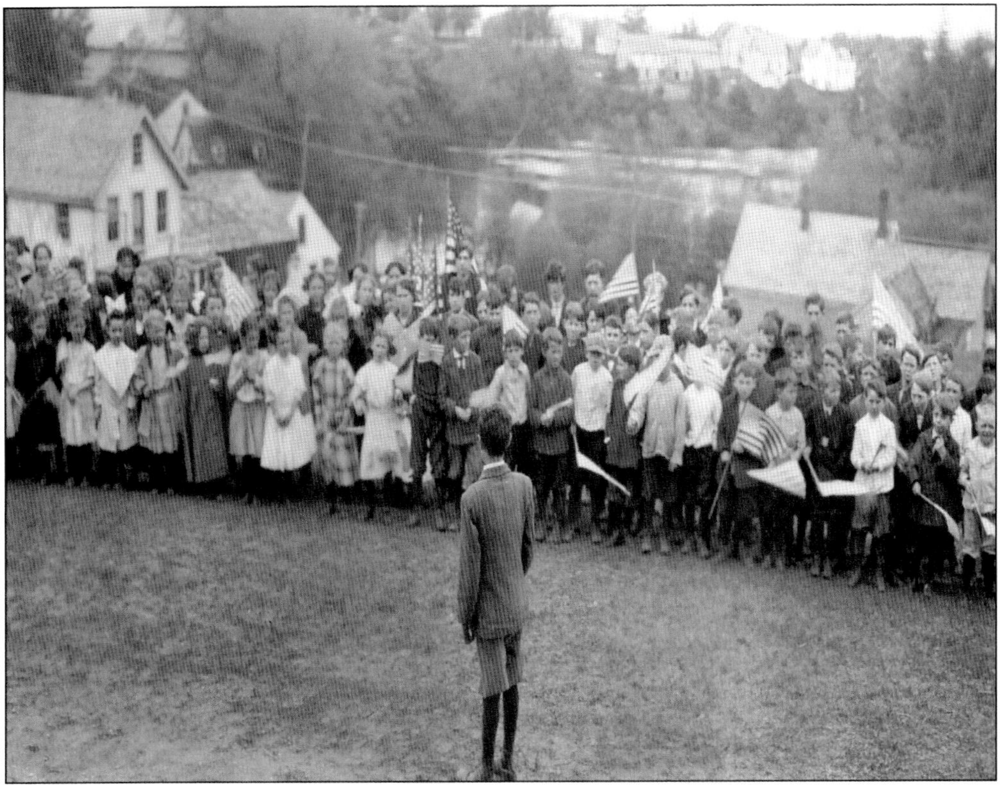

FLAGPOLE DEDICATION, 1914. Carl Miller is the boy shown speaking in the photograph above of the dedication of a new flagpole by the Wilton Grammar School. Information written on the back of the photograph suggested that it might also be a Memorial Day celebration.

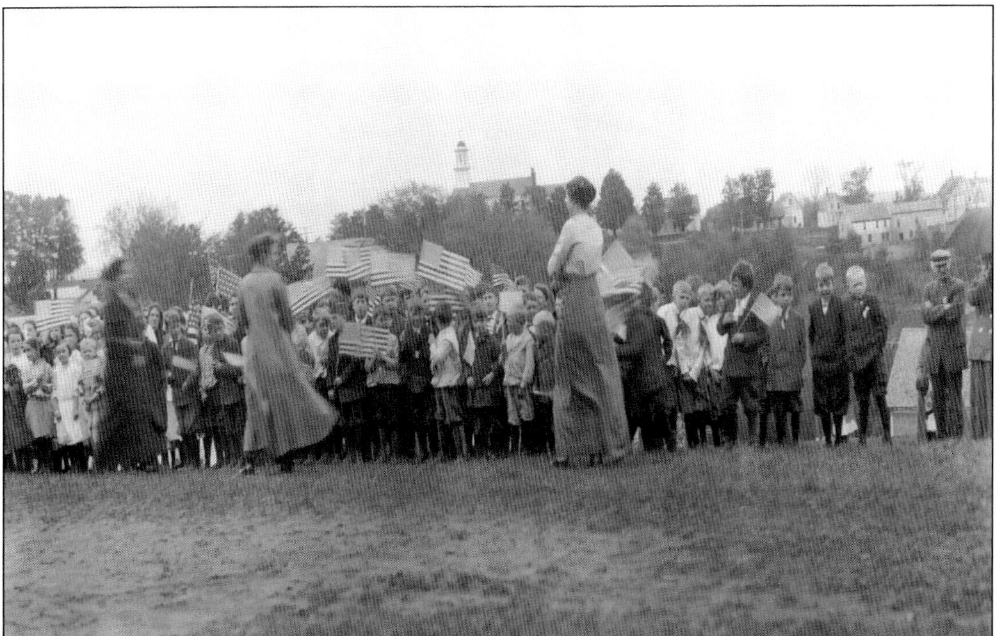

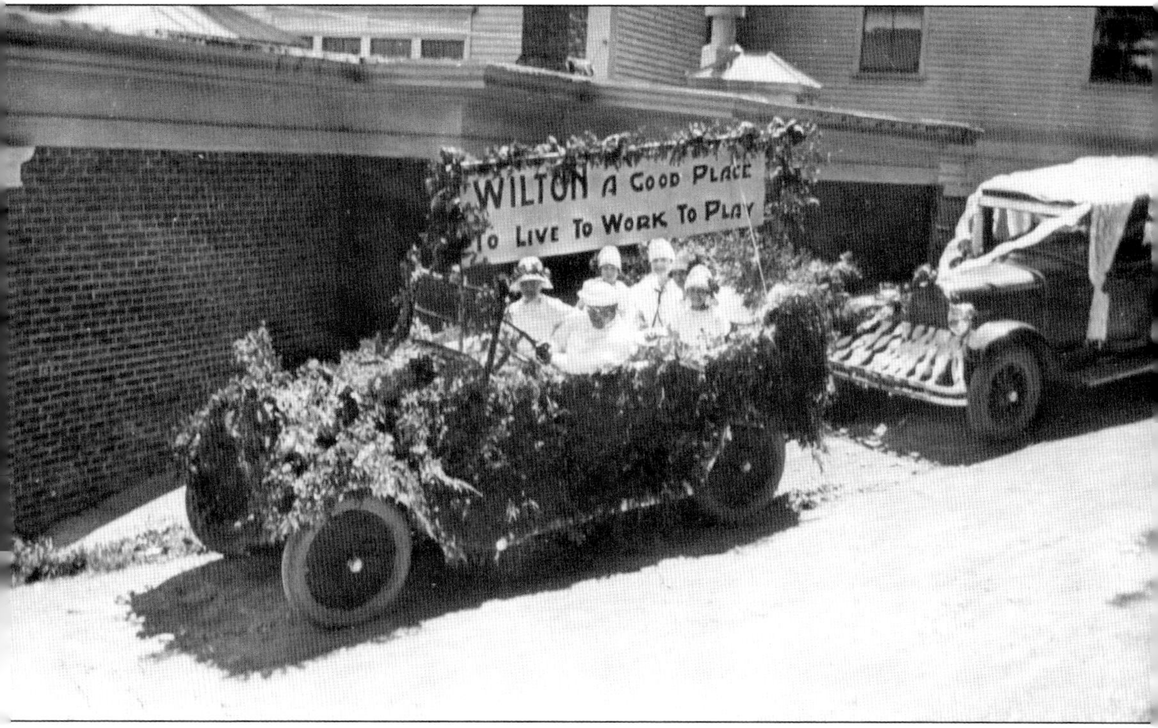

INDEPENDENCE DAY PARADE, JULY 4, 1919. On this day, a parade was held. This particular float worked the town motto into its theme, reflecting the sentiment of a town thriving in industry. Wilton was indeed "A Good Place to Live, to Work, to Play."

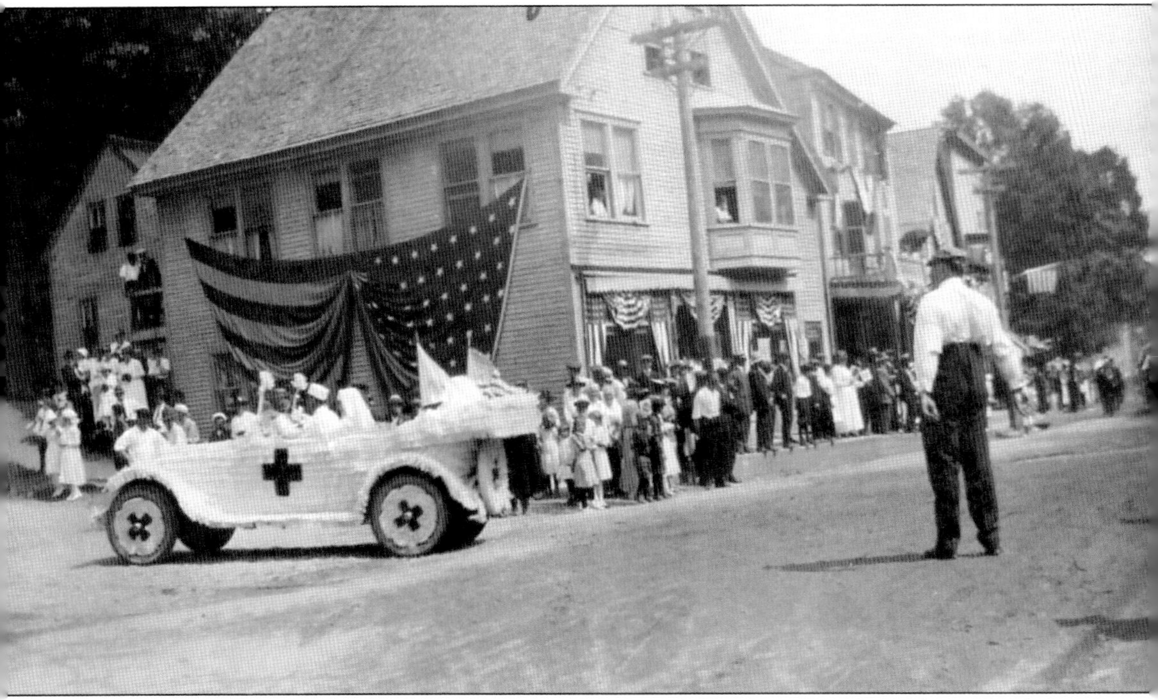

PRIZE-WINNING FLOAT, JULY 4, 1919. This was a float created by Mrs. E.H. Holman depicting the Red Cross. Mrs. Holman was awarded the first prize for her creativity and artistry. One can see many townspeople in attendance of this gala celebration. Some are even viewing the festivities from their upstairs windows.

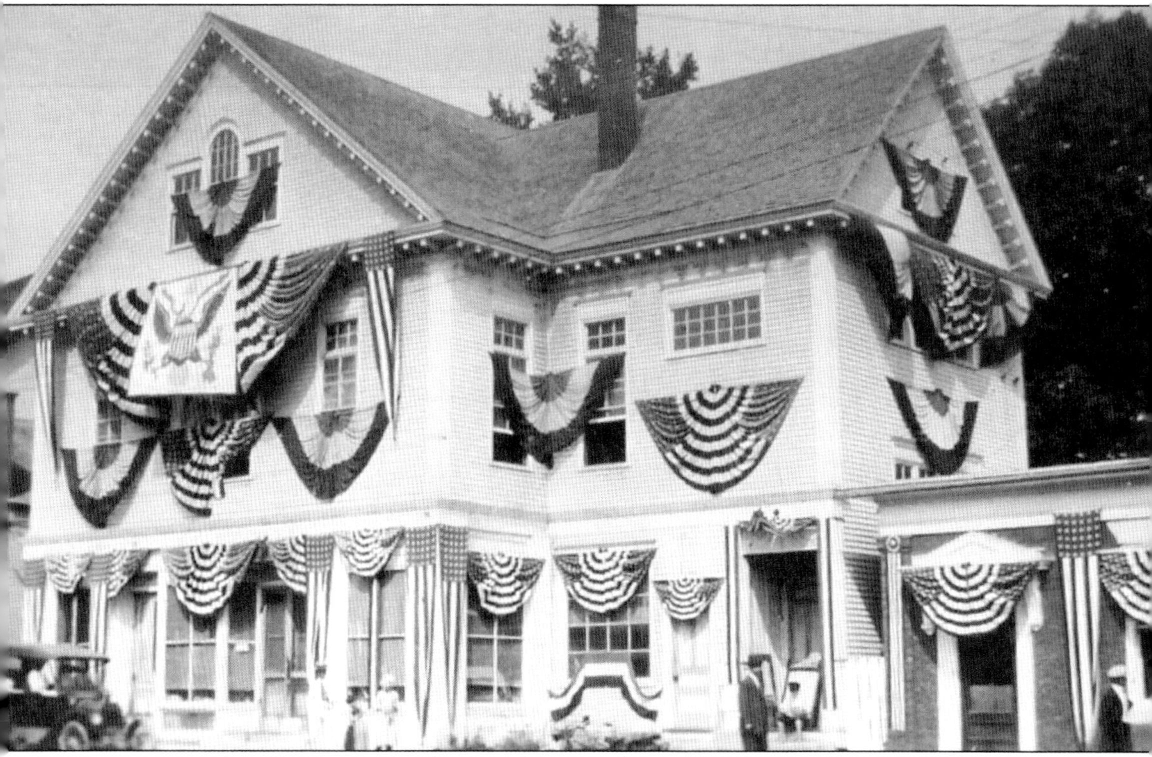

TOWN HALL, JULY 4, 1919. This is a photograph of the town hall all decked out in patriotic bunting for the celebration of the country's independence. At this time, J.E. Hiscock was the town clerk and treasurer. The selectmen were C.E. Miller, E. Merrill Bridges, and A.C. Adams.

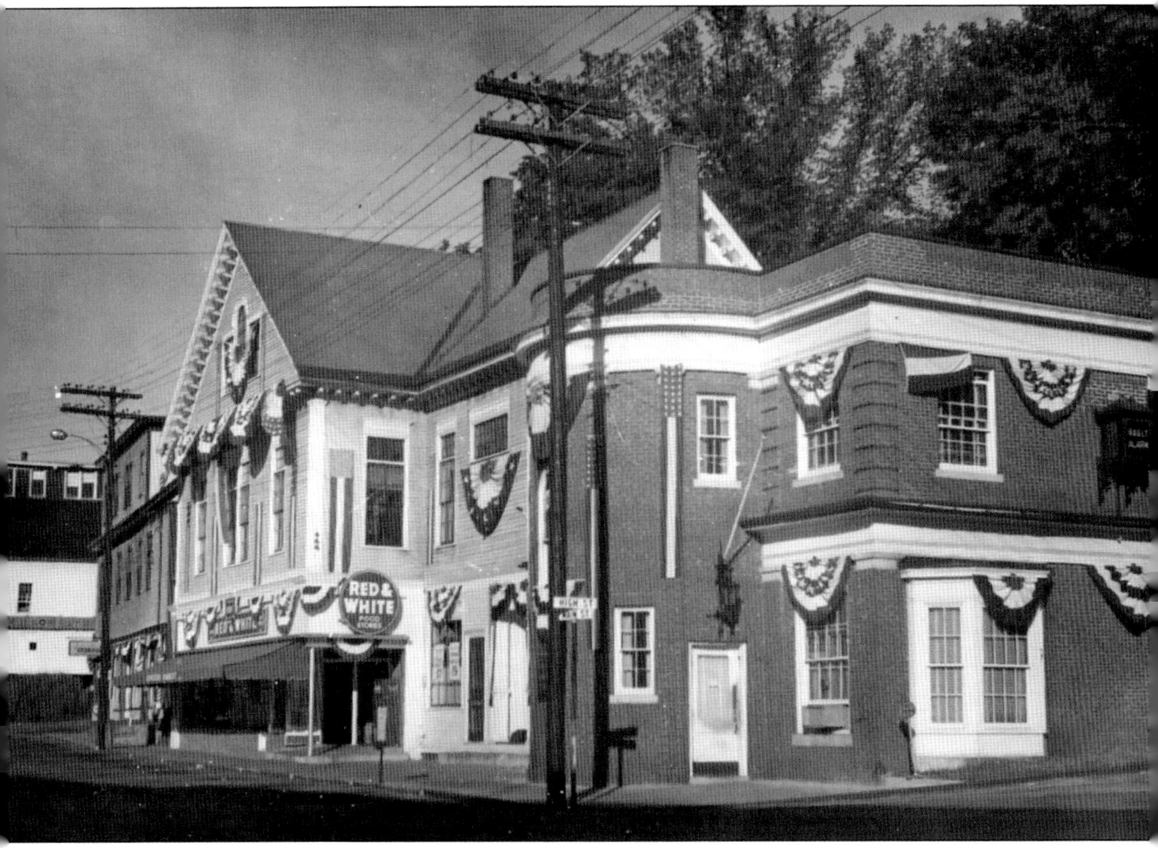

SESQUICENTENNIAL CELEBRATION, 1953. This photograph is of the intersection of Main and High Streets. Wilton Trust Company is on the corner. Fowler's Market, formerly the town hall, is in the center. The buildings are all decked out in patriotic bunting. In all, the sesquicentennial celebration lasted for five days in July 1953. Some of the events included the planting of the time capsule, a style show, a large parade (nearly two miles in length), fireworks, contests, and many other events. A sesquicentennial booklet was also published with pictures, articles, and historical sketches.

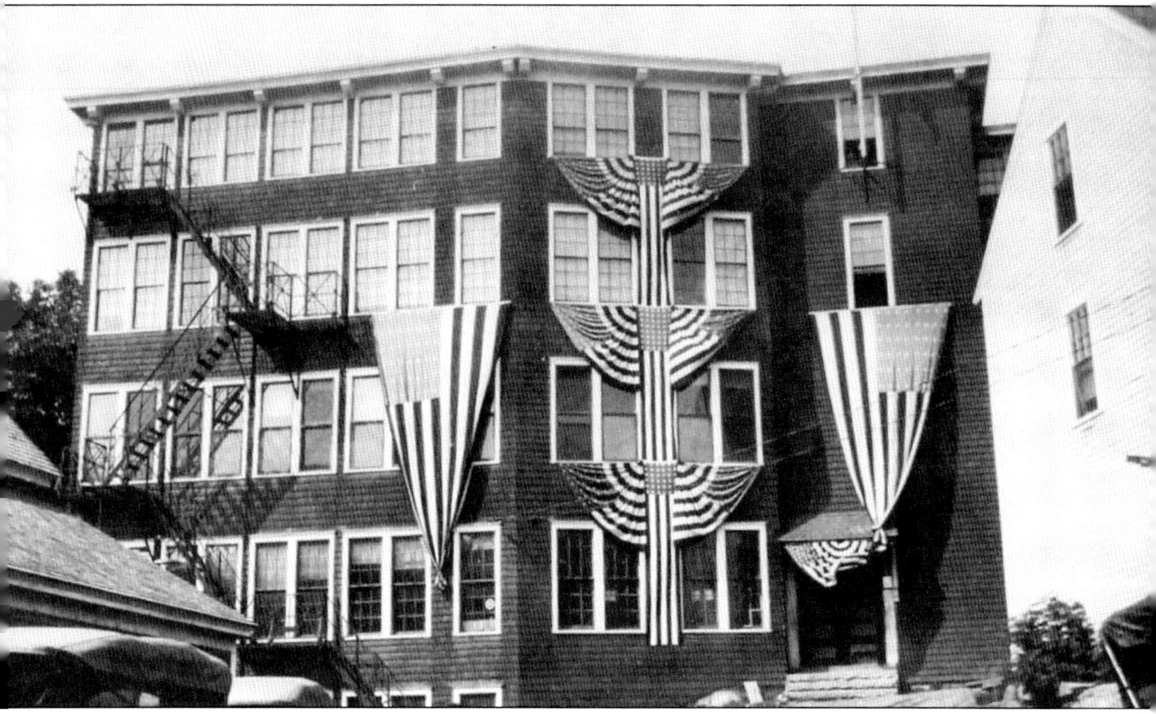

G.H. Bass & Co., July 4, 1919. What was known as Building No. 1 is shown here decorated with flags and bunting, adding to the spirit of this Independence Day celebration.

Five

Fires, Floods, and Storms

Every town has its share of naturally occurring events and disasters; Wilton is no different. Whether it was a snowstorm, flood, or raging fire, the local inhabitants endured through it. In the case of fires, oftentimes, people had to rebuild what was destroyed. Natural disasters like floods also wreak havoc on a small town, eroding infrastructure and damaging or destroying businesses and homes. Snowstorms, while typically just a temporary nuisance, can also cause great damage, as when snow accumulates after a snowy winter and causes structures to collapse. The following chapter presents events of note in Wilton's history.

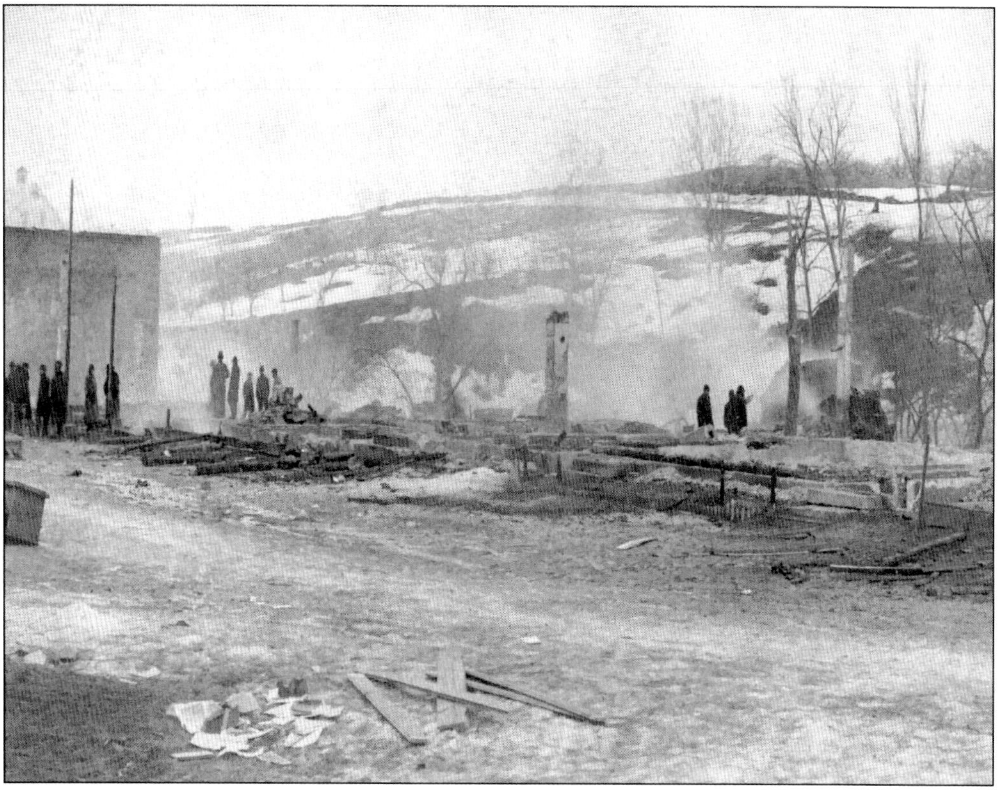

FIRE OF APRIL 2, 1893. This fire destroyed much of the south side of Main Street in Wilton. Flames were first seen at Bill Leavitt's Livery Stable when town folk were returning from church. The church bell rang to alert townspeople that there was a fire. There was not an organized fire department at the time. Soon, several men were seen carrying water buckets and ladders. The men ended up having to break down the doors to save the horses. The building containing hay and grain, however, could not be saved. The men tried to keep the fire from spreading to the opposite side of the street, but they were unable to halt it. Many of the businesses lost ended up being rebuilt.

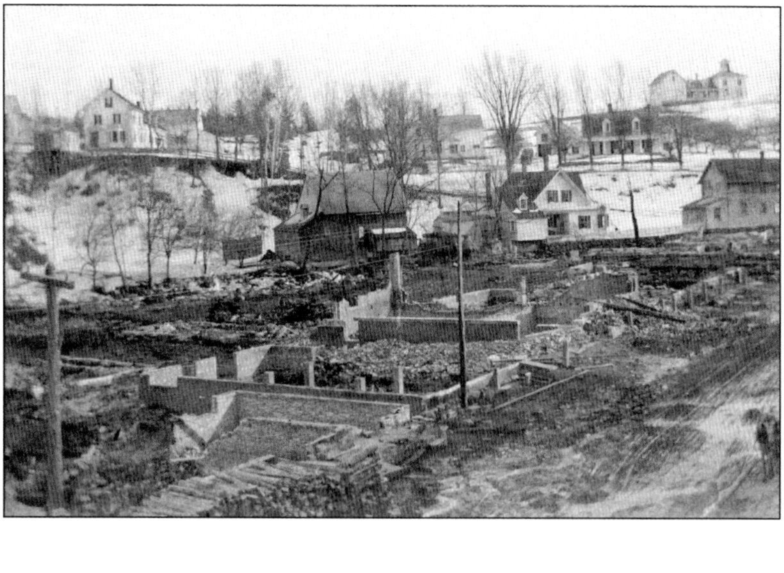

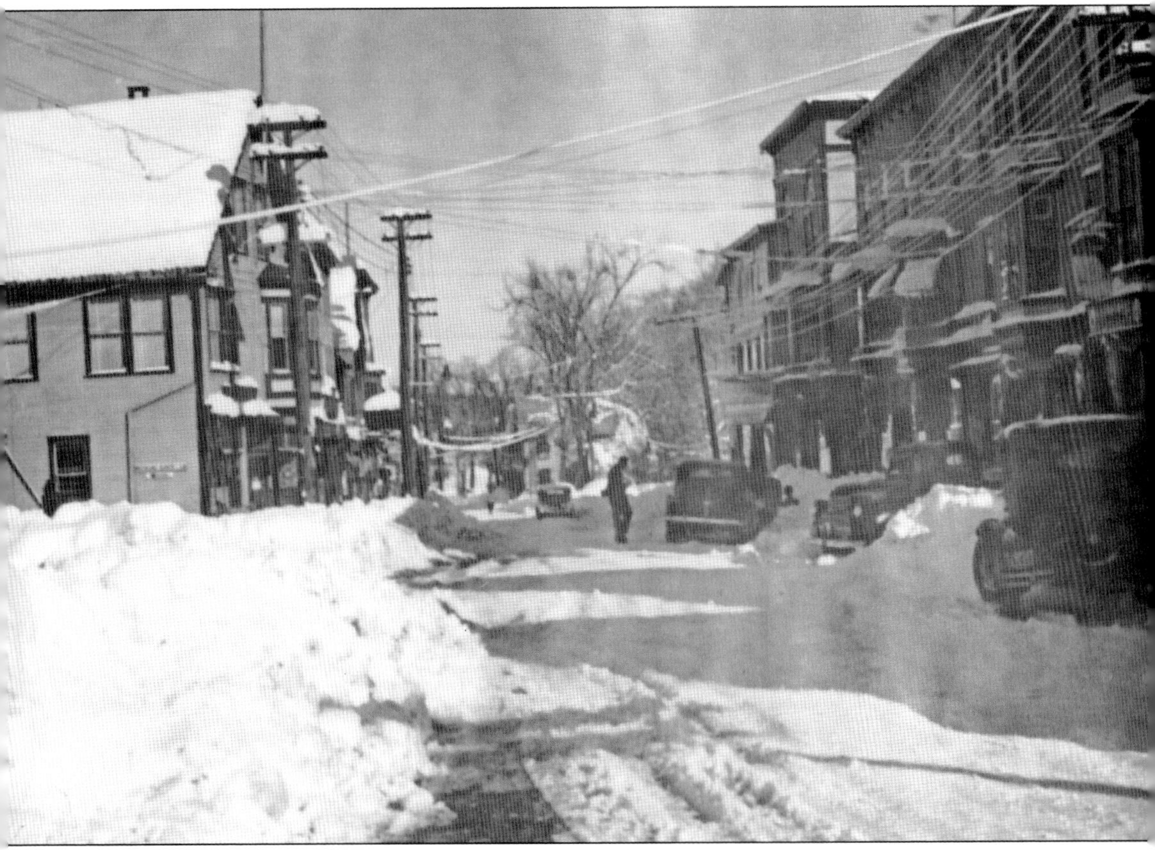

MAY SNOWSTORM, 1945. This photograph was taken of Main Street looking west in 1945 after a sizable snowstorm hit the town in May of that year. There were already leaves on the trees when the storm dismayed townsfolk, who believed winter was over. The photograph really shows the magnitude of the May 11th storm. There was a lot of heavy, wet snow on the wires and on the sides of the road. It looks like Main Street lost some parking spaces in the wake of this storm.

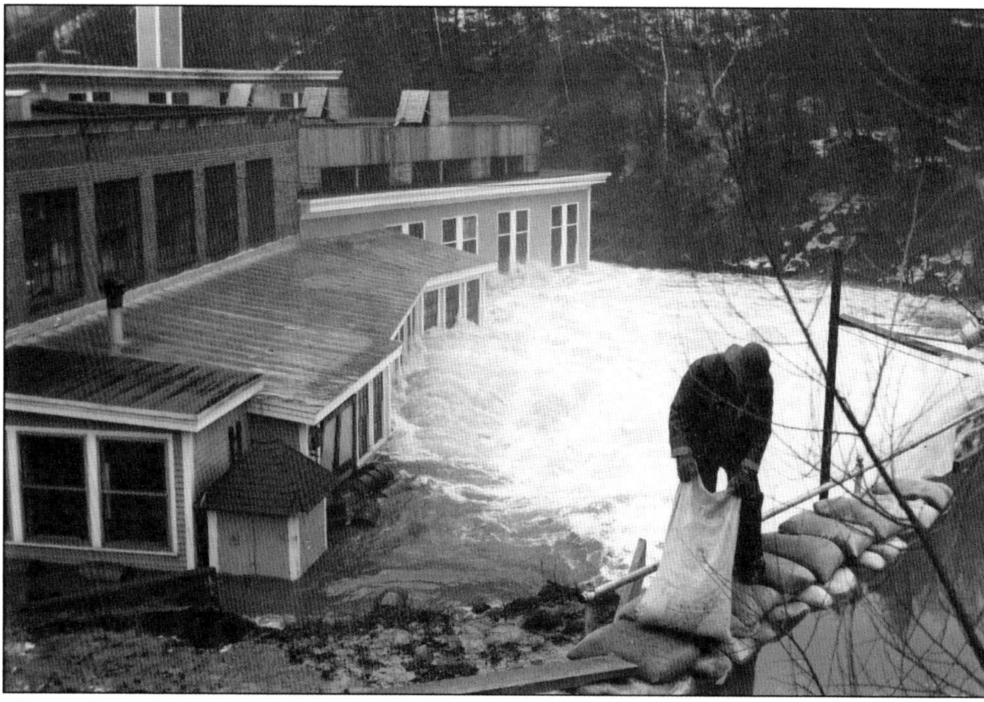

WILSON LAKE DAM, FLOOD OF MARCH 1953. This photograph is of the dam at the former Wilton Woolen Company in Dryden. This man appears to be placing sandbags along the dam to hold back the water. As one can see, however, the water has already reached the building. This photograph was taken by Harold Karkos.

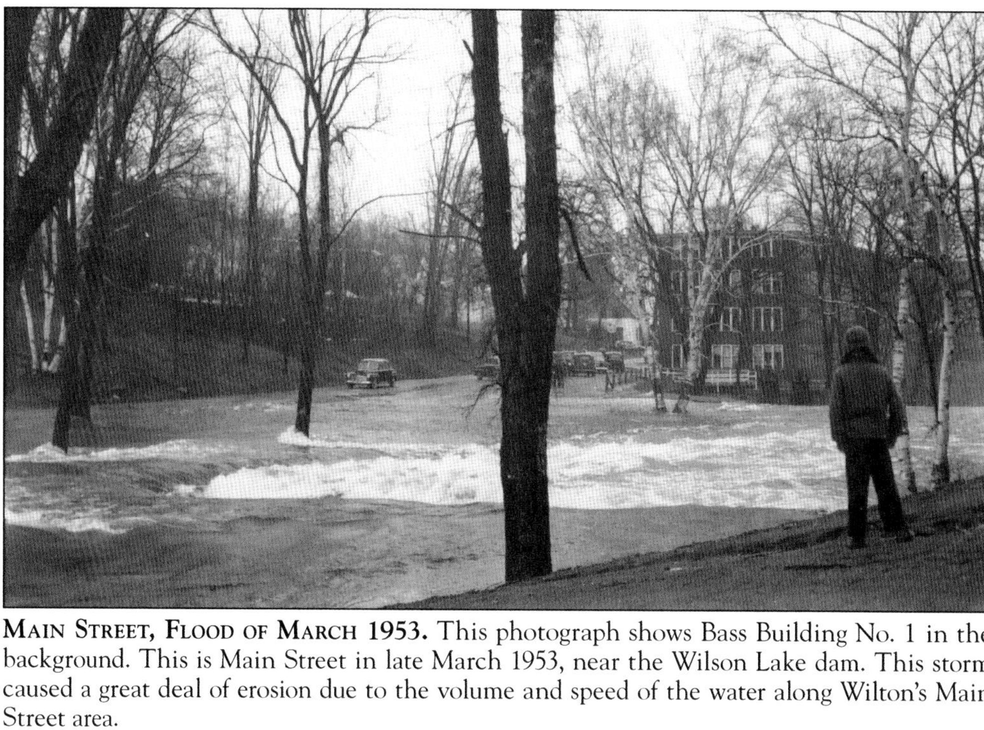

MAIN STREET, FLOOD OF MARCH 1953. This photograph shows Bass Building No. 1 in the background. This is Main Street in late March 1953, near the Wilson Lake dam. This storm caused a great deal of erosion due to the volume and speed of the water along Wilton's Main Street area.

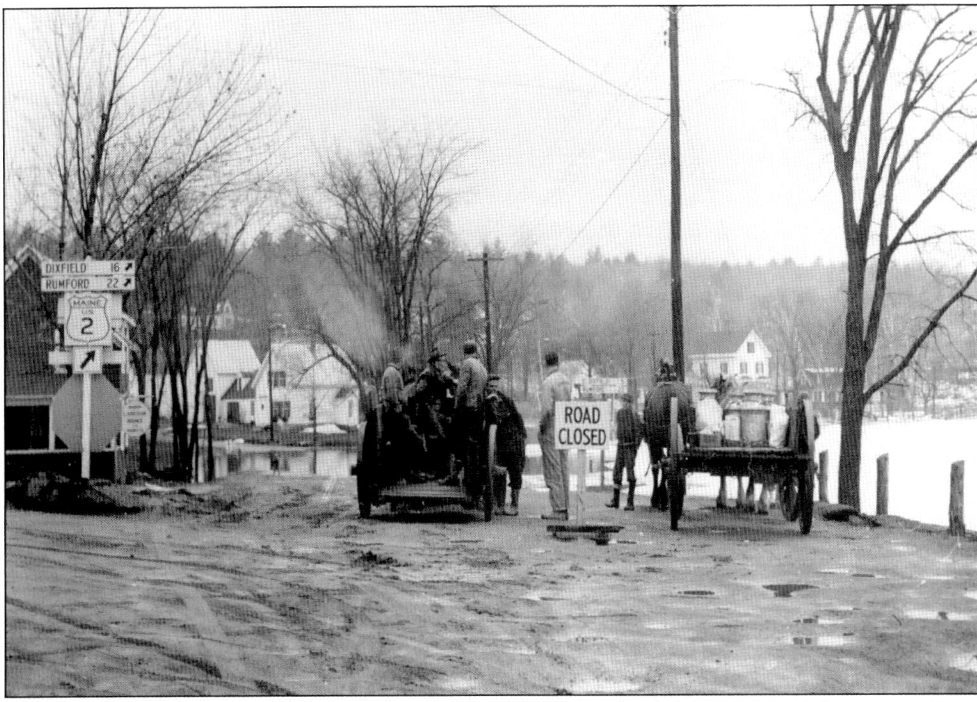

ROUTE 2, FLOOD OF MARCH 1953. This photograph of the flood shows Route 2 (now considered "Old Route 2" after a new road was constructed) flooded and closed. This photograph was taken by Harold Karkos.

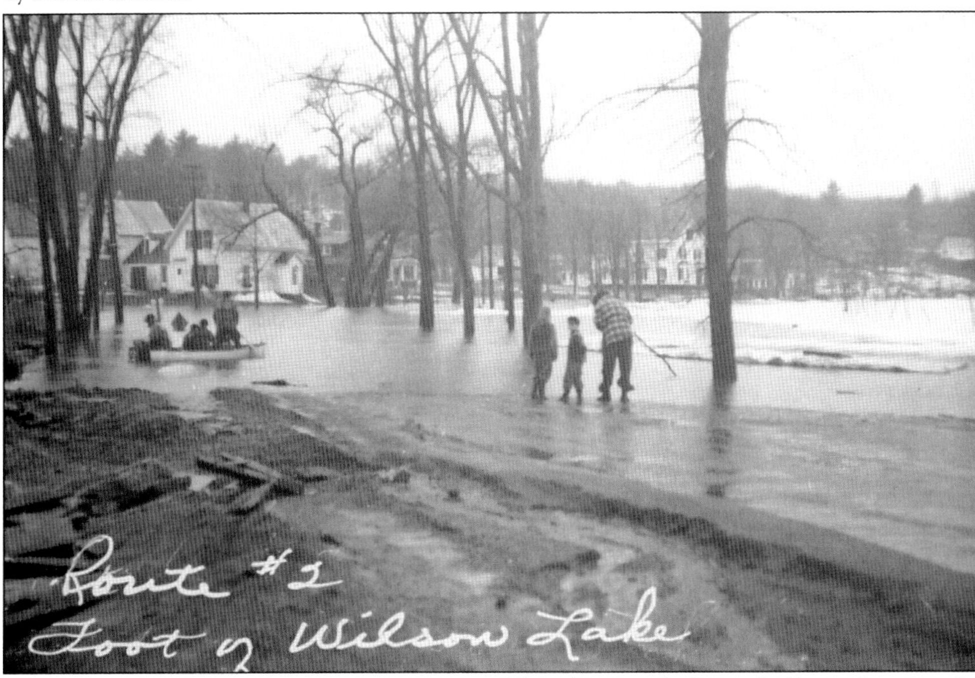

FOOT OF WILSON LAKE, FLOOD OF MARCH 1953. This photograph shows the Route 2 sign at the foot of Wilson Lake with all of its post in the water. One can also see people in their boats and spectators checking out the floodwaters.

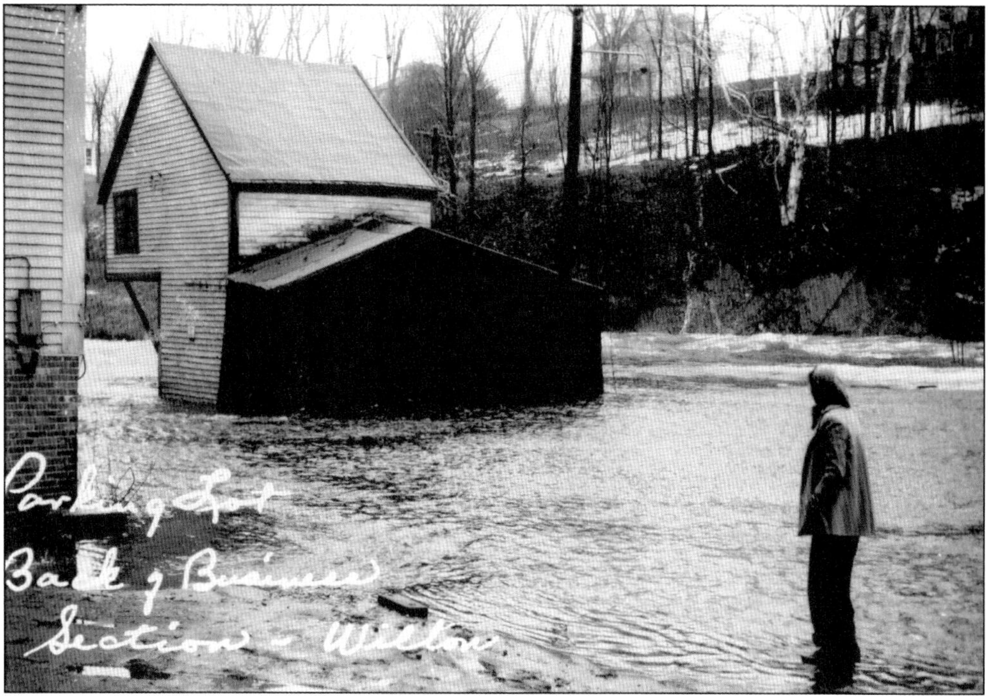

FLOOD OF MARCH 1953. The business section of downtown Wilton was flooded. This woman is checking out the damage and the flooded parking lot behind the business section.

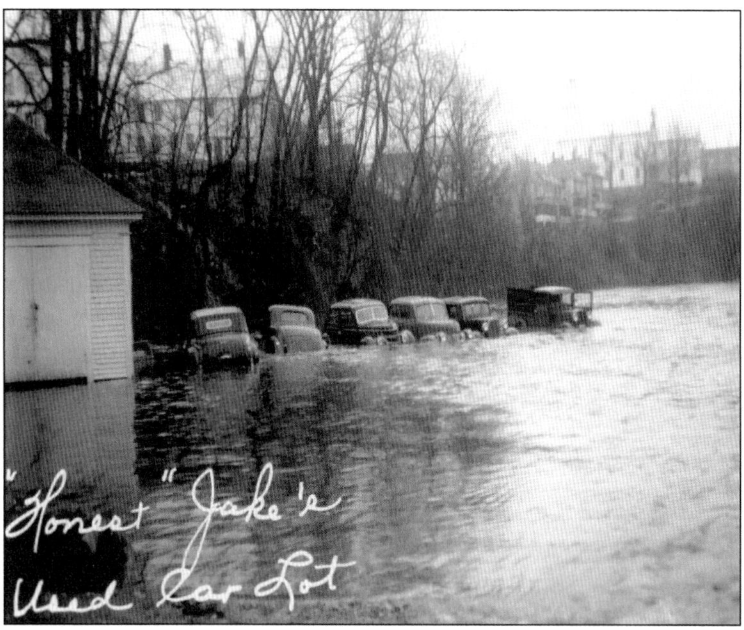

USED CAR LOT, FLOOD OF MARCH 1953. In this photograph, one can see a number of cars immersed in water, which is over their wheel wells in many cases. This photograph of "Honest" Jake's Used Car Lot on lower Main Street is just one instance of damage to a local business. A great deal of property was either damaged or completely destroyed in this flood.

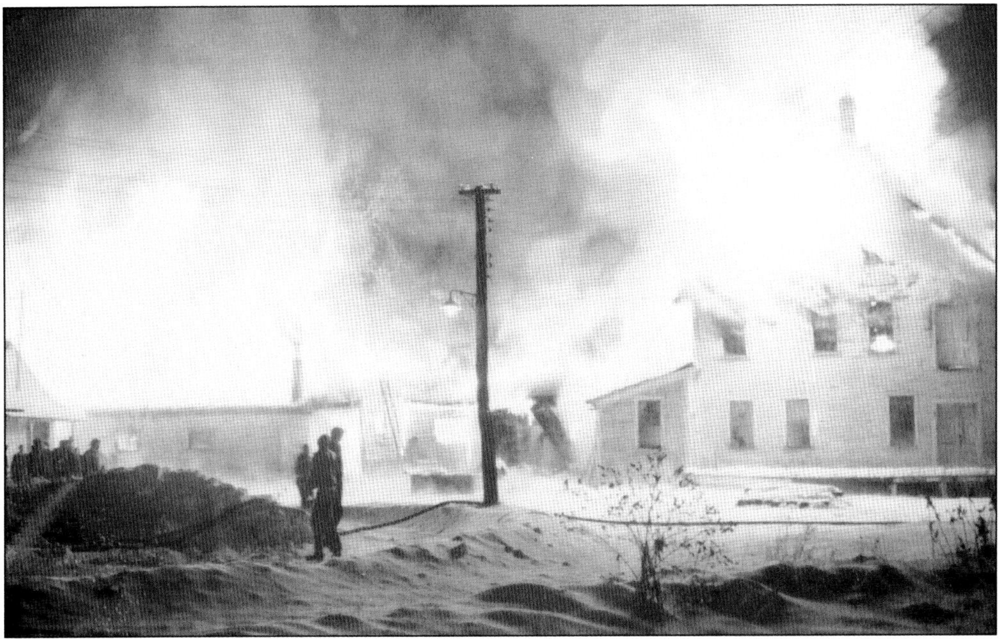

THOMAS & MARBLE CANNERY FIRE, 1960. This cannery, which was also known as Marble's Corn Cannery, burned and was destroyed on Christmas Eve, 1960. This business had been in town for decades. At another time, it was called Marble & Dingley Canned Goods.

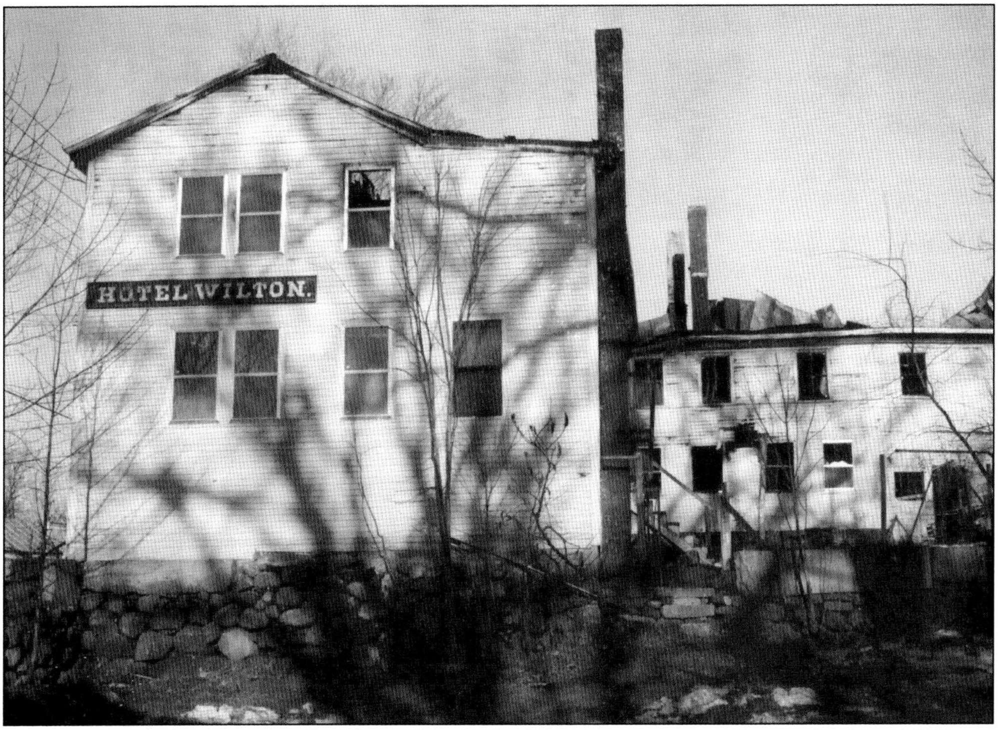

HOTEL WILTON FIRE, 1961. In November 1961, there was a massive fire at the Hotel Wilton, formerly Miller's Hotel. This is a photograph of the shell of the hotel, which was almost a complete loss after the November 21st fire.

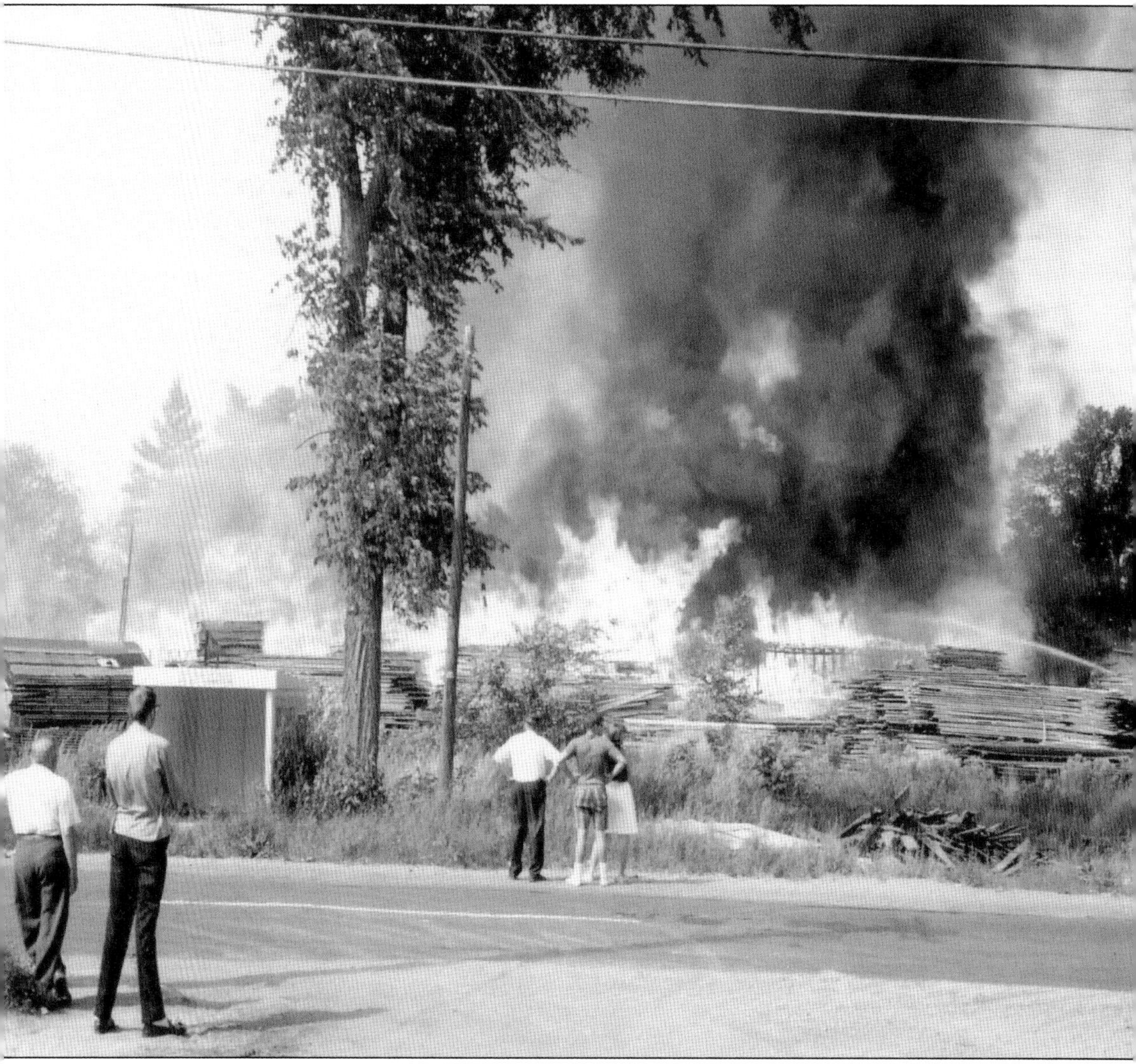

WILTON LUMBER COMPANY FIRE, C. 1965. This photograph of the Wilton Lumber Company fire was taken at the height of the blaze, at approximately 3:30 p.m. This photograph was made by Wilton Printed Products. The lumberyard was across from the end of Union Street in Dryden.

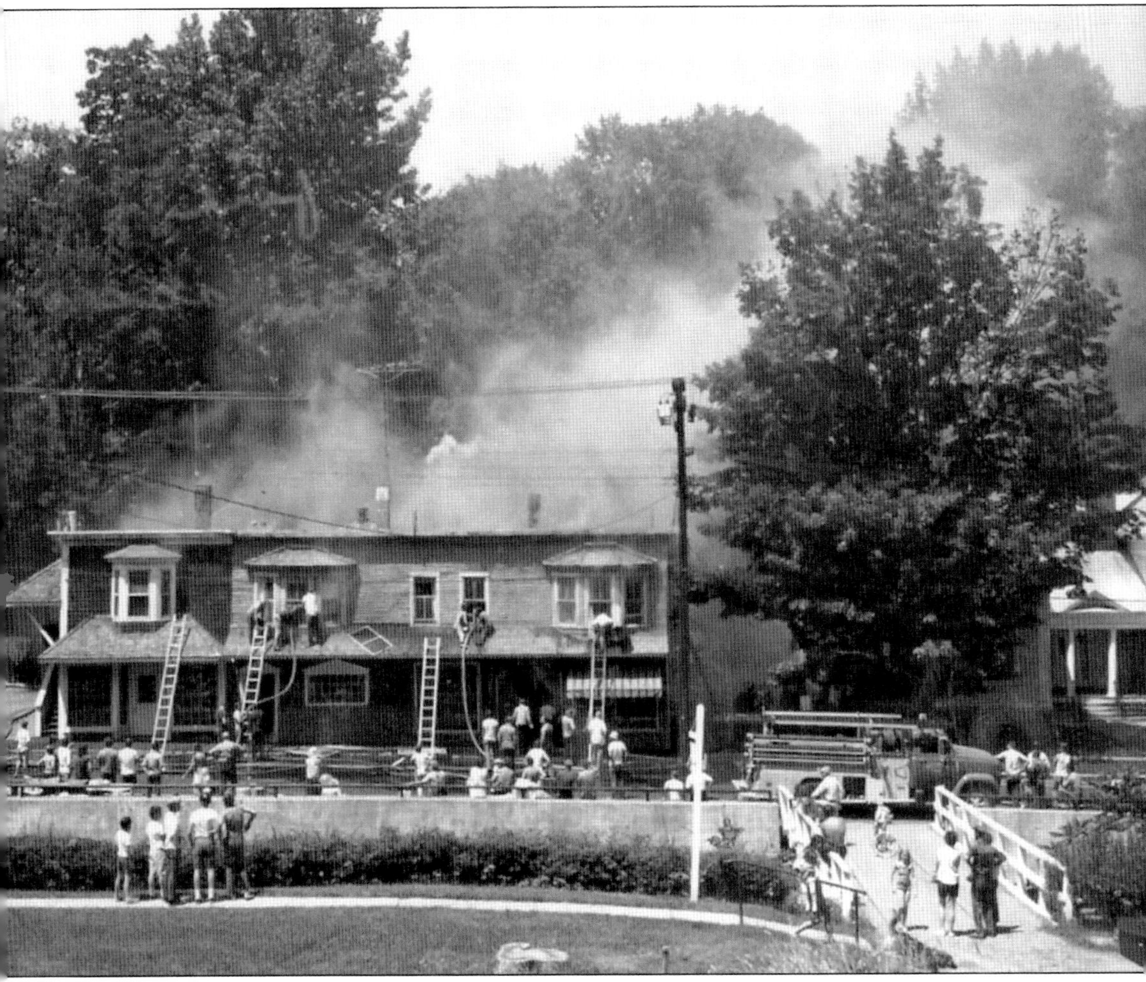

MAIN STREET FIRE, 1971. After this fire, only a shell remained of Dr. Robert Stoddard's wood-framed, two-story block, which housed his optometry office. According to an article in the July 10, 1971, *Lewiston Daily Sun*, the blaze started in Maillet's Jewelry Store. This shop was destroyed, as was Pam's Beauty Salon, on the ground floor, and two apartments on the second floor. Also ruined was the apartment of Louis and Tina Franchetti, over the antique shop. The two buildings were connected in front and by a connecting roof.

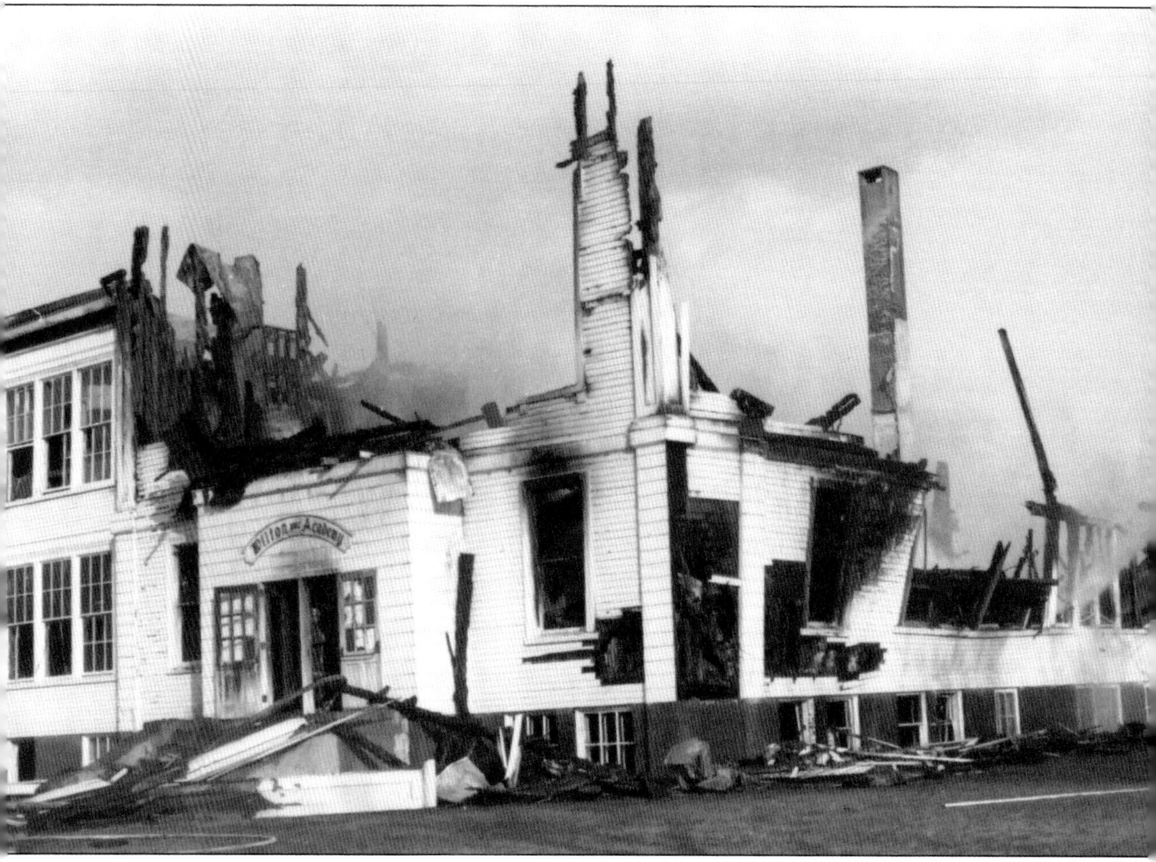

WILTON ACADEMY FIRE, MAY 10, 1980. Wilton Academy had at one time been called the Old Meeting House. In 1866–1867, it had been converted into a school. It was also used for the services of three churches until about 1930. Fire departments from Wilton and the neighboring towns of Jay, Farmington, East Wilton, and East Dixfield fought the fire, with over 114 firemen battling the blaze. They pumped over 400,000 gallons of water before the fire was extinguished that Saturday evening, according to the Monday, May 12, 1980, edition of the *Lewiston Daily Sun*. This photograph was taken by Carrol H. Merchant.

Six

Camp Kineowatha

Camp Kineowatha was a girls' camp established in 1912 on the shores on Wilson Lake. It was established by Elisabeth Bass and Irving G. McColl. This camp strived to offer the campers a variety of activities during the weeks from July 1 to September 1, when they attended camp. The youngest campers were eight or nine years old, and the oldest were in their late teens. The girls who attended camp here came from families of wealth and refinement. The camp offered a number of activities and opportunities throughout the summer. The girls enjoyed camping, hiking, swimming, boating, tennis, horseback riding, arts and crafts, games, charades, storytelling, dancing, pageants, costume parties, and assorted other activities.

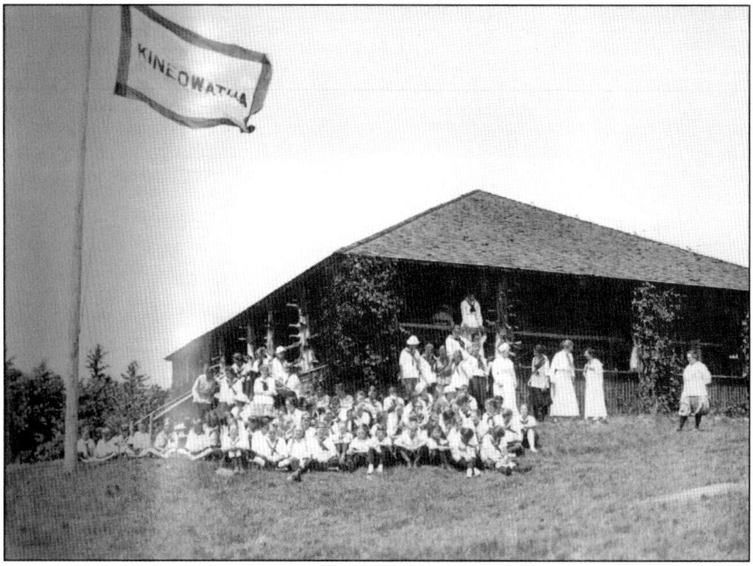

MAIN BUNGALOW, C. 1915. This is an impromptu photograph showing the Main Bungalow, which was used as headquarters and was the center of camp life at Camp Kineowatha. Many assemblies and other social functions were held here.

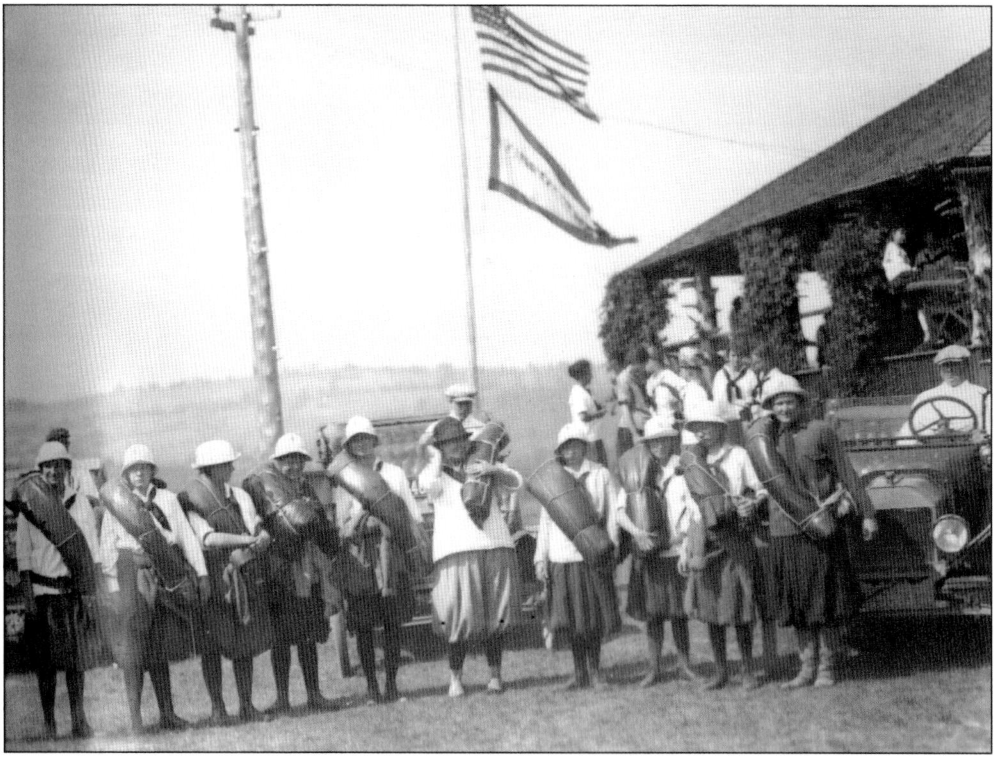

TENTING AND HIKING, C. 1915. The girls in this photograph are getting ready to go to Mount Blue. They would travel by automobile to the foot of the mountain and then climb up and spend the night at the top.

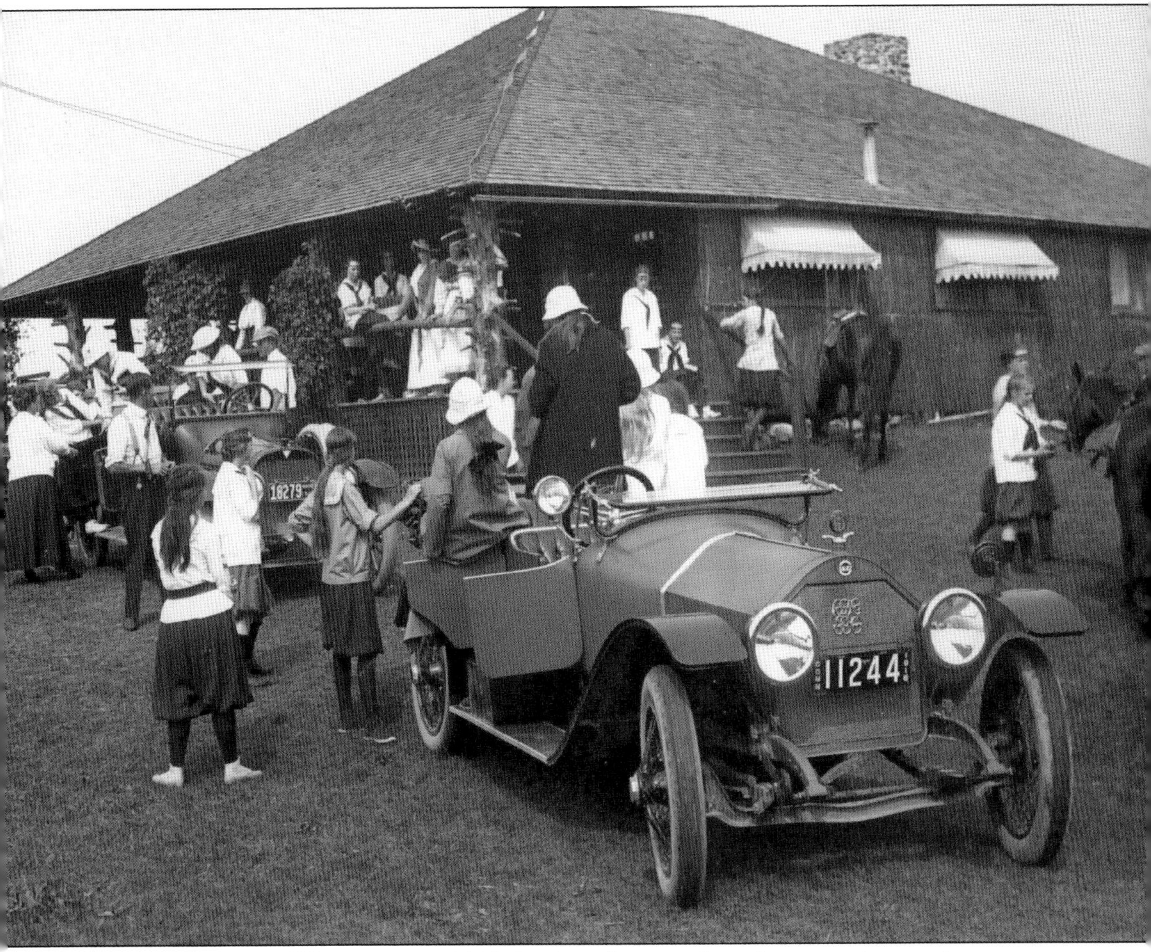

CAMPING ON MOUNT WASHINGTON, 1915. In this photograph, girls are getting ready to go to Mount Washington. Two councilors and 10 girls went to this camp via automobile every week. After a week, another group would go, and so on. This was one of many enriching trips offered to the girls attending Camp Kineowatha. .

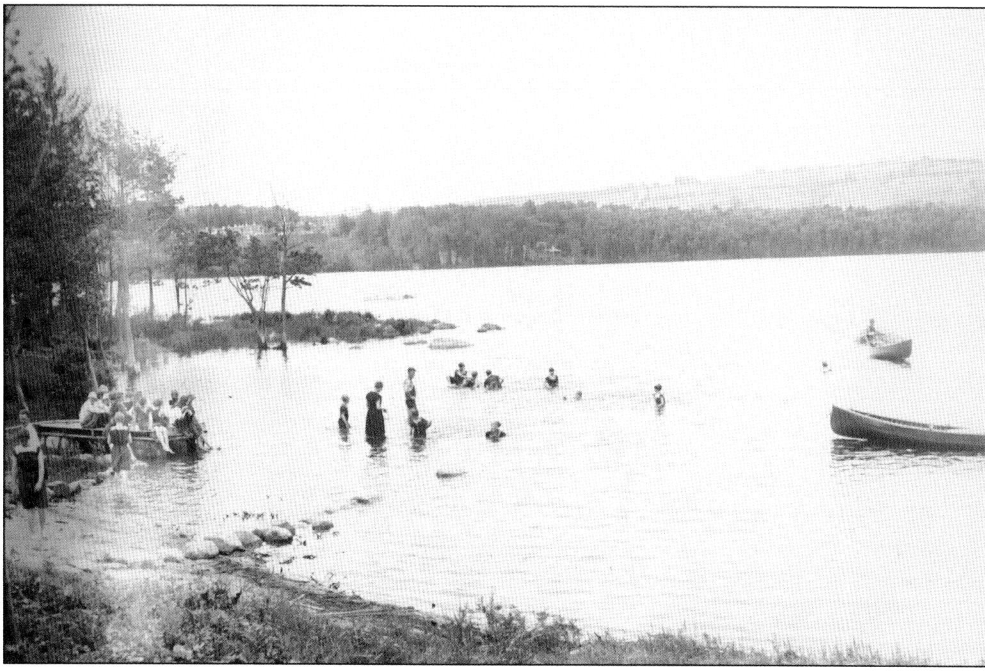

Swimming Lessons, c. 1915. These photographs show the girls getting swimming lessons in Wilson Lake. The photograph above is of a beginner's class, with some of the campers and instructors in the water. Also visible are a couple of canoes, which campers or instructors are paddling. The photograph below shows another swimming lesson, with the girls practicing their swimming moves.

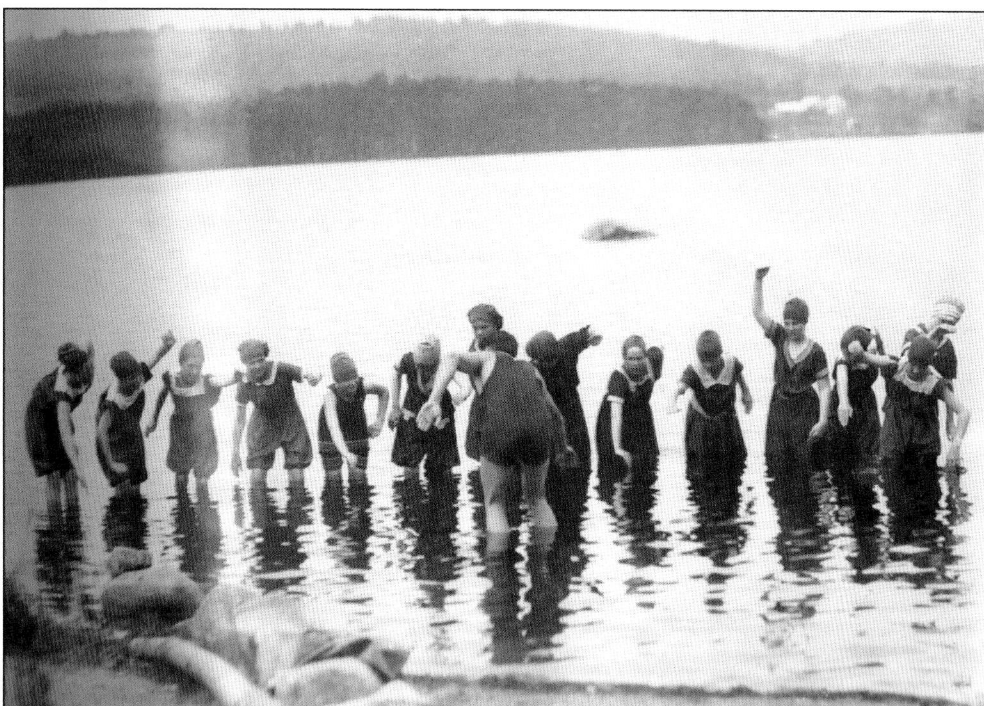

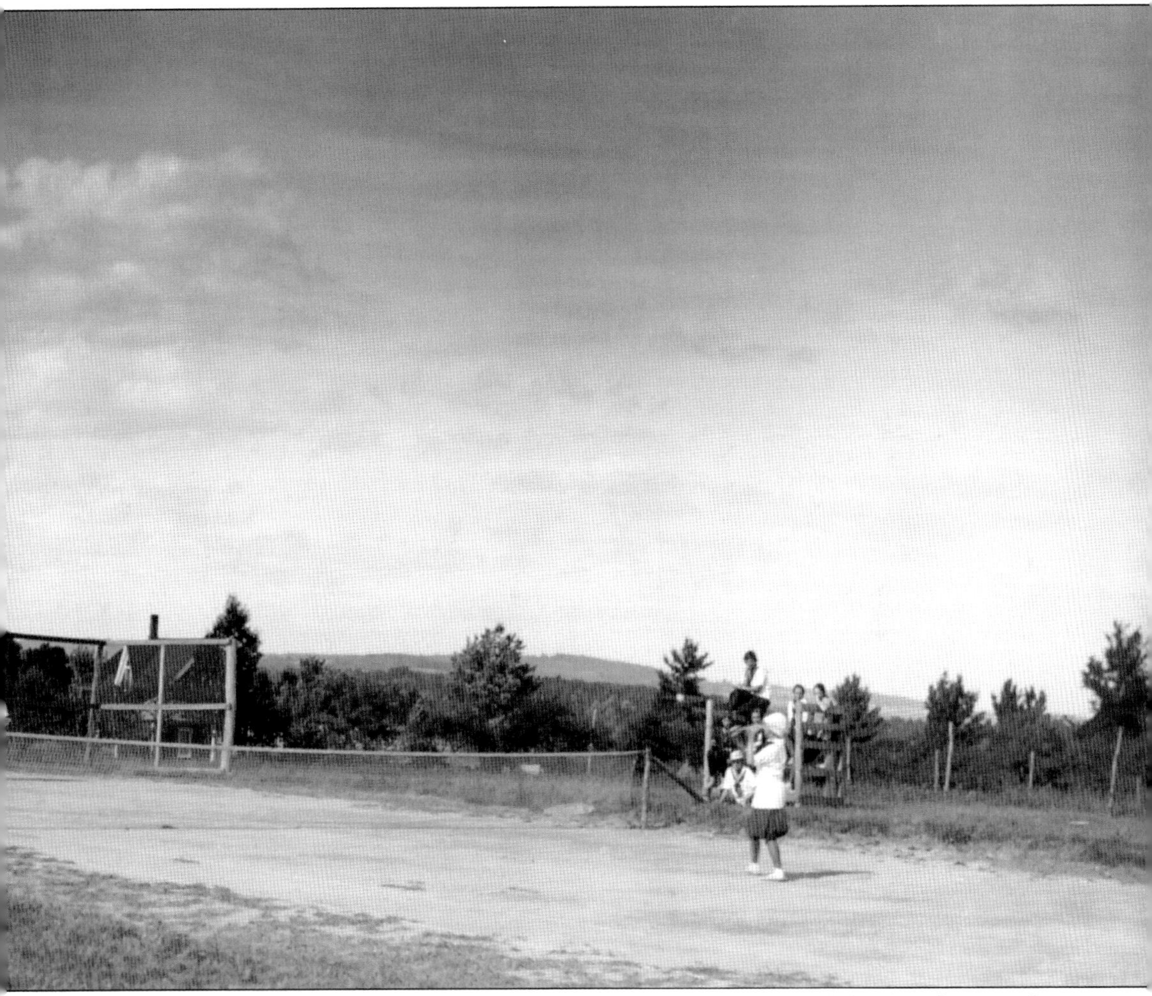

TENNIS, C. 1915. At Camp Kineowatha, sports were at the center of camp life. This photograph shows two girls playing a game of tennis on one of the three clay courts, which saw nearly constant use. One can also see other campers in the bleachers watching the game.

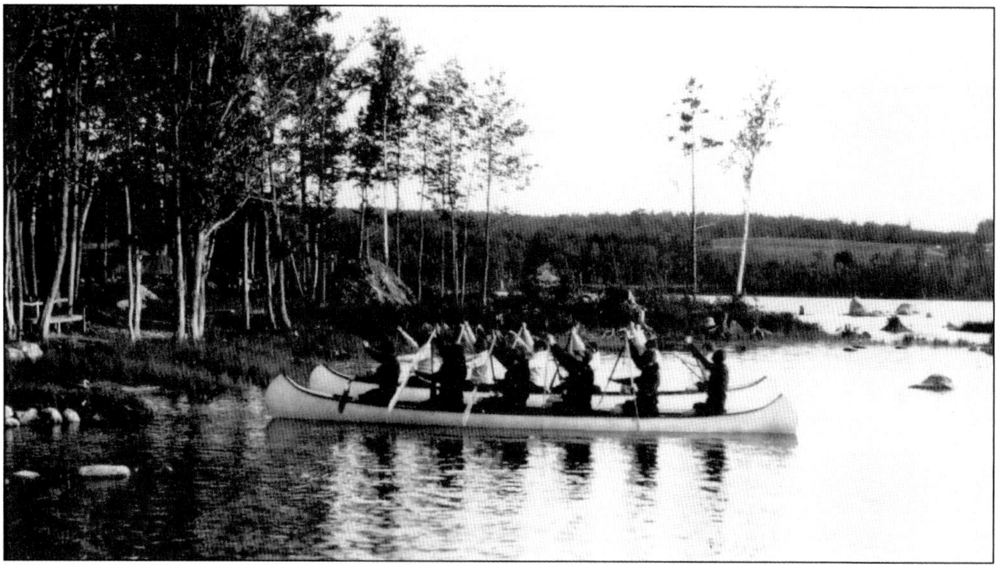

WAR CANOES, C. 1915. The image on this postcard was published by Herbert E. Glasier. Boating, particularly canoeing and sailing, was enjoyed by the campers at Camp Kineowatha. The type of canoe they are using here is called a war canoe.

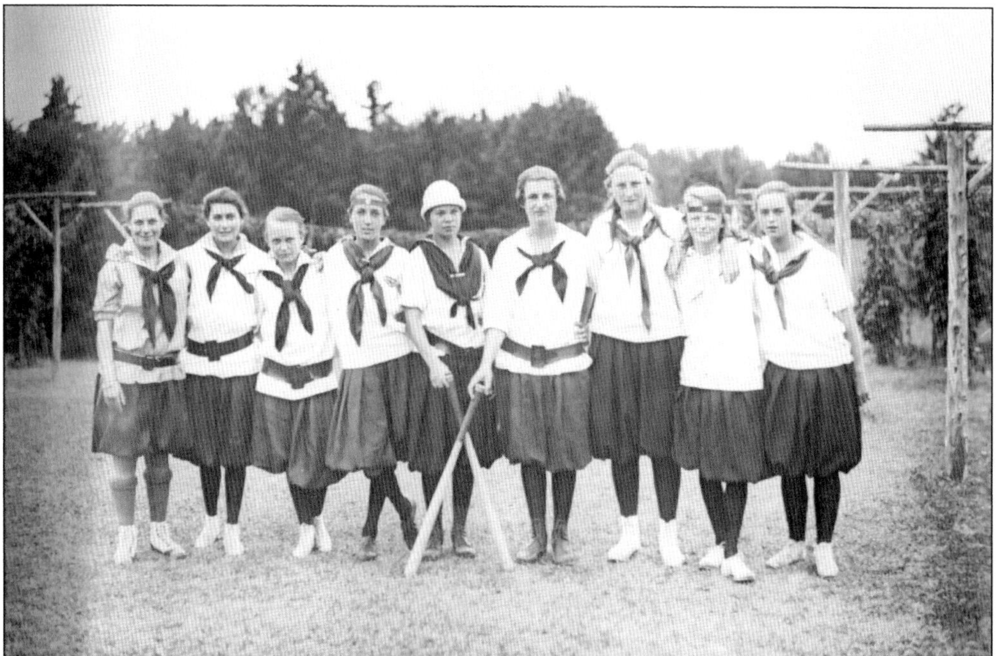

BASEBALL, 1920S. This is a photograph of the girls' baseball team. During gala week, the girls played against the Camp Kineo boys. This was an event looked forward to by both the boys and the girls.

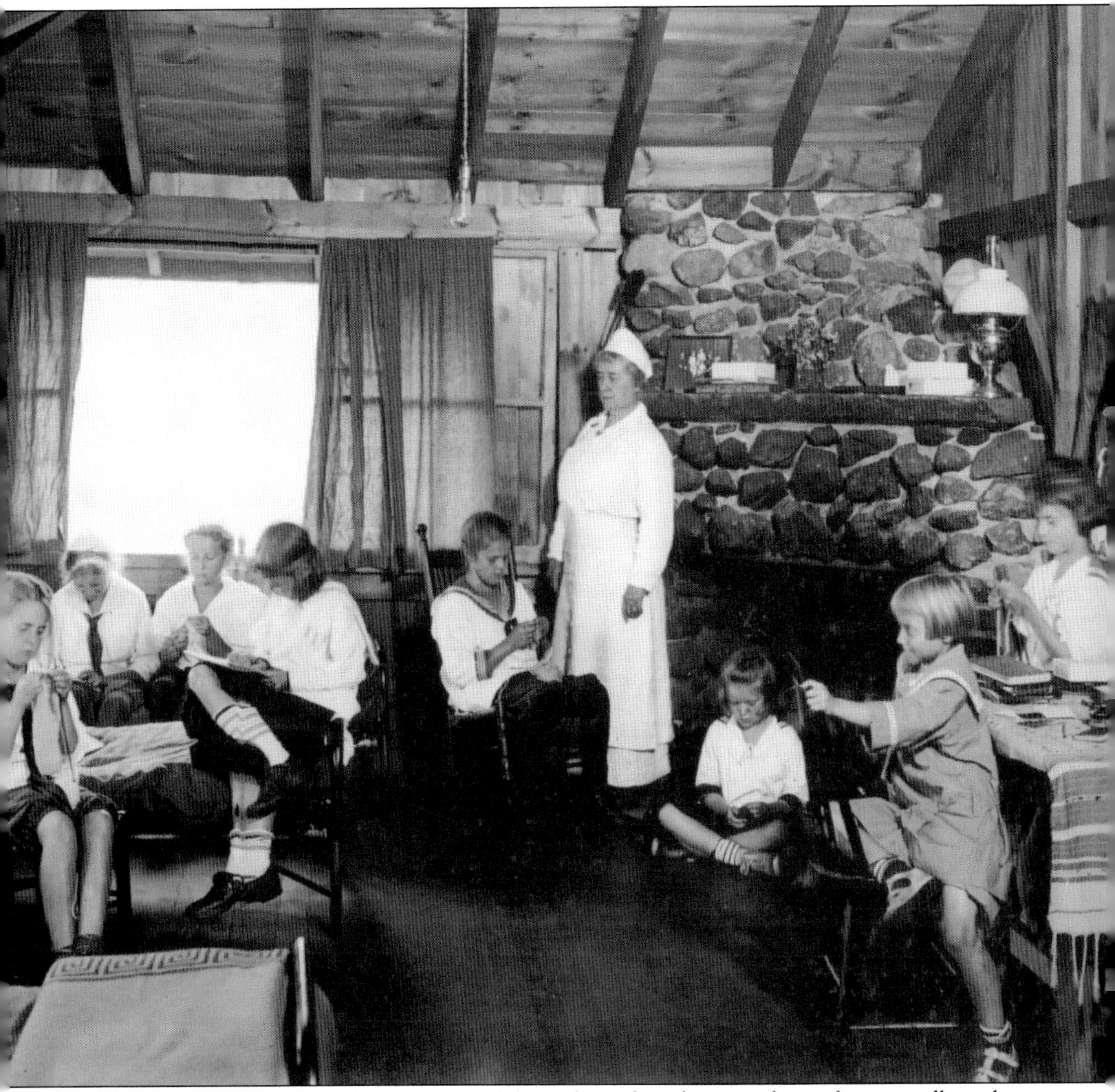

JUNIOR LIVING BUNGALOW, 1920S. Many of the girls in this photograph are doing needlework. This particular bungalow was known as the Junior Living Bungalow. It was described as "a real summer home with all the modern comforts and conveniences." Thus, it was a real home away from home for the girls. This bungalow housed 10 juniors and two counselors.

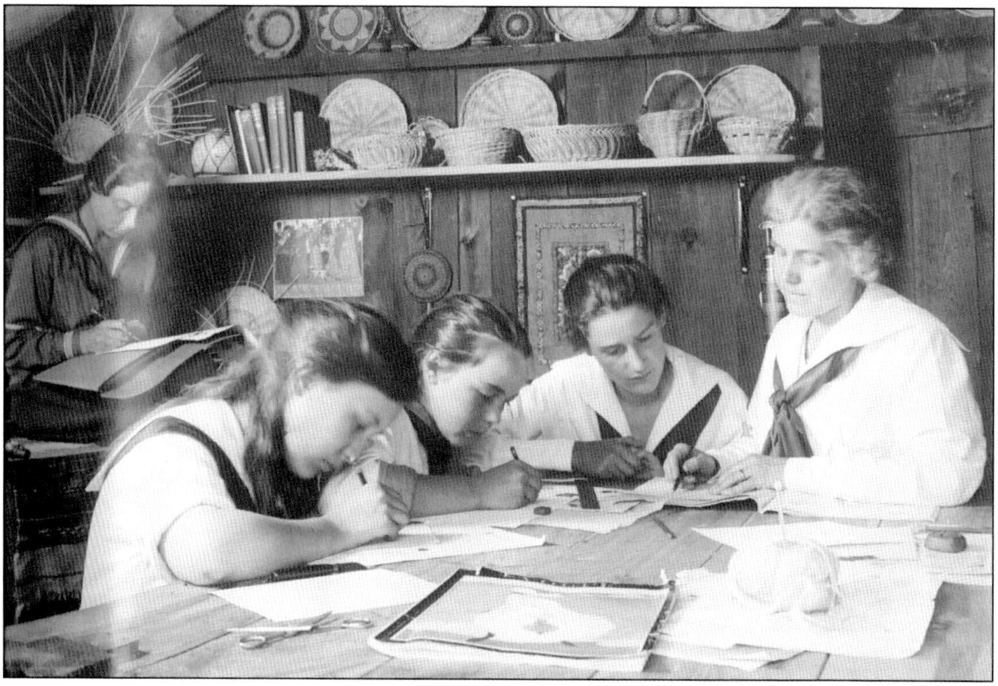

ARTS AND CRAFTS, C. 1915. While sports were very central to camp life, so, too, were more creative activities. In the photograph above, girls are in a sketching class. All of the baskets and ornamental work on the walls were made by the girls. In the photograph below, the girls are taking part in a leatherwork class. They have the same instructor for both of these classes.

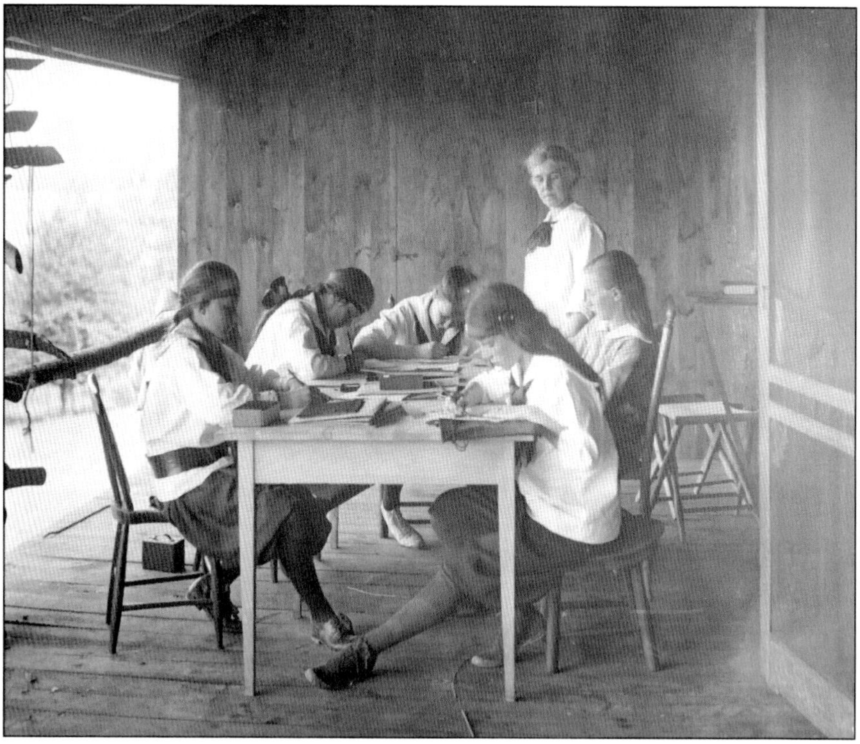

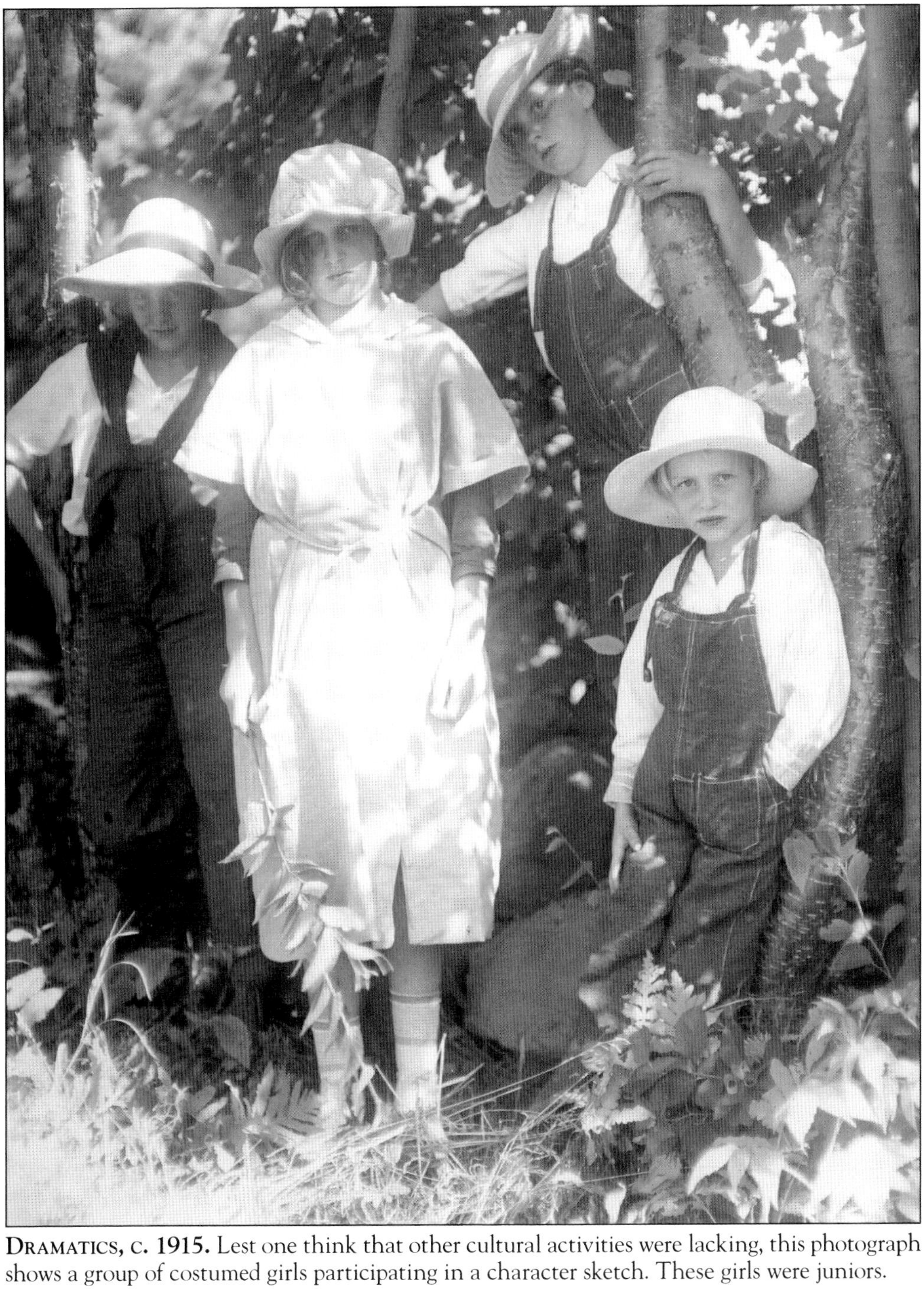

Dramatics, c. 1915. Lest one think that other cultural activities were lacking, this photograph shows a group of costumed girls participating in a character sketch. These girls were juniors.

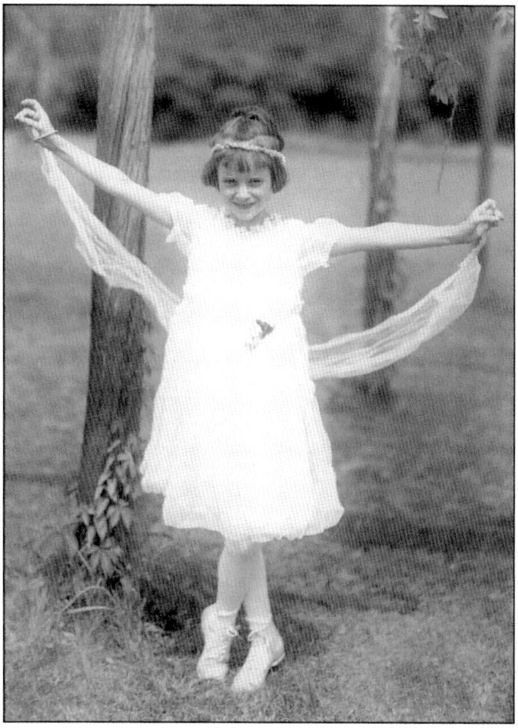

Costumes, c. 1915. The girls don more costumes in these two photographs: party and pageant costumes. The girls enjoyed a well-rounded camping experience.

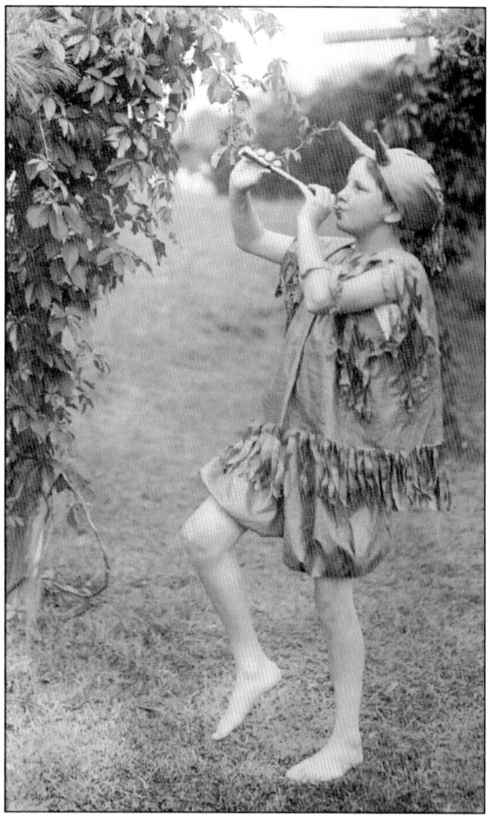

The Bungalets, c. 1915. This is a photograph of a fireplace in one of the camper bungalows, or, as they were often called, bungalets. These cabins were where the campers lived. Each bungalet was equipped with modern plumbing, electric lights, hot and cold running water, and a fireplace.

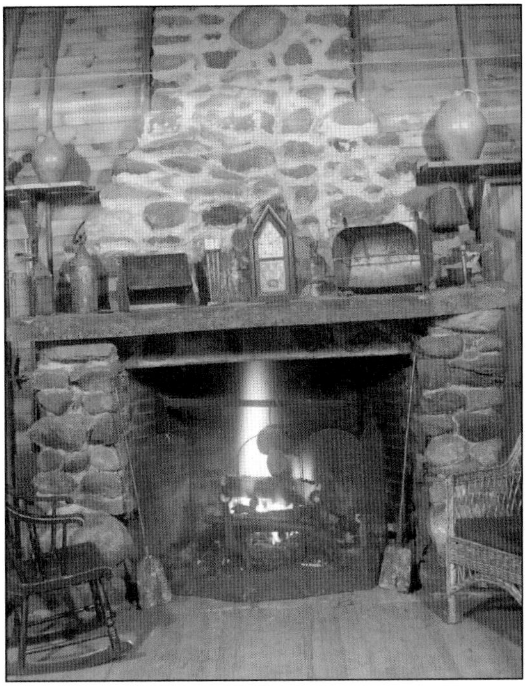

Sleeping Quarters, 1915. This is an example of sleeping quarters for the campers. This is of the interior of the senior bungalow. The camp supplied good spring beds, mattresses, blankets, sheets, pillows, slips, and the like for the girls. While rustic, the bungalows still had many amenities.

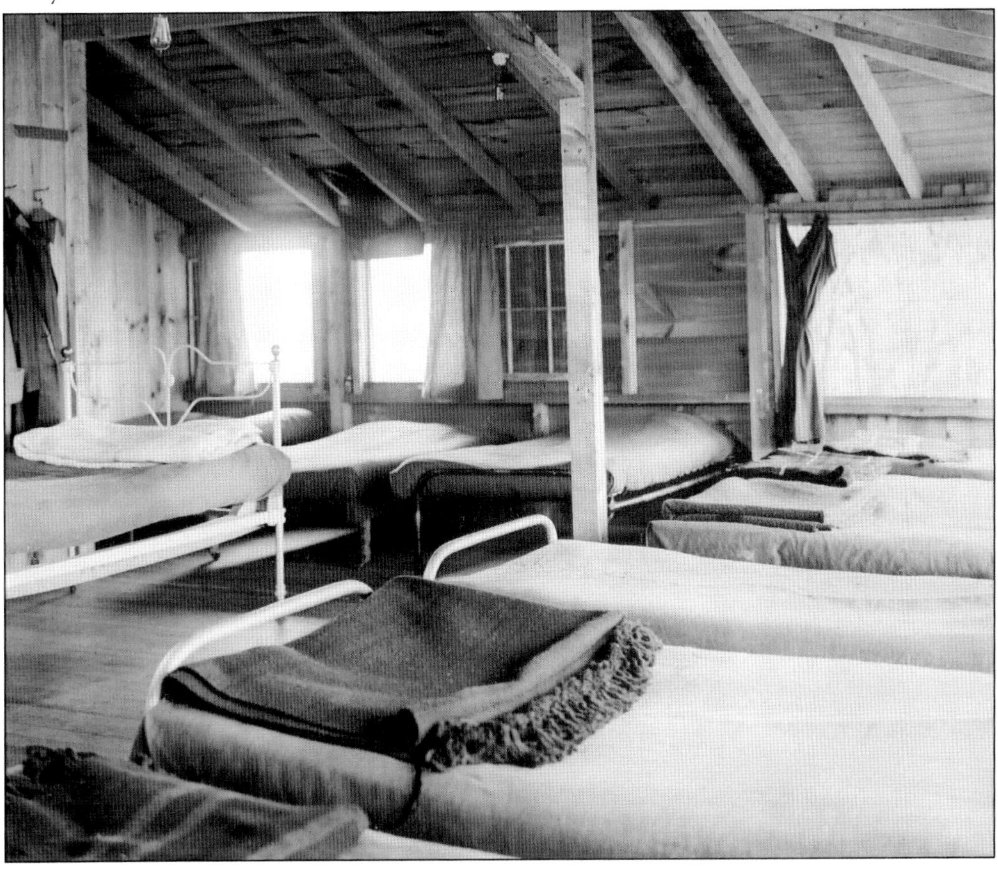

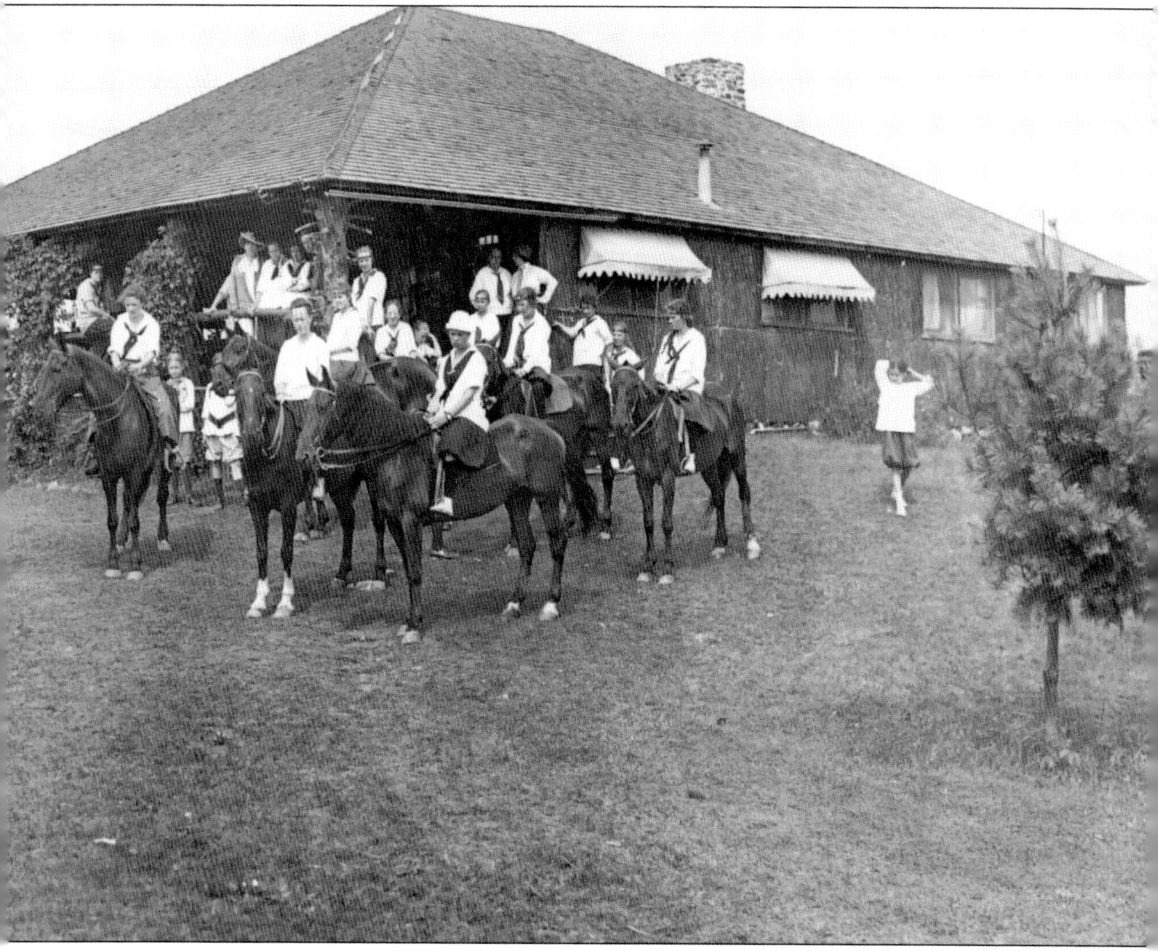

HORSEBACK RIDING, 1912–1920. These campers are off for a long ride on horseback. Horseback riding was a much-loved activity of the girls at Camp Kineowatha.

Seven

HOME AND FAMILY

Wilton is not without homes of note that have been owned by prominent citizens in the town's history. Some of the dwellings were quite humble, and others were more extravagant. Some of the homes of note are those of Abraham Butterfield, Herbert E. Houghton, and Dr. William J. Trefethen. The Fenderson House is another well-known residence in town, as are the Orie Miller House and the residence of Cyrus N. Blanchard. The most extravagant home is that of George Goodspeed. Other homes of perhaps lesser note are also included in this chapter to give a well-rounded image of some of the town's dwellings.

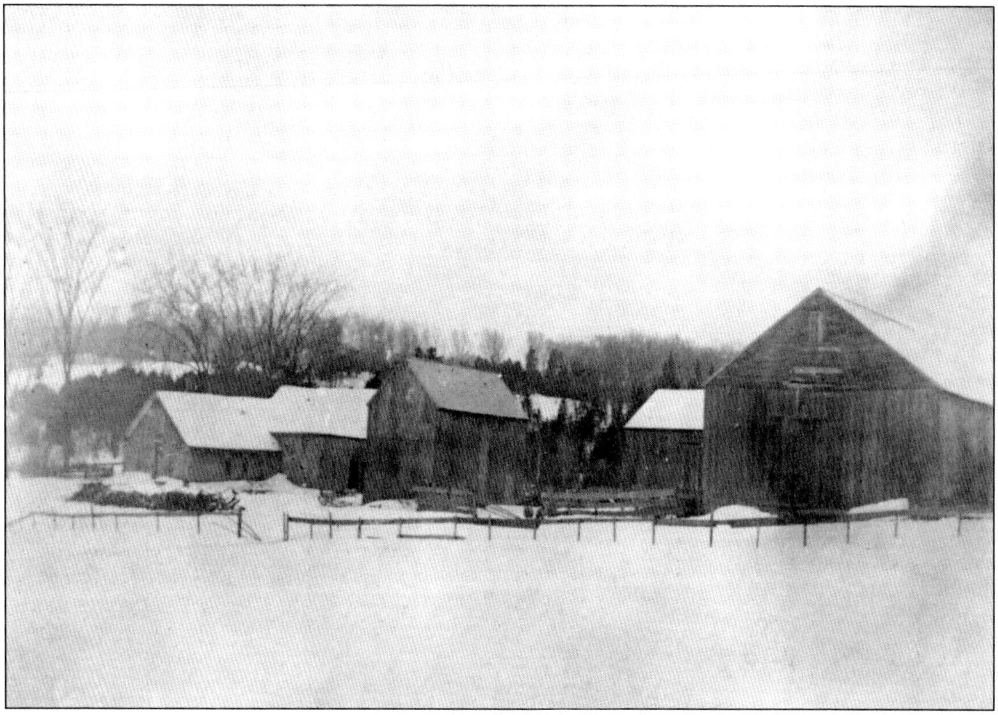

ABRAHAM BUTTERFIELD HOUSE, EARLY 1900S. This was the Abraham Butterfield home and farm, on McCrillis Corner Road in East Wilton. It was one of the many farms in the area at the time. Butterfield's family, consisting of Amelda, Nettie, Bessie, and George, resided here. Abraham was the chairman of a committee to secure the town's incorporation. He offered to pay all necessary expenses of incorporation if he could name the town after his native town of Wilton, New Hampshire. The committee agreed, and Wilton was incorporated as the 149th town in the commonwealth of Massachusetts on June 22, 1803. The home was owned in the 1900s by Frank and Dorothy Beedy. Frank was a woolen weaver at the woolen mill.

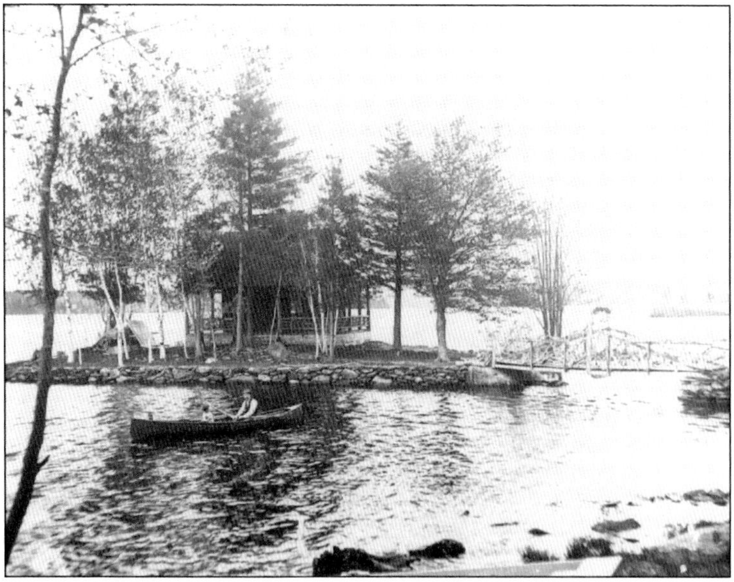

ISLAND COTTAGE, c. 1920. This island cottage on Wilson Lake was once owned by the Monroe sisters of North Jay. The two people in the photograph are having a leisurely paddle in their canoe. This camp was later owned by Rev. Lawrence Washington in 1977.

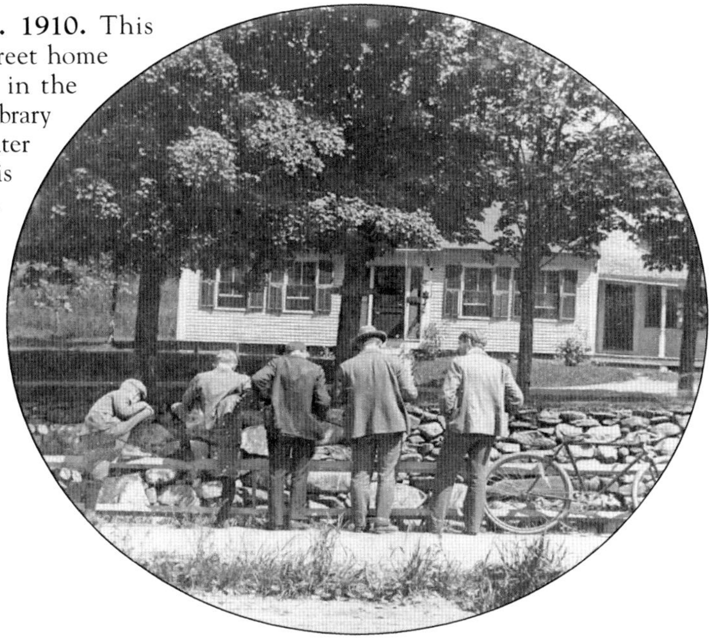

MAIN STREET HOME, C. 1910. This photograph of a Main Street home shows the Wilton Bridge in the foreground, near where the library is today. The home was later moved to High Street. It is difficult to say for certain what these men were doing, but something in Wilson Stream seems to have captured their attention. They could be fishing.

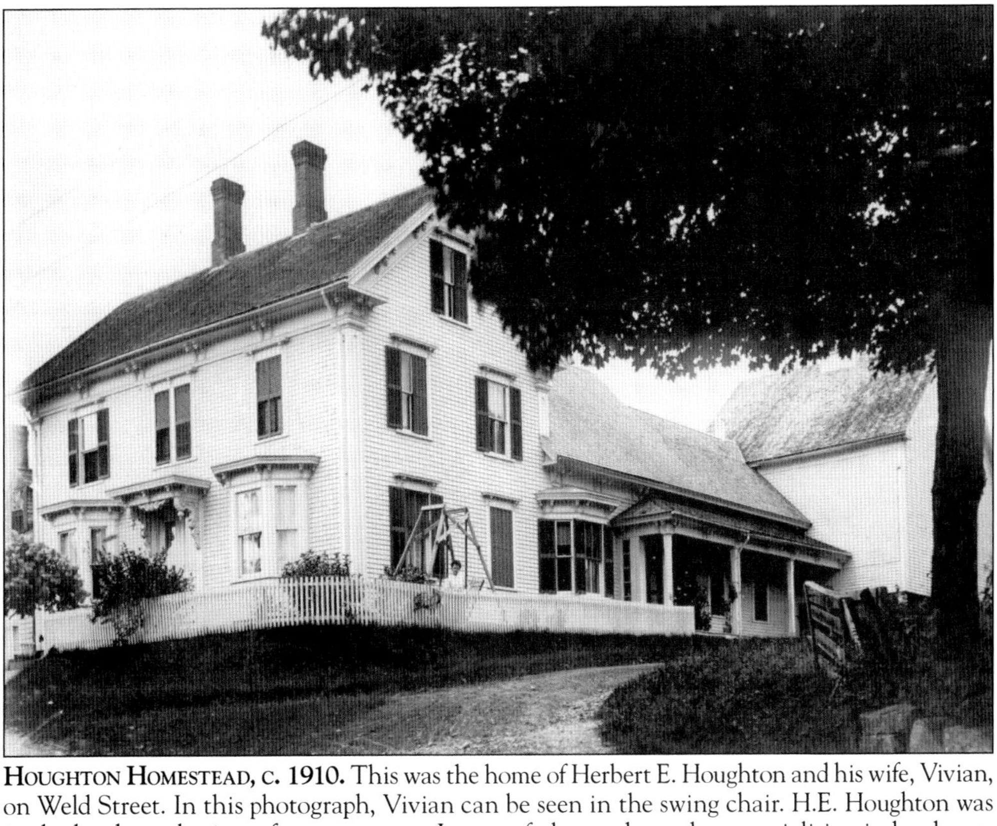

HOUGHTON HOMESTEAD, C. 1910. This was the home of Herbert E. Houghton and his wife, Vivian, on Weld Street. In this photograph, Vivian can be seen in the swing chair. H.E. Houghton was in the hardware business for many years. It was a father-and-son shop specializing in hardware, bicycles, and repairing. He also specialized in stoves, agricultural implements, tin, carriages, sleighs, and the like, according to the *Maine Register* of 1919–1920.

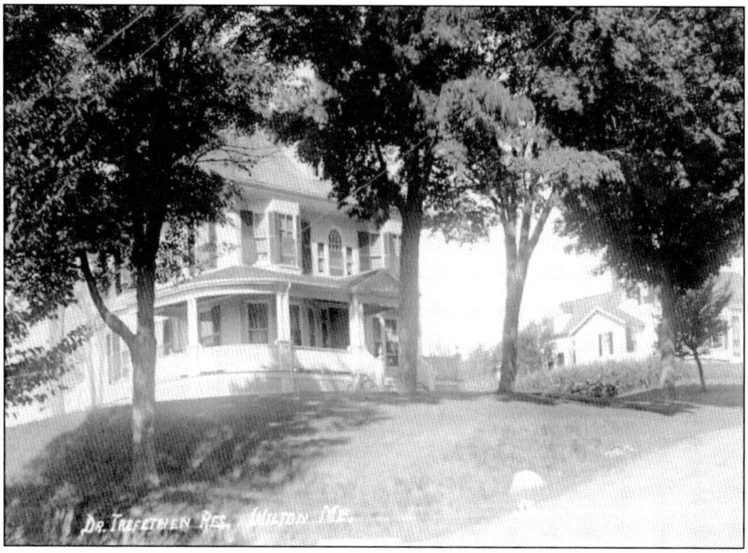

Dr. Trefethen Residence, Early 1900s. Dr. William J. Trefethen was a physician and surgeon who provided his services to Wilton for many years. Later, this home was owned by Heber Purington.

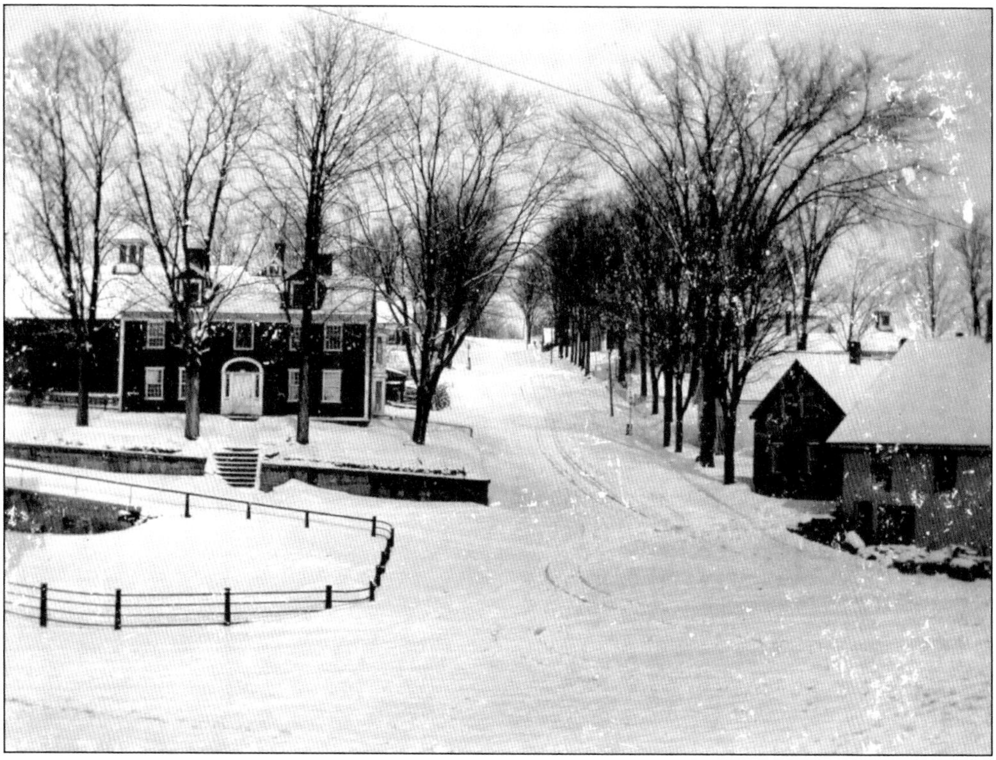

Fenderson House, Early 1900s. This house was originally built to be a tavern by a Mr. Moulton. He sold it to Col. Charles Morse, who then made it into a dwelling and presented it to his daughter as a wedding gift. In 1846, Cyrus Fenderson, postmaster and orchardist and the grandfather of Edna Fenderson, purchased it, and it stayed in the family until 1953, after Edna's death. At that time, it was offered to be used as a parking area by her sister Fannie Fernald and her nephew Cyrus Fernald. This gift was accepted at a special town meeting on Friday, June 12, 1953.

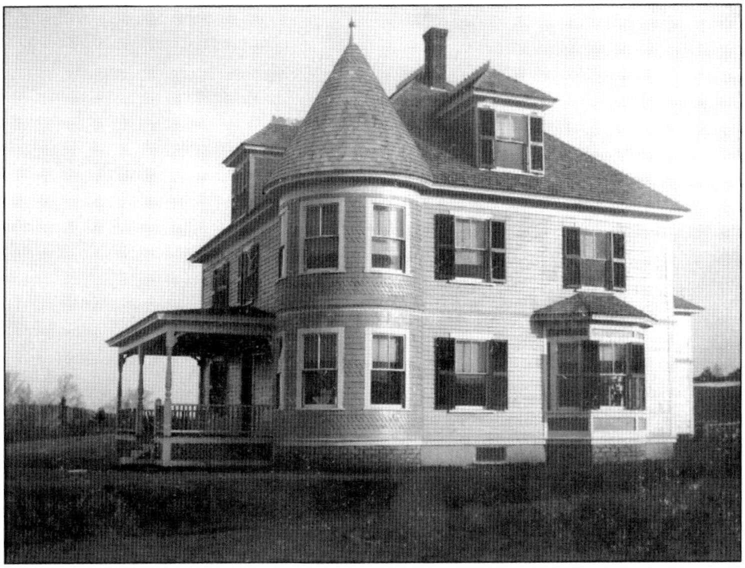

Orie Miller House, Early 1900s. This was the home of Orie Miller, a manufacturer of harnesses and saddlery hardware for horses. He was also a dealer in horse clothing, trunks, and bags.

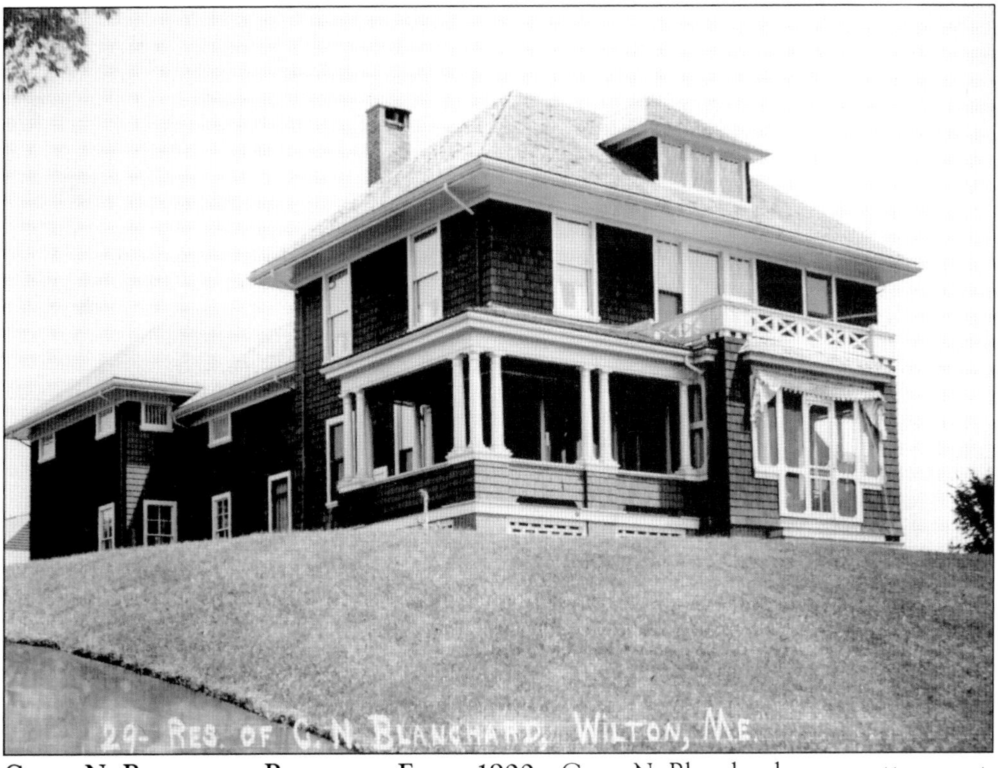

Cyrus N. Blanchard Residence, Early 1900s. Cyrus N. Blanchard was an attorney-at-law, disclosure commissioner, and notary public in Wilton. He lived in this house with his wife, Florence.

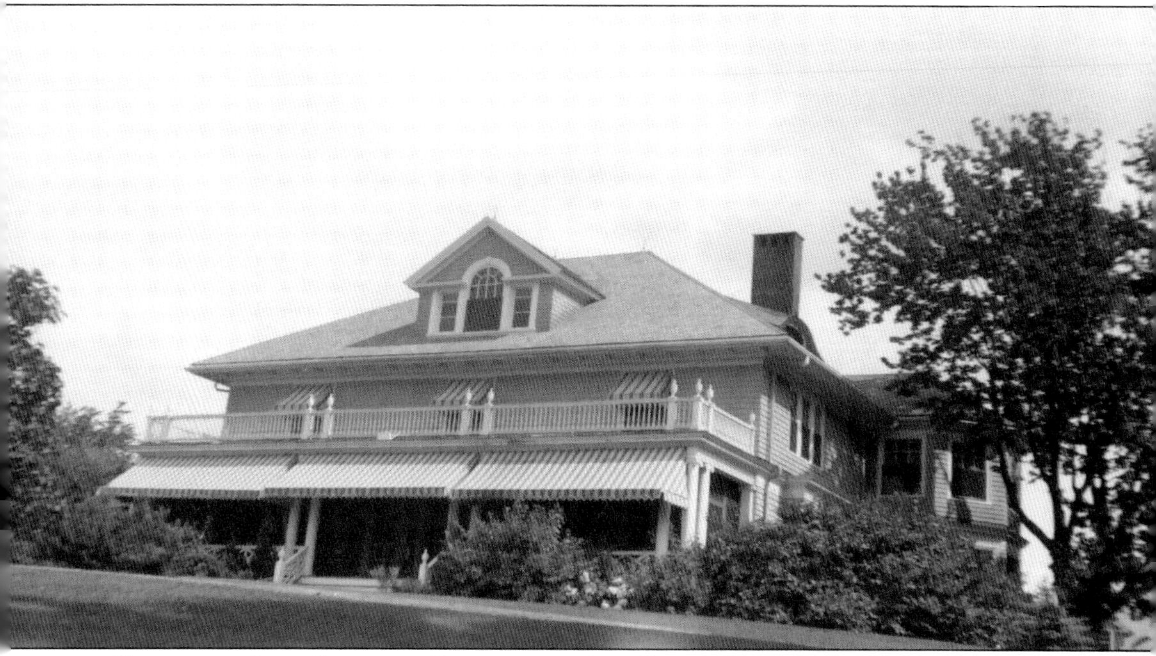

George and Inez Goodspeed Residence, 1930s. George Goodspeed was a wool manufacturer and mill man with Wilton Woolen Company. He lived in this house with his wife, Inez, and their three children, Elanor, George, and Frances. Later, the home was owned by Inez and Jack Davis and, later still, by Peggy Hodgkins.

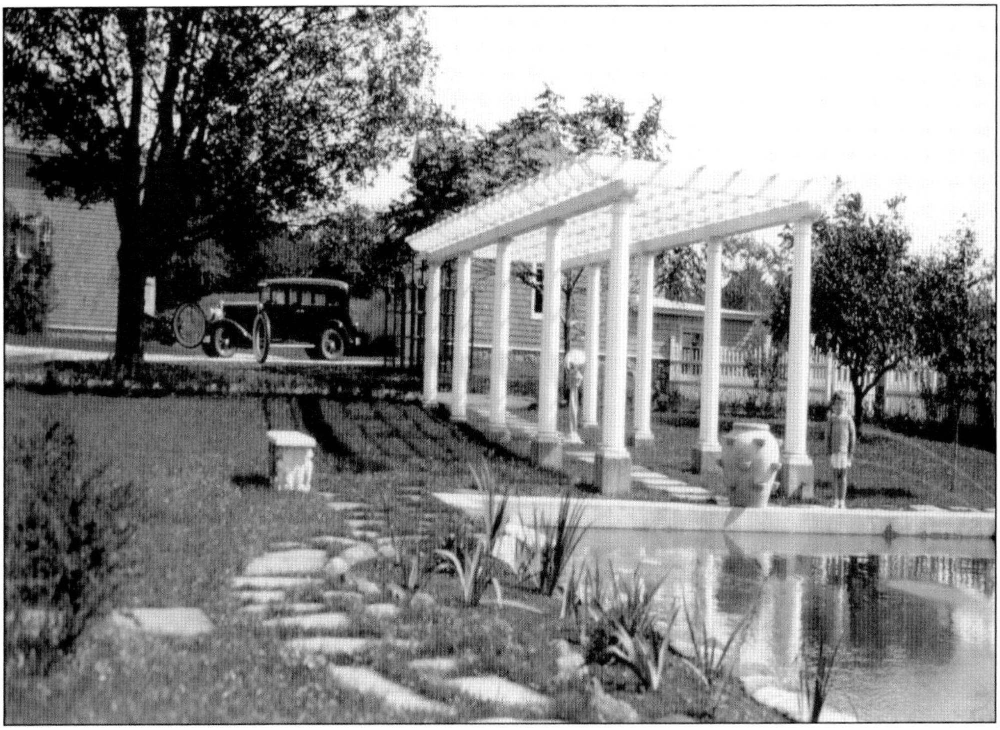

The Grounds of the George and Inez Goodspeed Residence, 1930s. These photographs show the beautiful grounds at the Goodspeed residence. A note on the back of the photograph suggests that the little girl in the photographs was very likely George and Inez Goodspeed's daughter Frances. These photographs show elaborate landscaping with fountains, benches, fences, and other structures.

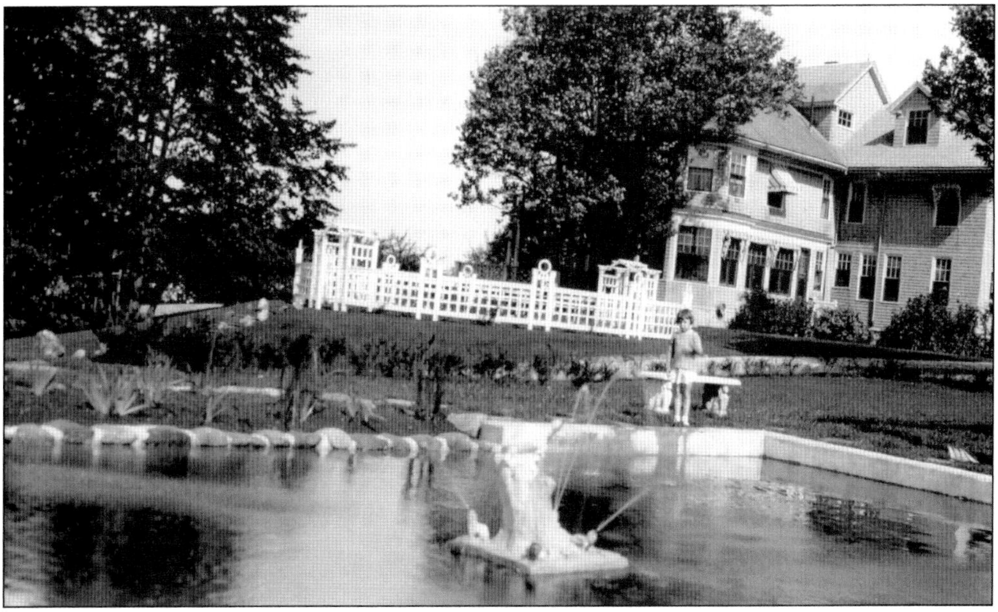

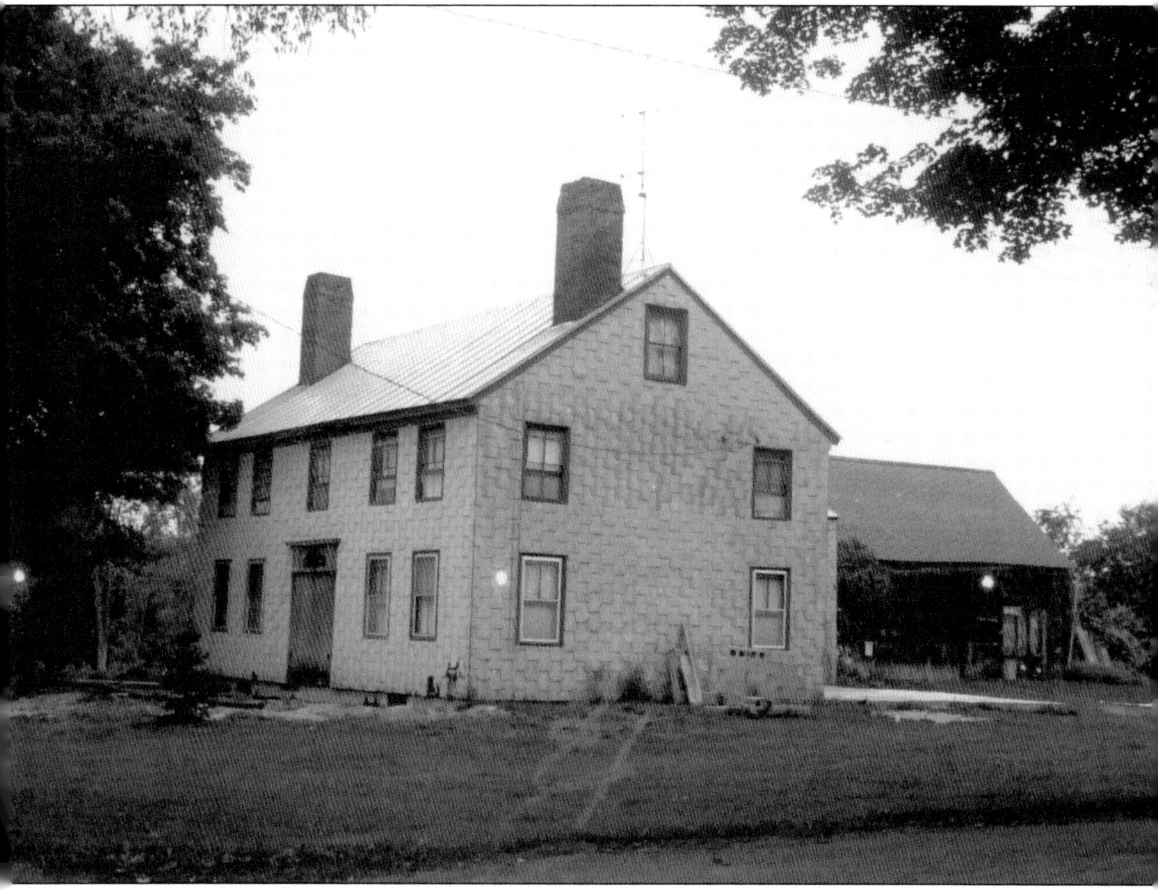

BUTTERFIELD HOME, C. 1950. It has been said that this is the oldest house in Wilton. It was constructed in the 1790s. The first town meeting was held here. It was also a stagecoach station at one point in time.

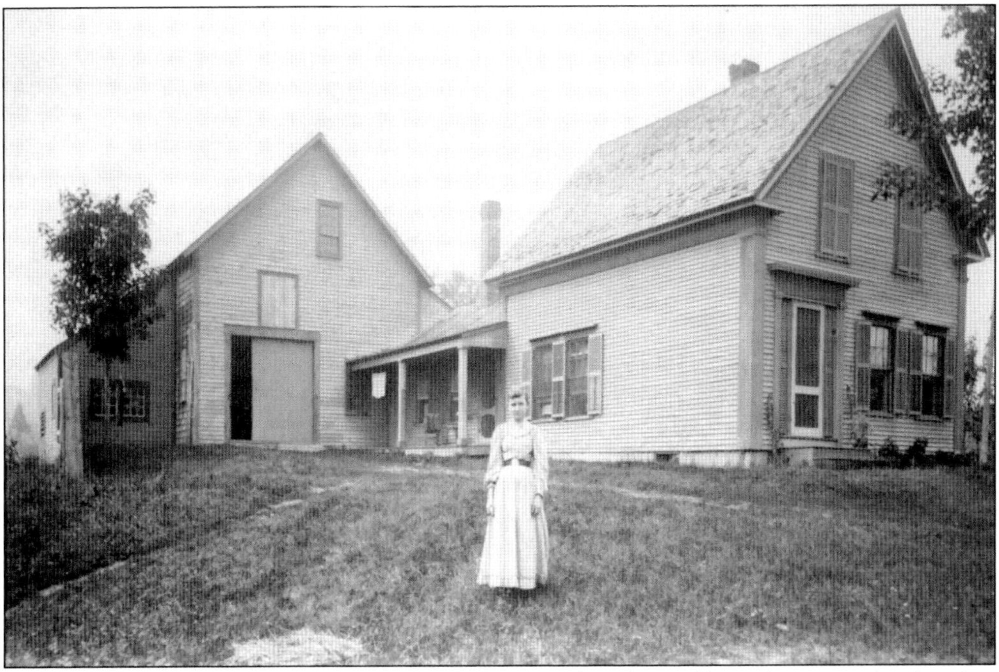

Ola Calden Home, c. 1900. This photograph is of Viola "Ola" Calden, who was a schoolteacher in town. Her home was on Depot Street in Dryden.

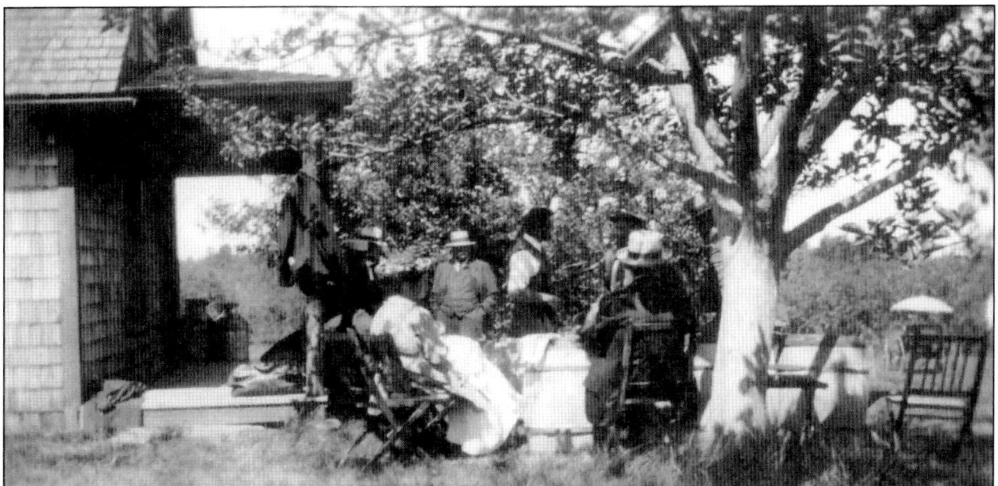

Family Gathering, c. 1900. This is a photograph of a family gathering at what appears to be a farm as evidenced by the apple barrels and milk jugs in the photograph.

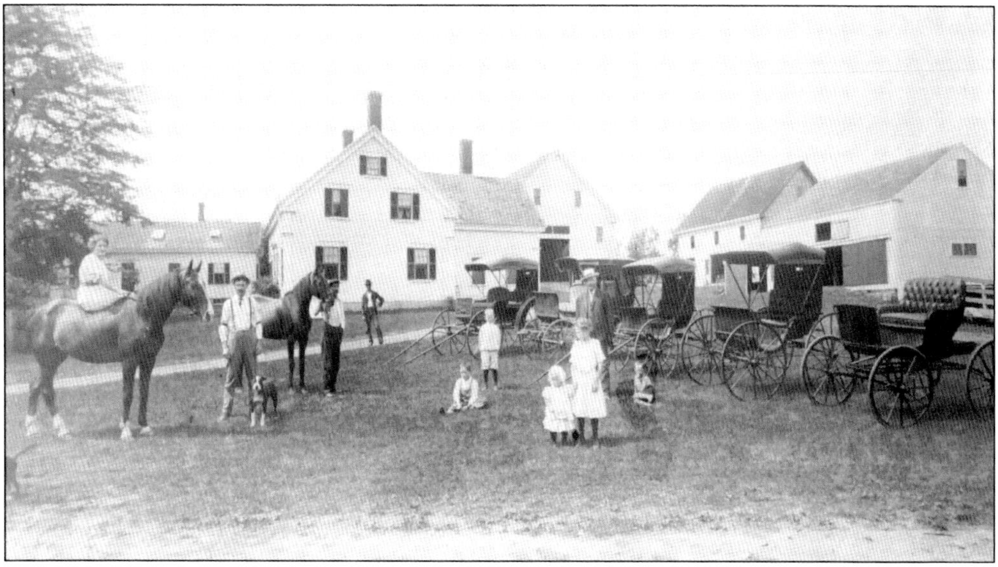

JOHN BLANCHARD'S PLACE, EARLY 1900S. John Blanchard was the son of Charles F. Blanchard, who was a farmer and cattle dealer. This residence was located at Wilton Notch at the turn of the 20th century.

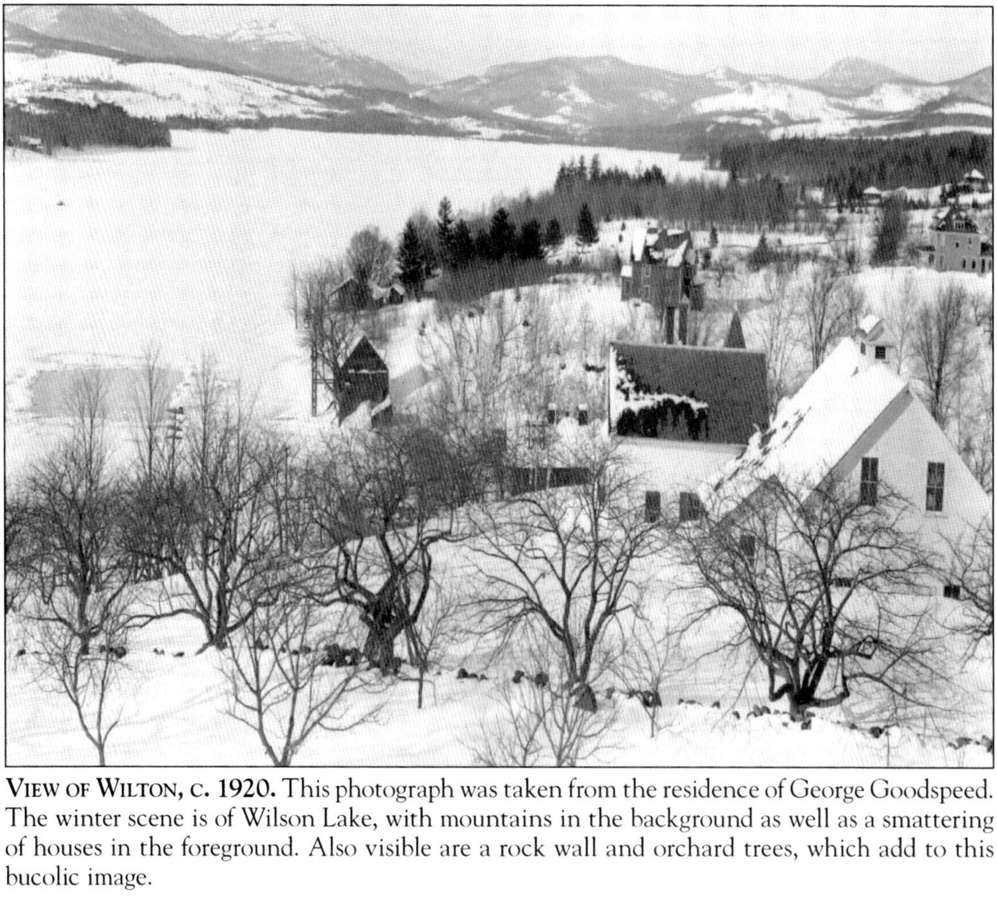

VIEW OF WILTON, C. 1920. This photograph was taken from the residence of George Goodspeed. The winter scene is of Wilson Lake, with mountains in the background as well as a smattering of houses in the foreground. Also visible are a rock wall and orchard trees, which add to this bucolic image.

Eight

Streets and Villages

This chapter's focus is on the streets as they once looked, as well as the villages in the town of Wilton. There were a number of villages that made up the town of Wilton. There were separate post offices for each village. The following villages were all part of Wilton at one time: East Wilton, Dryden, Wilton, Wilton Notch, and part of East Dixfield. For the purposes of this book, this chapter will focus most on Wilton Village, East Wilton, and Dryden. One more item of note is the town square in Wilton Village and how it changed over time. This chapter covers select images from the town's evolution.

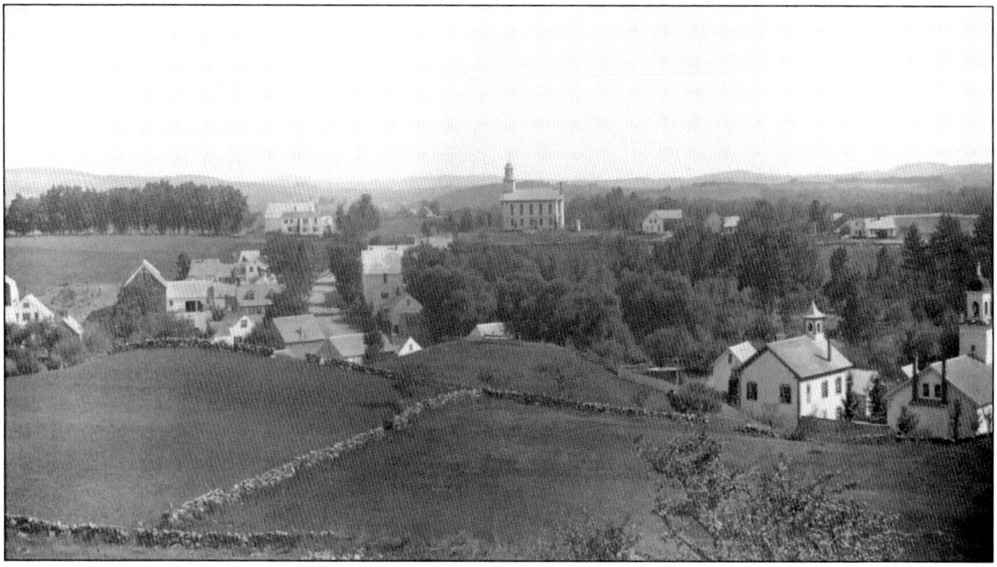

Pastoral View of Wilton Village, Early 1900s. The major landmarks in this photograph are the Methodist church (far right) and the schoolhouse (far right), which was built in 1870 at the cost of $3,045. In the distance on the hill is the Wilton Academy. Behind the church and school, farmland is divided by rock walls. This photograph was taken by A.O. Reed of Brunswick, Maine.

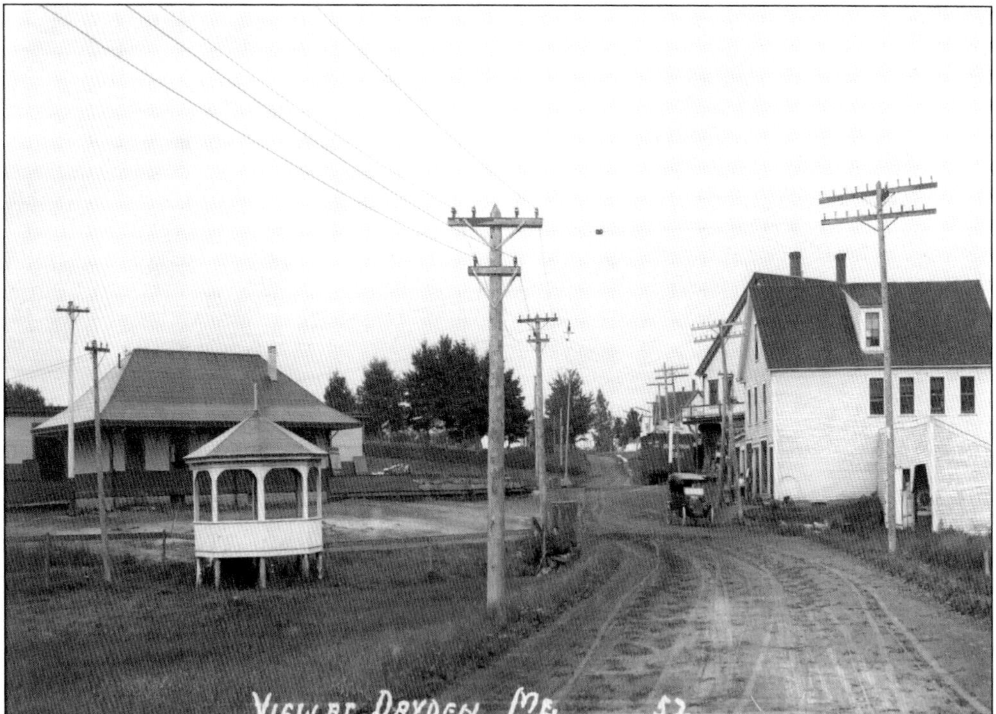

Dryden Train Depot, c. 1910. This is the railroad depot in Dryden, a village within Wilton. The railroad crossing by the B.F. Stanley Store is visible in this photograph, as is a railroad car for the Grand Trunk Railroad, which came through Wilton at that time.

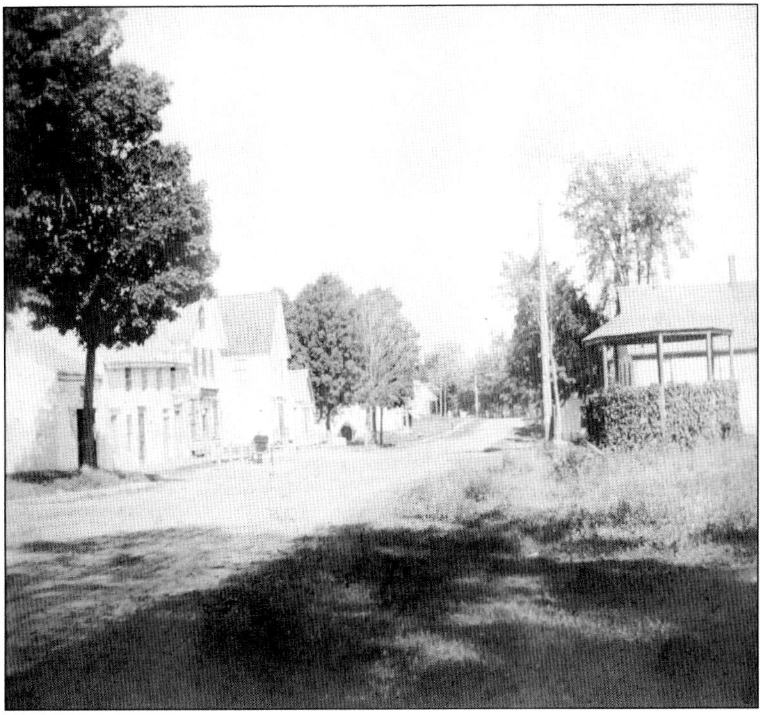

EAST WILTON VILLAGE, AUGUST 1900. East Wilton was the first part of Wilton to be settled. Seen here is a road through Wilton in the early 1900s. One can see a gazebo on the right, and, on the left, a carriage is parked in front of what was likely a business.

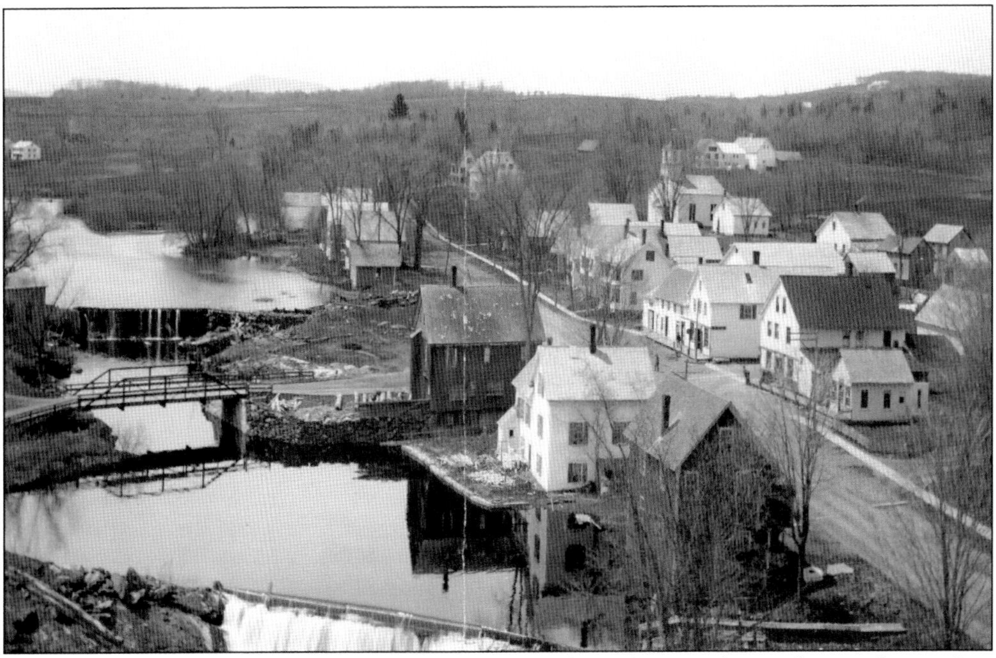

EAST WILTON VILLAGE, EARLY 1900S. This photograph is of East Wilton village and was taken from the Walker Woolen Mill. One can see the upper and lower dam here. At this time, East Wilton was a very prosperous village. During its peak years, in the late 1800s and early 1900s, it was bigger than Wilton Village. Waterpower was used to run the mills here.

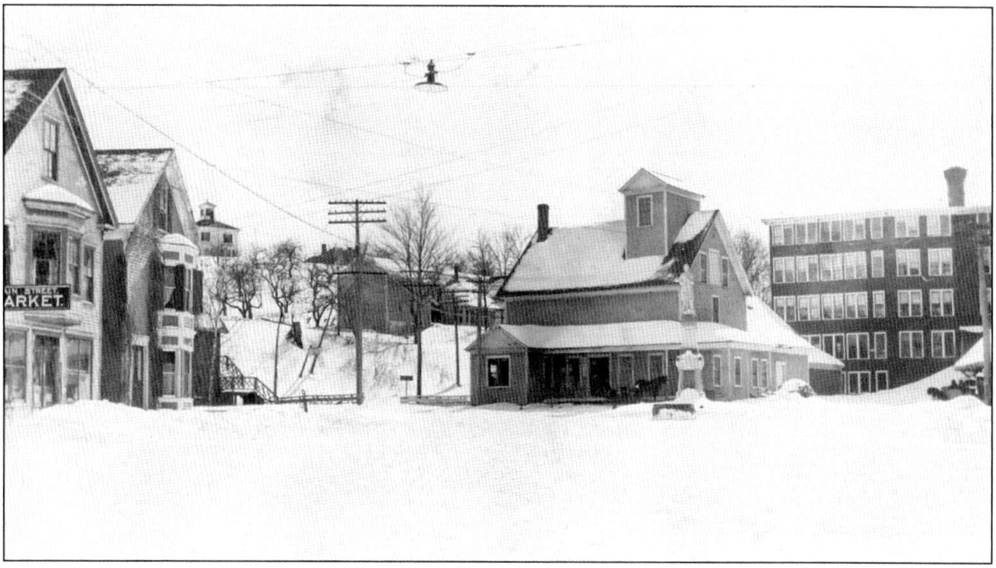

Town Square and Monument, 1913–1915. The G.R. Fernald & Co. Grist Mill, where flour and grain were processed, is visible in this photograph. A horse is hitched up in front of the mill. One can see the Main Street Market in the foreground. Also in the foreground is the Soldiers' Monument, which was presented to the town by the Grand Army of the Republic. The soldier in the monument is wearing the uniform of a Civil War soldier. In addition, there is a horse trough in front of the monument.

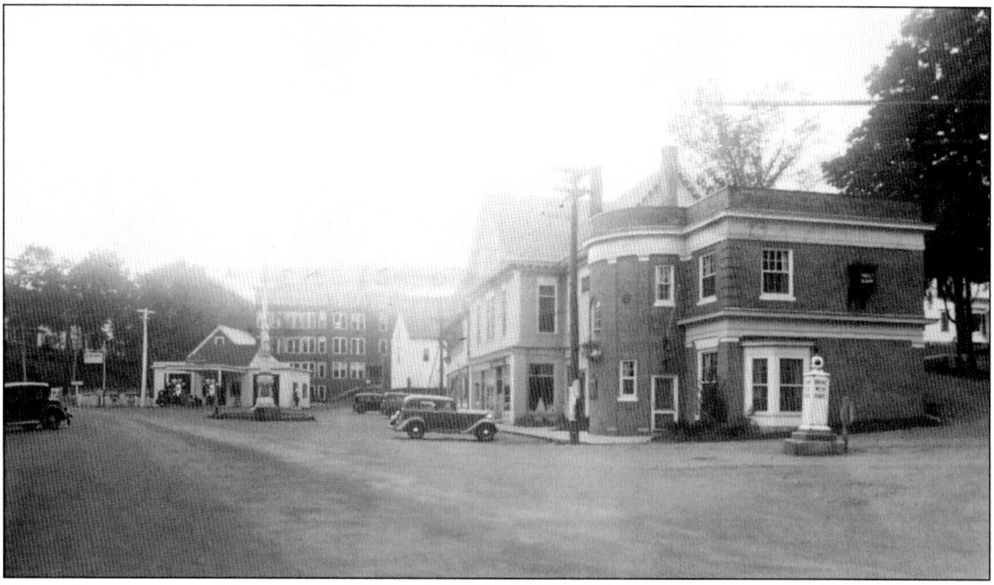

Town Square and Monument, 1930s. This photograph shows numerous changes from the previous one. There is no longer a horse trough in front of the monument, as it is now the age of the automobile. Rather than horses tied up in front of stores, vehicles are parked. The gristmill has been torn down, and there is now a different business there, the Brookside Filling Station, which was established in 1931 and provided Socony gasoline.

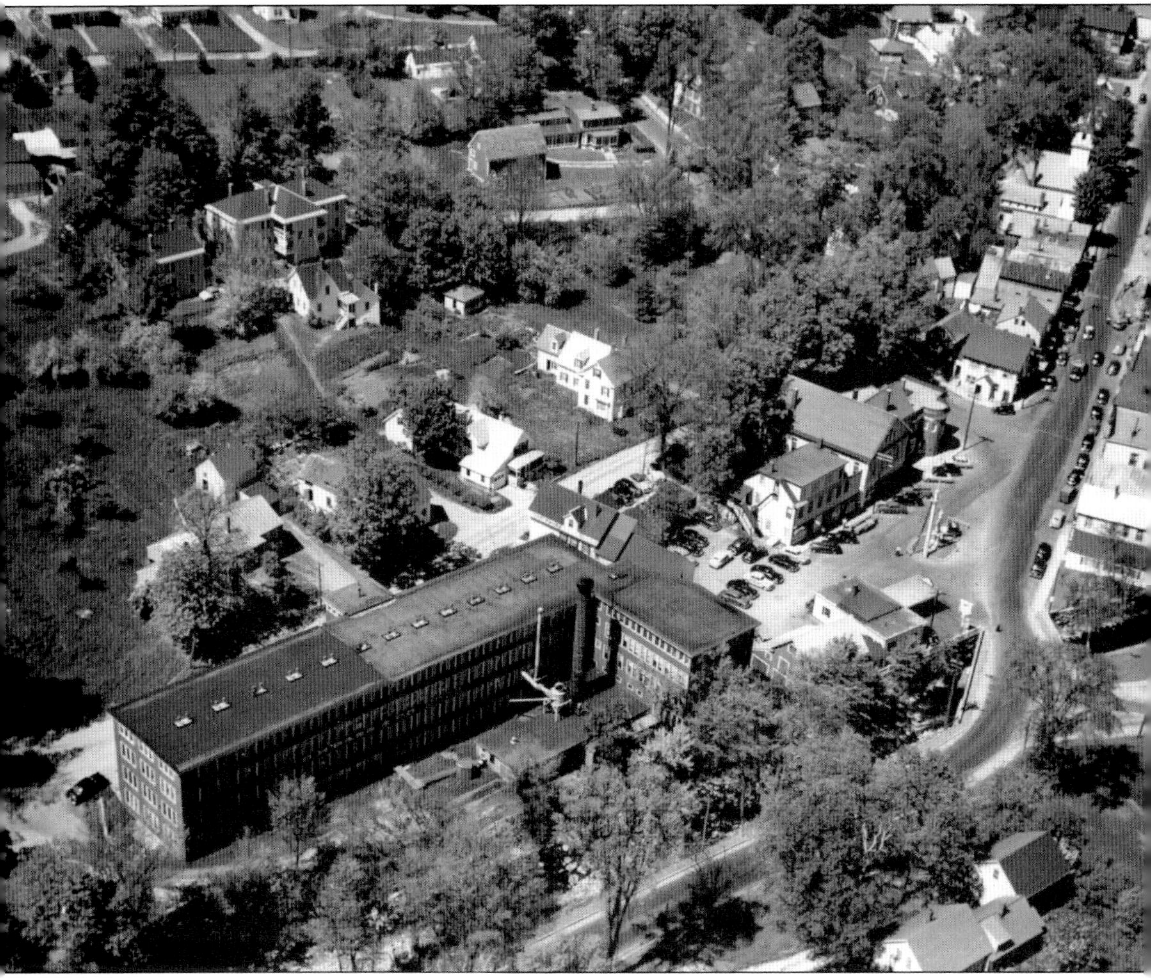

Aerial View of Wilton Village, c. 1953. This photograph, taken from the air by the Luce Studio in Farmington, is of Bass Building No. 1 and the surrounding Wilton village in 1953. At the time this photograph was taken, more than 200 men and women were employed here making Bass Outdoor Footwear, which included Sportocassins, Weejuns, quail-hunting boots, and ski boots.

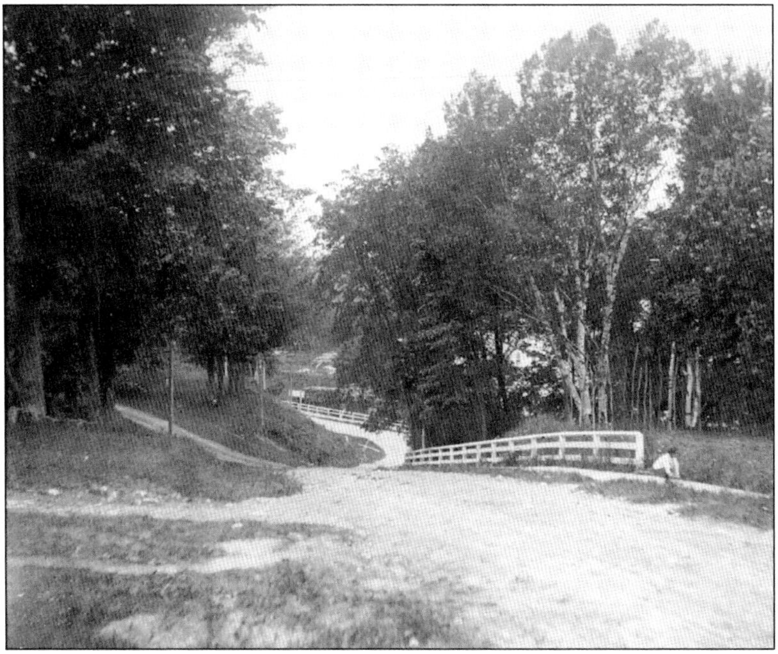

Bass Hill, Before 1900. This is a photograph of the area called Bass Hill in Wilton before the new Bass factory was built. Later, the factory would be a very prominent feature at the bottom of the hill.

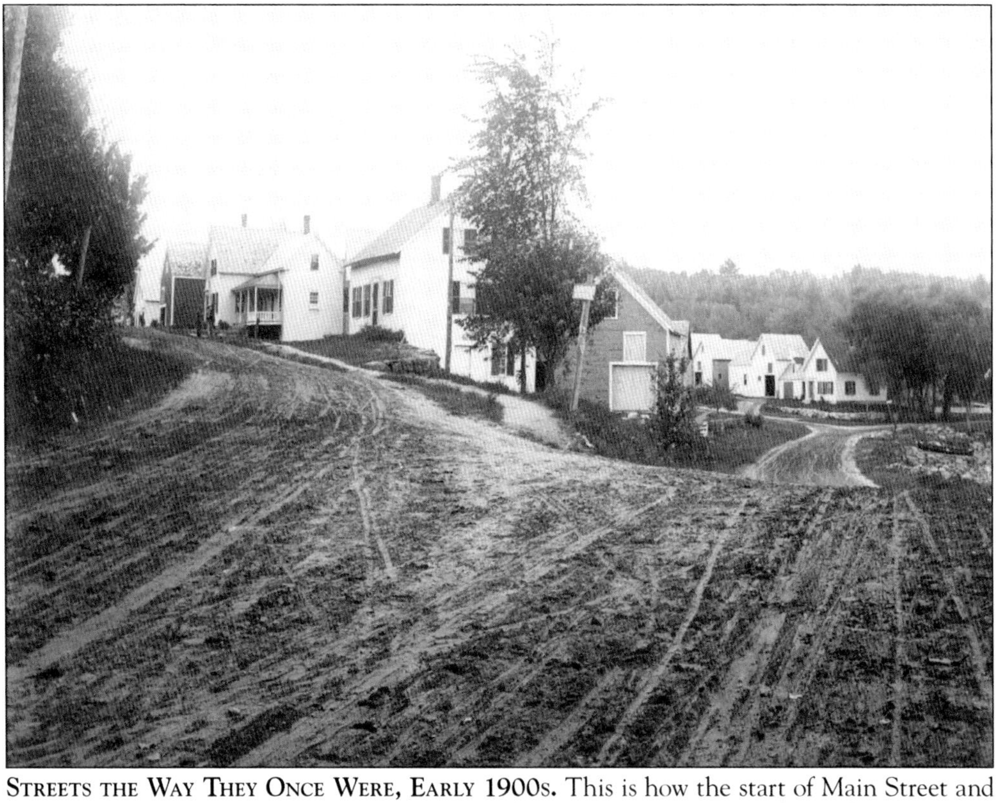

Streets the Way They Once Were, Early 1900s. This is how the start of Main Street and Old Route 2 looked early in the 20th century. Old Route 2 went along the shore of Wilson Lake, making for a scenic walk, ride, or drive. This road was later renamed Lake Road.

Nine

RECREATION

The town of Wilton has had a number of recreational opportunities to offer its residents. Wilson Lake has always been the center of recreation, whether for swimming, boating, or picnicking. It also provided a splendid backdrop for photographers, with the mountains in the distance. Other types of seasonal recreation such as camping and sleigh racing were enjoyed as well. Campers mostly came from out of town to enjoy the peace of being in the country and the recreational activities available to them. Other sports enjoyed were ice-skating, basketball, tennis, and bowling. Not every form of recreation was sport, as Wilton also had its own movie theater, where many locals enjoyed evening movies and matinees. Wilton has always been a good place to play.

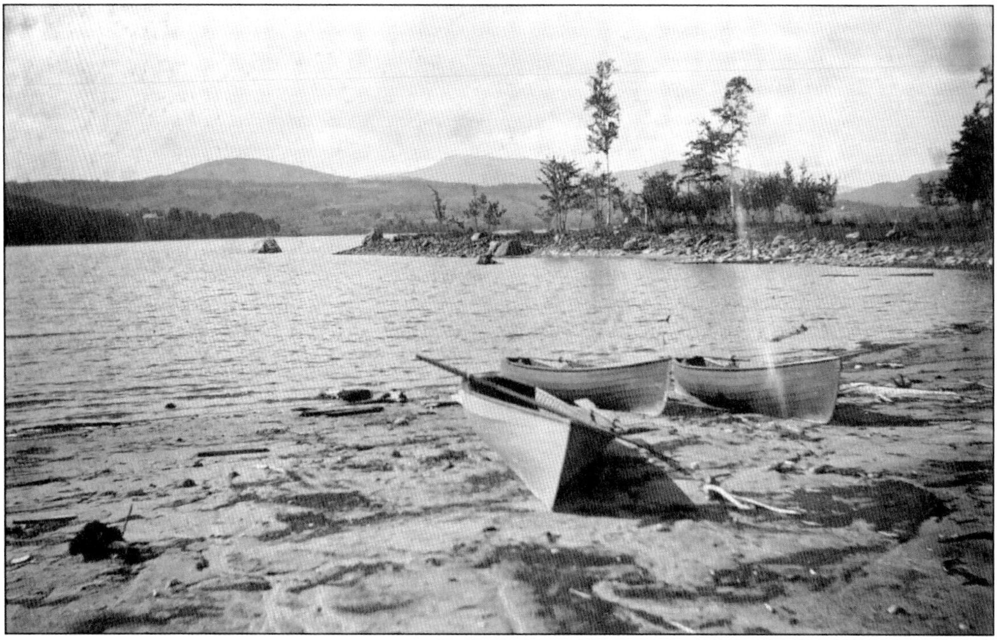

WILSON LAKE, LATE 1800S. These photographs provided two different views of Wilson Lake from its shore. Many people have commented on the splendid mountain backdrop and the mirror-like surface of the water. Many boaters and photographers would concur.

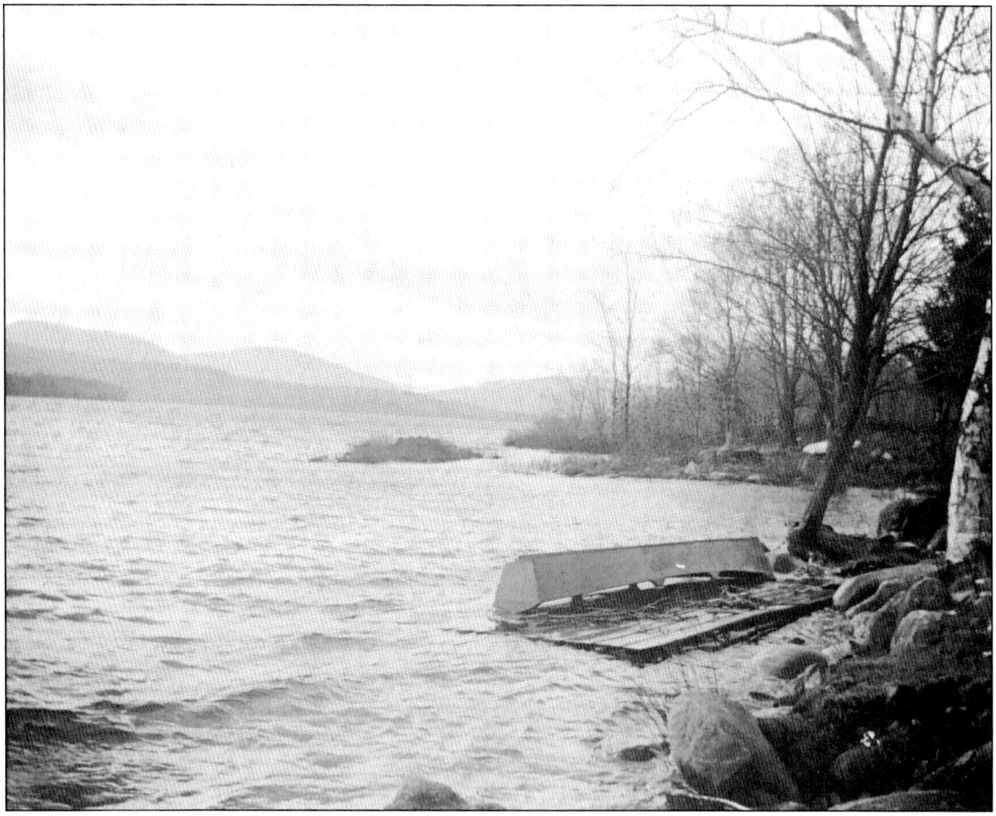

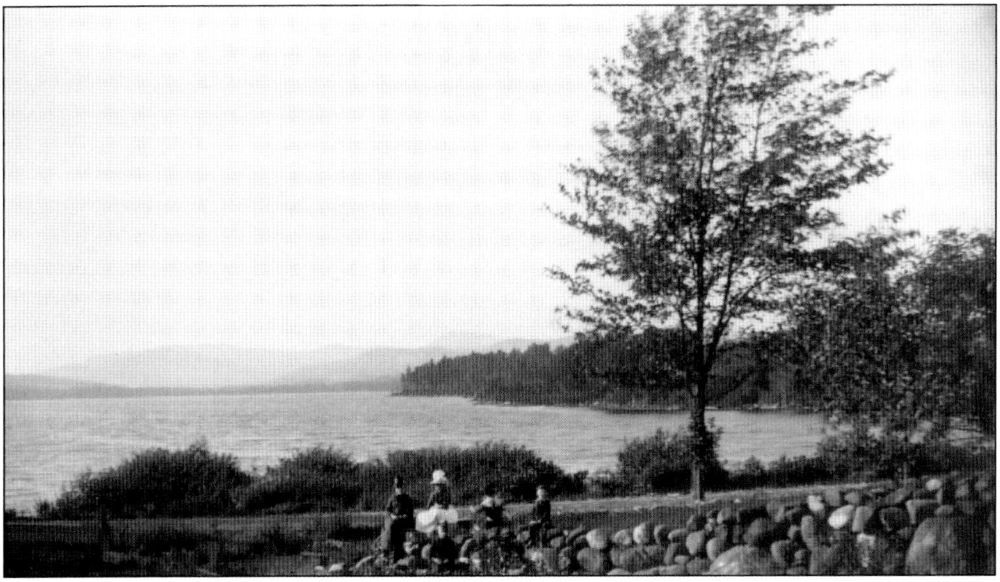

BY THE LAKE, C. 1900. Many picnickers over the years have enjoyed an outing with the peaceful rolling mountains and clear, sparkling water as a backdrop. This photograph was taken by A.O. Reed of Brunswick.

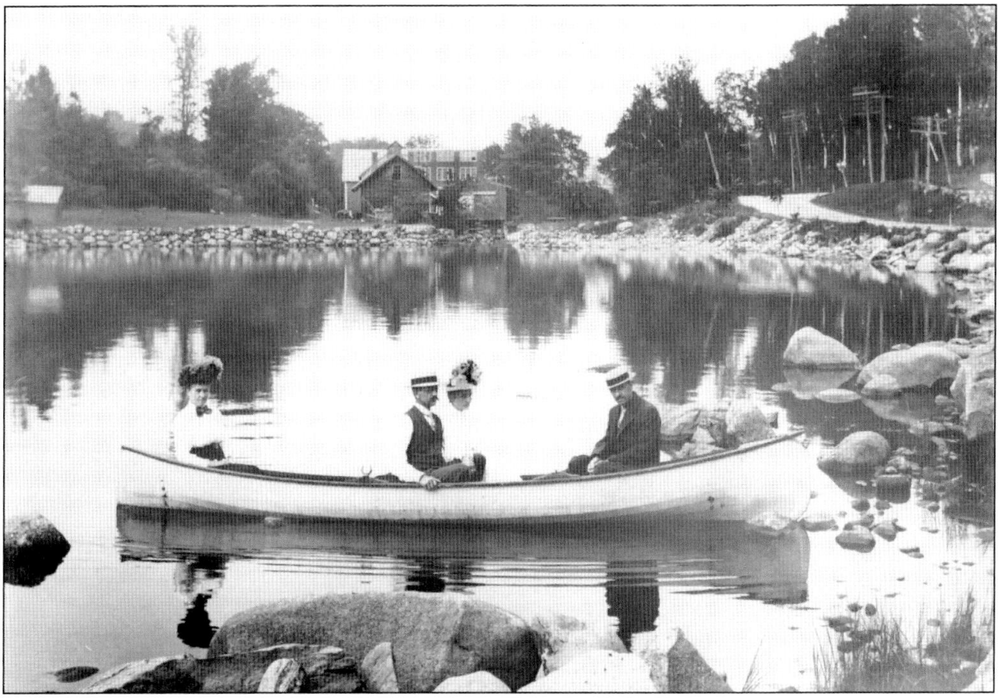

WILSON LAKE OUTING, SUNDAY, JULY 24, 1910. Wilson Lake is the most noted natural feature in Wilton. It has been noted for the mirror-like reflections on its calm waters. In this photograph, people can be seen enjoying a Sunday outing in their canoe. They are very well dressed, perhaps having gone to church that morning. They are all wearing hats, with the women's hats being quite spectacular, perhaps having been made by local milliner Emma Magrath. Bass Shoe and the gristmill are visible in the background of this image.

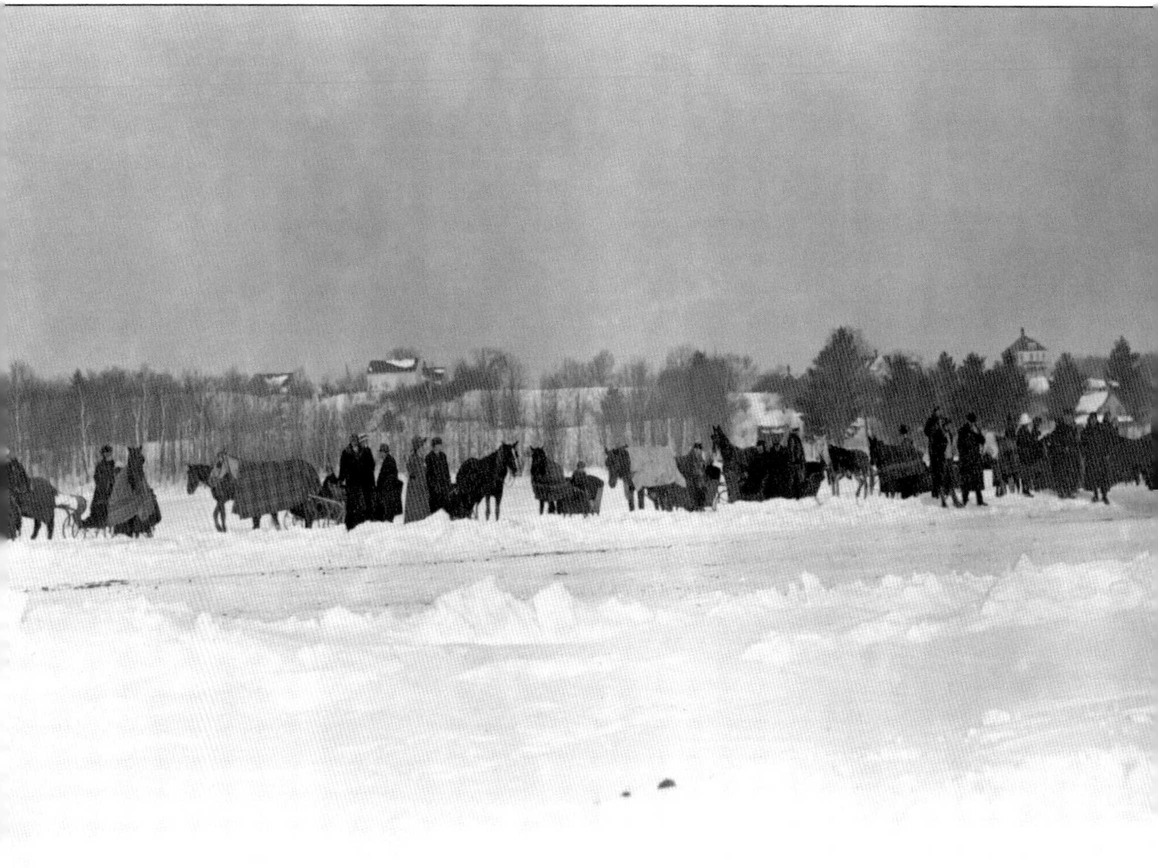

Sleigh Races, Late 1800s. Racing sleighs on Wilson Lake was a popular winter sport. Here, an area of ice has been cleared on the lake for the races. There are a number of sleighs in this photograph. The people and horses alike are wearing warm clothing. There is a sprinkling of residences on the hill in the distance. The Alton Farnum residence can be seen on the right.

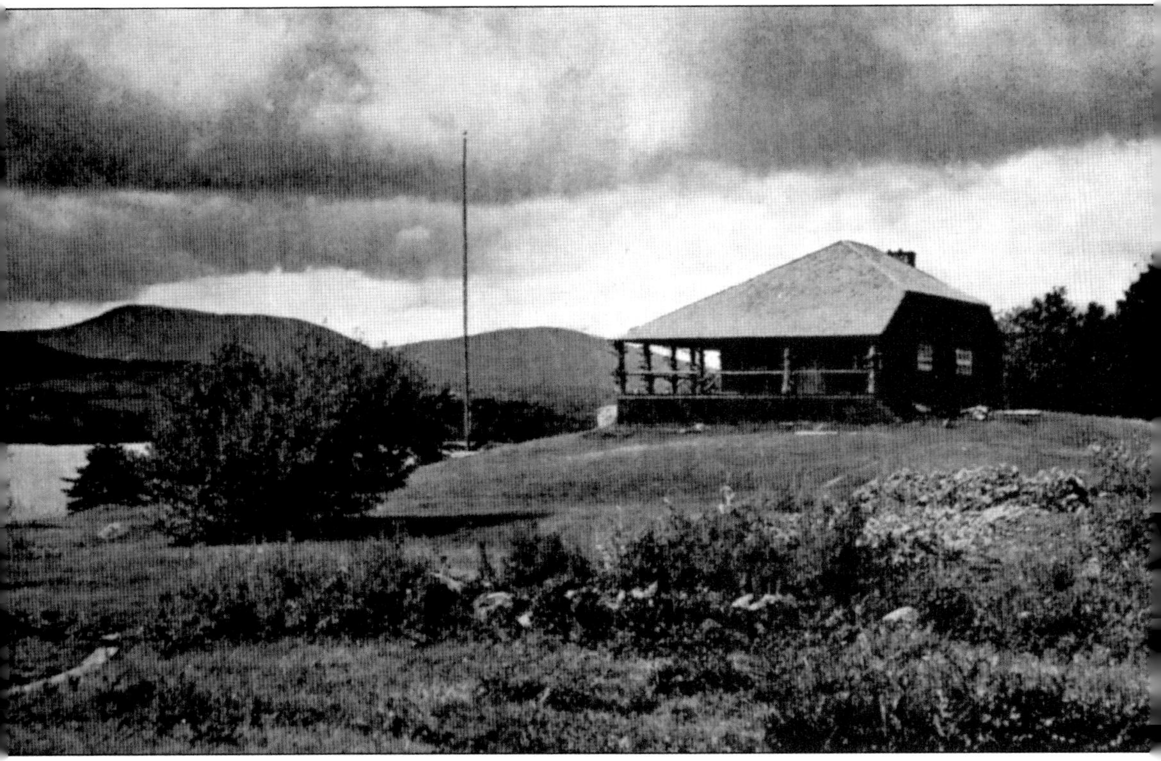

BLUE MOUNTAIN CAMPS, 1906. This would later be known as Kineowatha Camps, on the shores of Wilson Lake. The Blue Mountain Camps were created for both families and individuals. Wilson Lake was known for great fishing at this time. The salmon and bass fishing were both excellent. The camp was advertised in the *Boston Evening Transcript* of May 12, 1909, as being a great place to bathe, canoe, do mountain climbing and enjoy "fresh vegetables from our gardens, milk and cream from our Jersey cows." The camps were open from June to October.

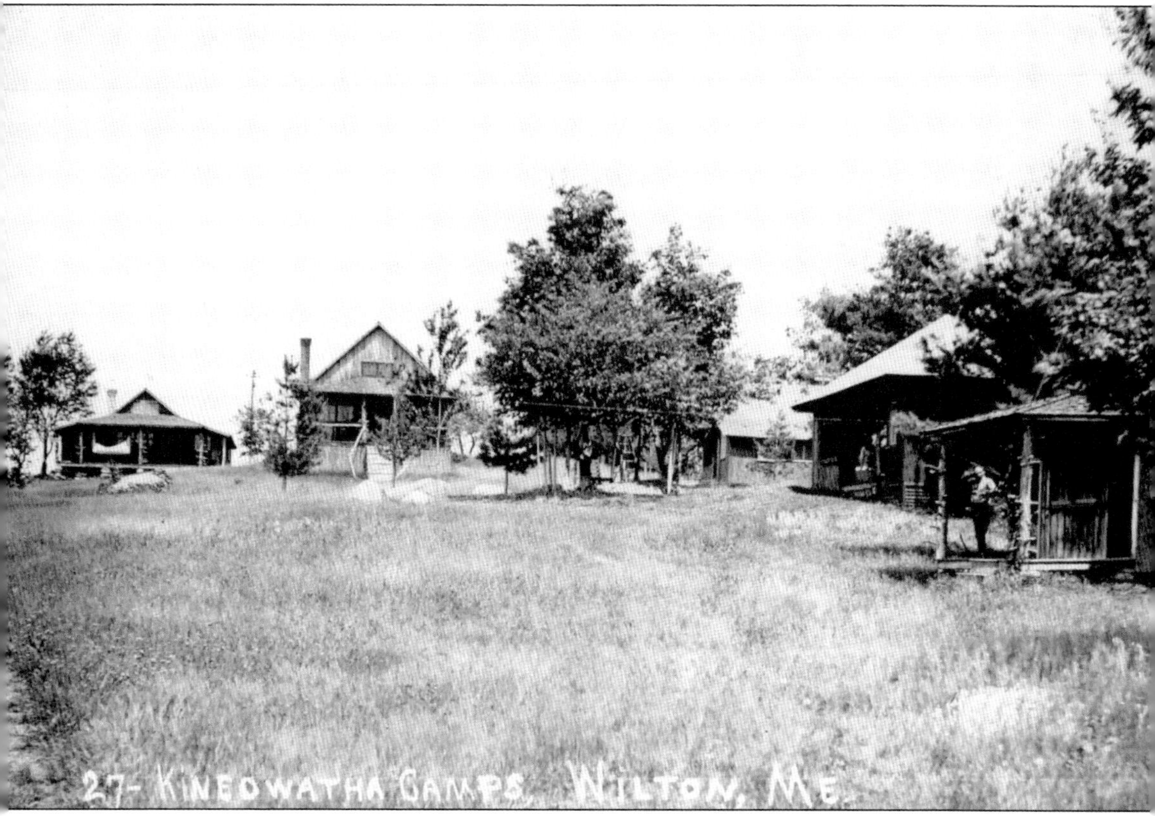

BLUE MOUNTAIN CAMPS CABINS, EARLY 1900S. The Blue Mountain cabins had a great deal to offer. One cabin featured a kitchen and a dining area. Other cabins, which were smaller, contained one, two, or three rooms and would accommodate two to four people. Each cabin had comfortable beds, furnishings, and a fireplace. A newspaper article about the opening of the camps wrote, "This lovely spot with its pure mountain air, pure spring water, pure food and fresh vegetables from the garden; milk, cream, eggs, and butter from the farm, and altogether healthful out-of-door life, has been chosen as best adapted to development of both voice and health."

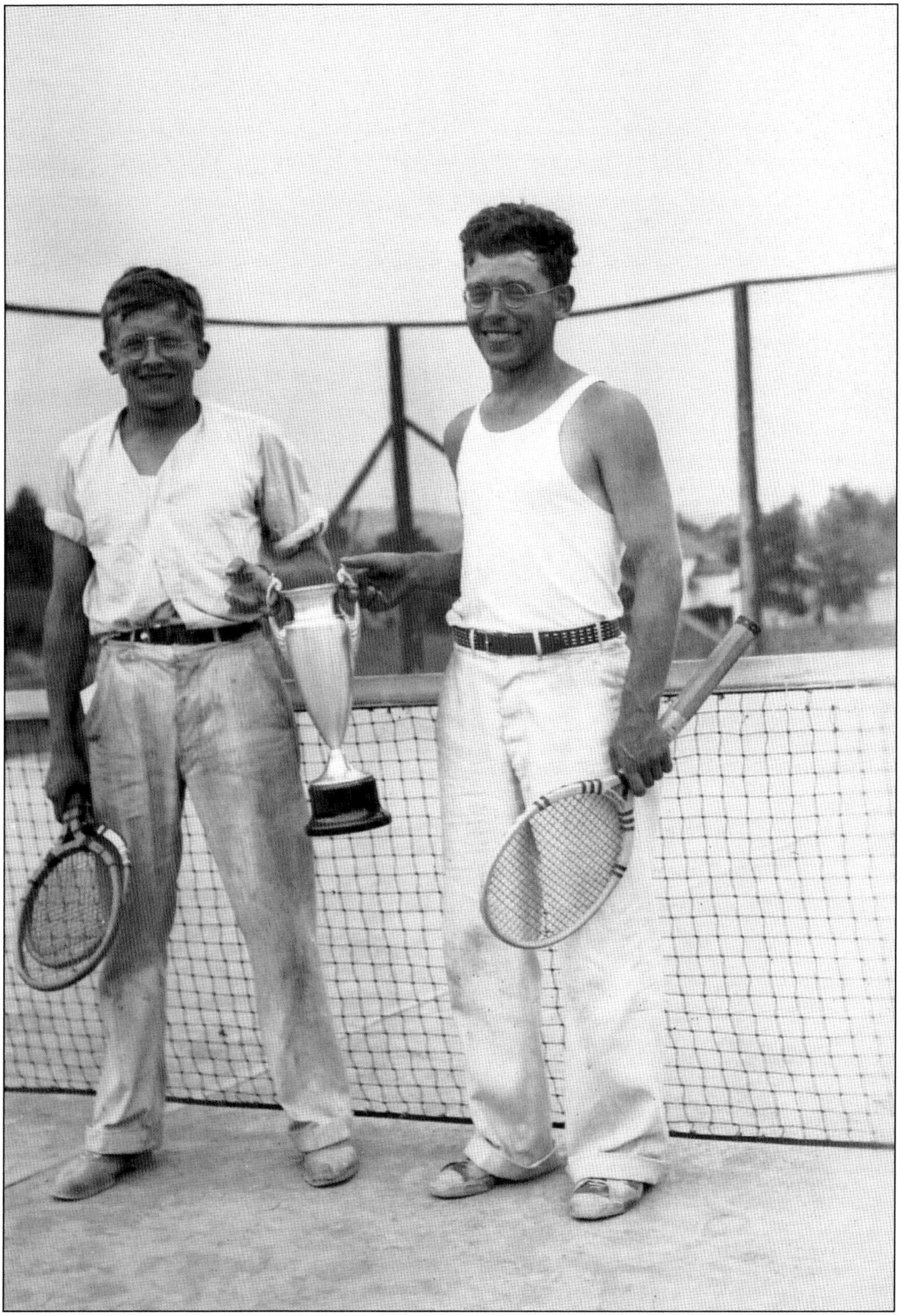

TENNIS TOURNAMENT, 1934. In this tennis match, Stanley Williams defeated Francis Karkos in three sets, 6-3, 6-4, 6-3, to win the first leg (and trophy) of the George F. Goodspeed Tournament. This was part of the extensive recreation program offered in the town at the time.

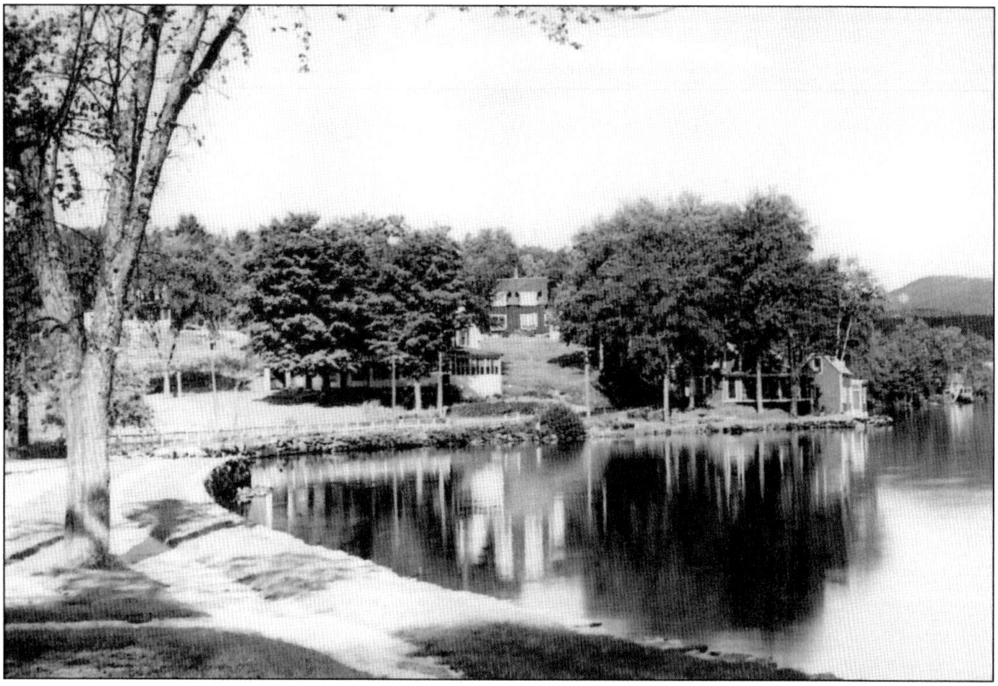

Wilson Pond, c. 1940. Known mostly as Wilson Lake, this body of water is two miles in length and half a mile wide. It has a maximum depth of 60 feet and seven miles of shoreline. At one time, there were floating islands at the head of the lake. This was a tourist attraction for many years. The first camp was built on Wilson Lake in 1896.

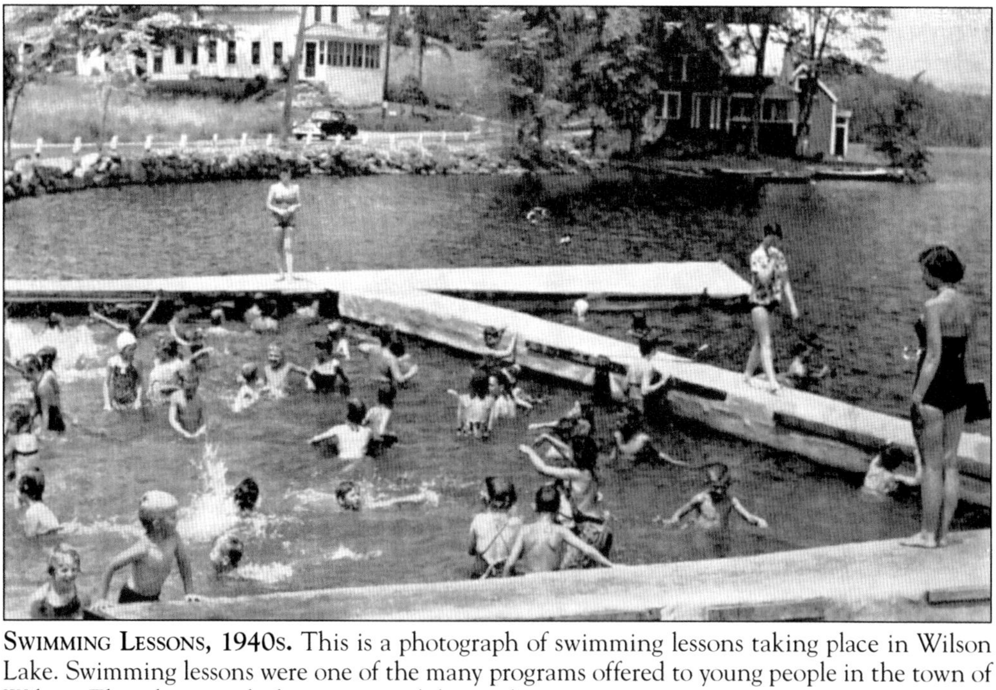

Swimming Lessons, 1940s. This is a photograph of swimming lessons taking place in Wilson Lake. Swimming lessons were one of the many programs offered to young people in the town of Wilton. This photograph shows a typical day in the town swimming program.

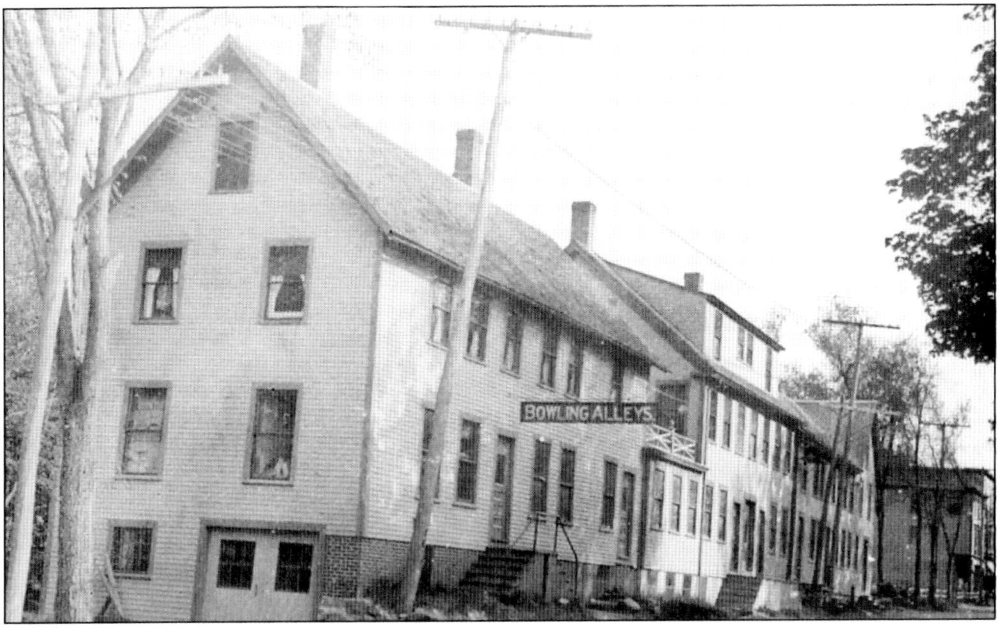

BOWLING ALLEYS, C. 1940. The Bass Block included bowling alleys for many years. Bowling alleys would later open at Meadow Lanes in East Wilton, and this one would close. This was also said to be a billiard hall. These sports added to the opportunities for recreation in this area at the time.

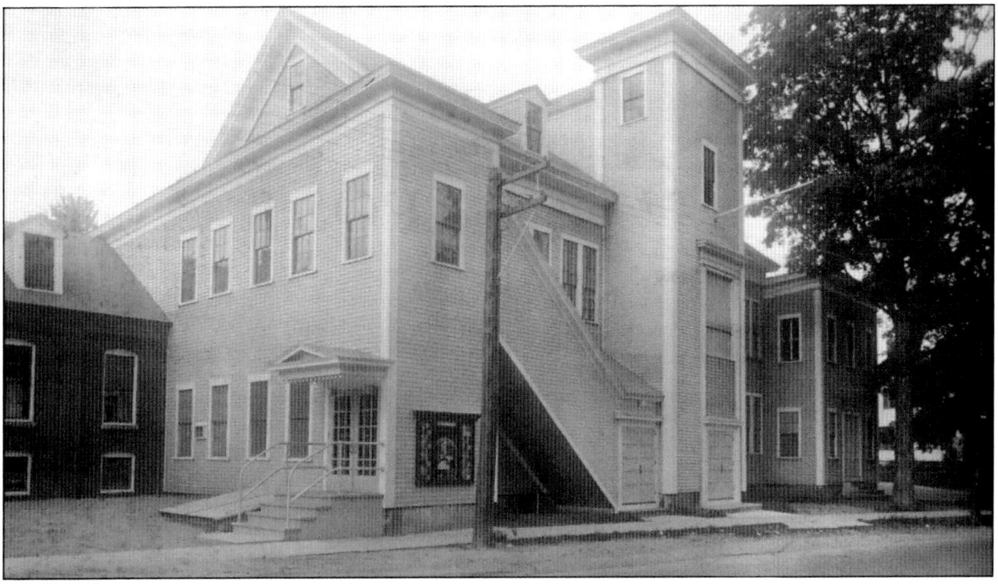

WILTON THEATER, C. 1950S. This theater was on Main Street across from the fire station in Wilton and was part of the community building given to the town by George Goodspeed in 1935. The theater was downstairs, and there was a basketball court and dance hall upstairs. This building was formerly Dimon Furnel's woolen mill, and, later, the Wilson Woolen Company's Main Street branch. At the time this photograph was taken, W.P. Dufour was the manager of the theater.

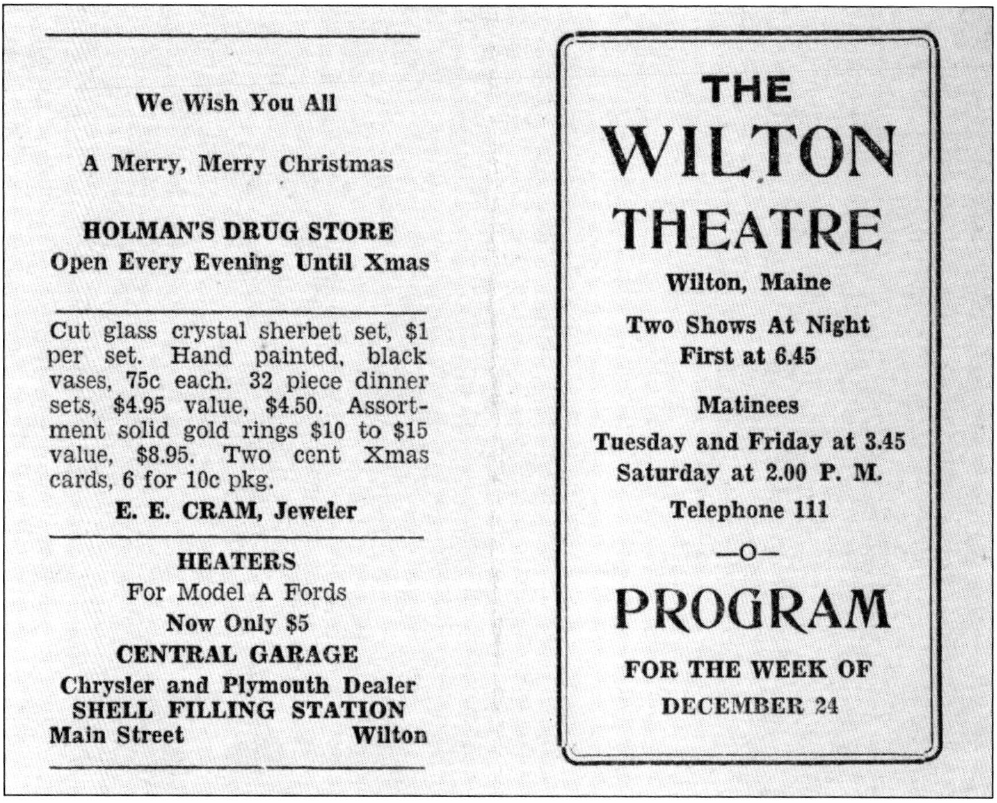

We Wish You All

A Merry, Merry Christmas

HOLMAN'S DRUG STORE
Open Every Evening Until Xmas

Cut glass crystal sherbet set, $1 per set. Hand painted, black vases, 75c each. 32 piece dinner sets, $4.95 value, $4.50. Assortment solid gold rings $10 to $15 value, $8.95. Two cent Xmas cards, 6 for 10c pkg.

E. E. CRAM, Jeweler

HEATERS
For Model A Fords
Now Only $5
CENTRAL GARAGE
Chrysler and Plymouth Dealer
SHELL FILLING STATION
Main Street Wilton

THE
WILTON
THEATRE
Wilton, Maine

Two Shows At Night
First at 6.45

Matinees
Tuesday and Friday at 3.45
Saturday at 2.00 P. M.
Telephone 111

—o—

PROGRAM

FOR THE WEEK OF
DECEMBER 24

WILTON THEATER MOVIE PROGRAM, 1934. The photograph above shows the outside of the theater program for the week of December 24, 1934. The second photograph is of the inside of the program. The theater offered a number of movies every week, with two shows nightly and matinees on three days. The auditorium seated about 400 people.

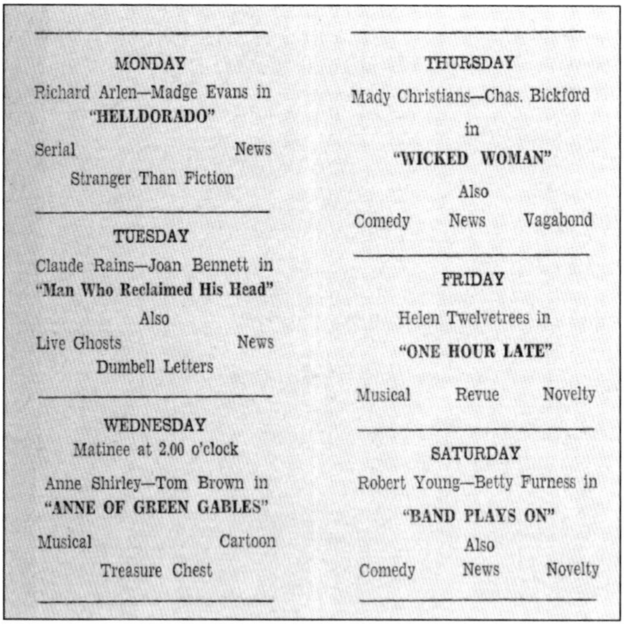

MONDAY
Richard Arlen—Madge Evans in
"HELLDORADO"
Serial News
Stranger Than Fiction

TUESDAY
Claude Rains—Joan Bennett in
"Man Who Reclaimed His Head"
Also
Live Ghosts News
Dumbell Letters

WEDNESDAY
Matinee at 2.00 o'clock
Anne Shirley—Tom Brown in
"ANNE OF GREEN GABLES"
Musical Cartoon
Treasure Chest

THURSDAY
Mady Christians—Chas. Bickford
in
"WICKED WOMAN"
Also
Comedy News Vagabond

FRIDAY
Helen Twelvetrees in
"ONE HOUR LATE"
Musical Revue Novelty

SATURDAY
Robert Young—Betty Furness in
"BAND PLAYS ON"
Also
Comedy News Novelty

Ten

Community

This last chapter includes numerous elements of importance to the town of Wilton's history and development. It will focus on education, primarily the Wilton Academy. It will also focus on churches in the town, including the development of their congregations and the evolution of their buildings. Additional elements important to the community such as the bank and the post office will be touched upon. The development of a town library was also instrumental to the town and community, as were other community resources and services, like the fire station. A few people of note are also included in this chapter, as well as modes of transportation, including horses and buggies, the railroad, and the automobile.

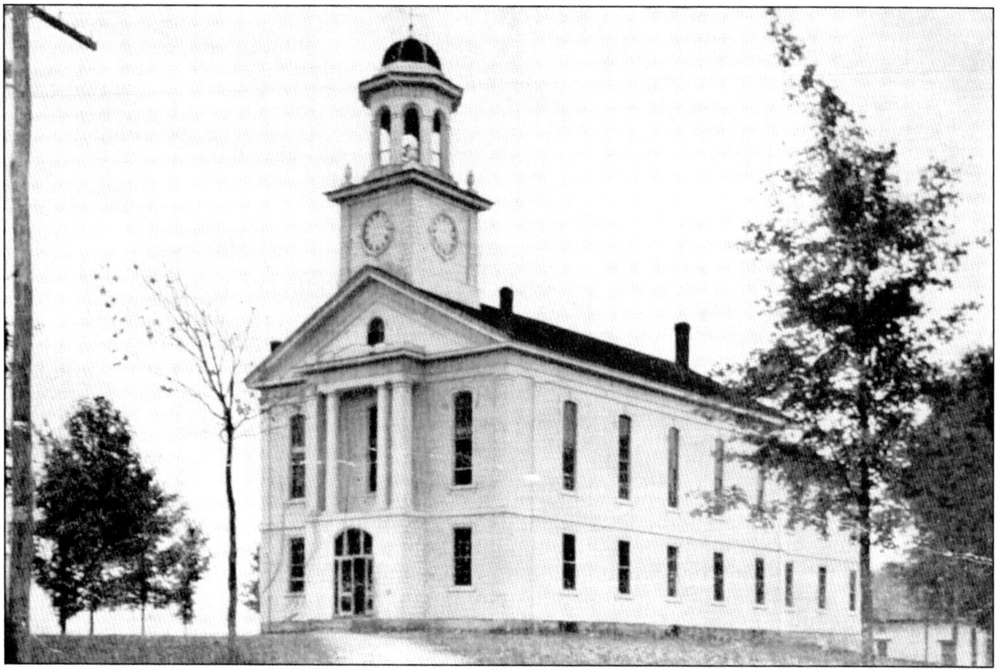

Wilton Academy, Early 1900s. This photograph postcard was published by Mrs. A.S. Magrath (Emma) and postmarked 1907. Wilton Academy was started on September 10, 1867. From 1895, the academy served as the free high school for the residents of Wilton. The school was accredited in 1901. Drew Harthorn was principal from 1894 to 1905 and then again from 1907 to 1912.

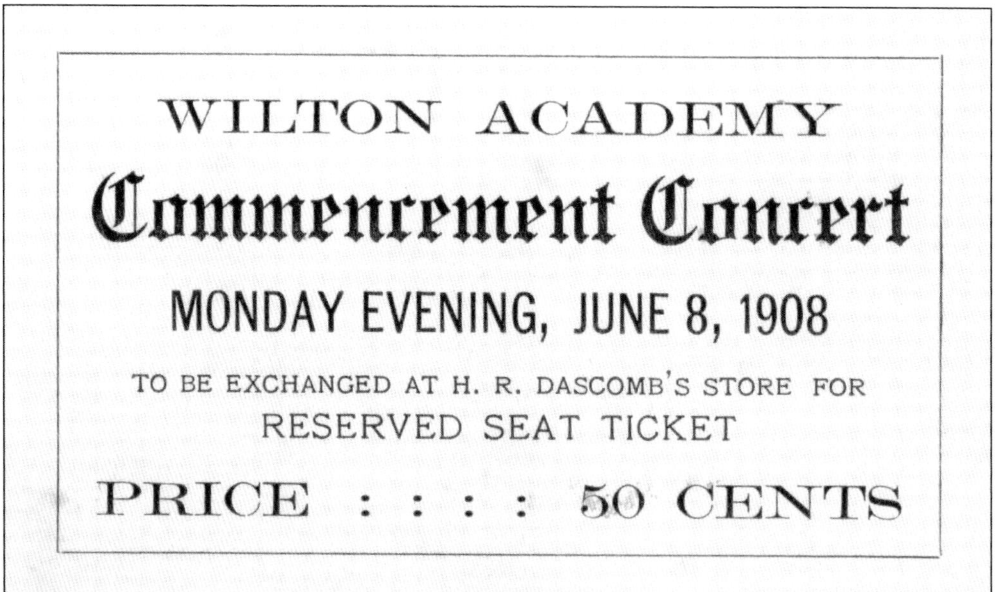

WILTON ACADEMY

Commencement Concert

MONDAY EVENING, JUNE 8, 1908

TO BE EXCHANGED AT H. R. DASCOMB'S STORE FOR

RESERVED SEAT TICKET

PRICE : : : : 50 CENTS

Wilton Academy Commencement Concert, 1908. This item had to be taken to the H.R. Dascomb Store and exchanged for a reserved seat for the commencement concert on June 8, 1908.

WILTON ACADEMY LUNCH LINE, 1950s. This photograph was taken in the lunch room at Wilton Academy. Of note are the glass milk bottles. The lunch ladies are serving the hot lunch to the students.

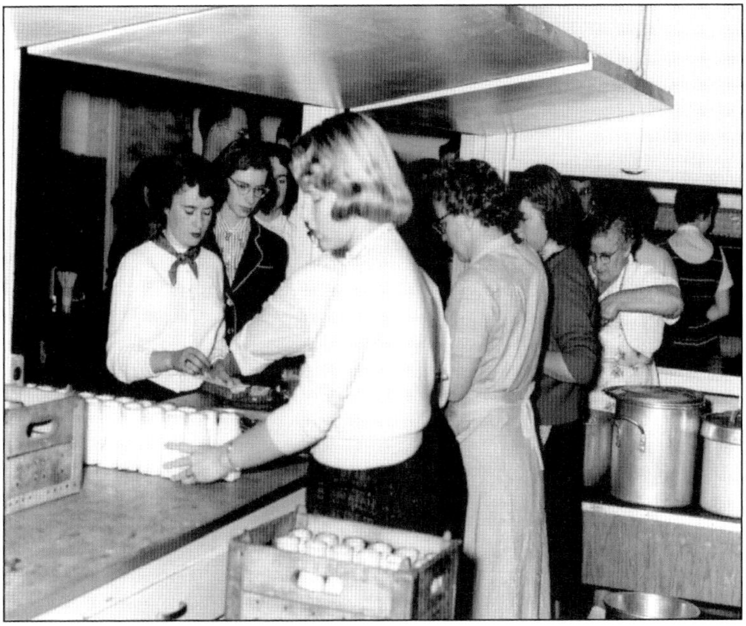

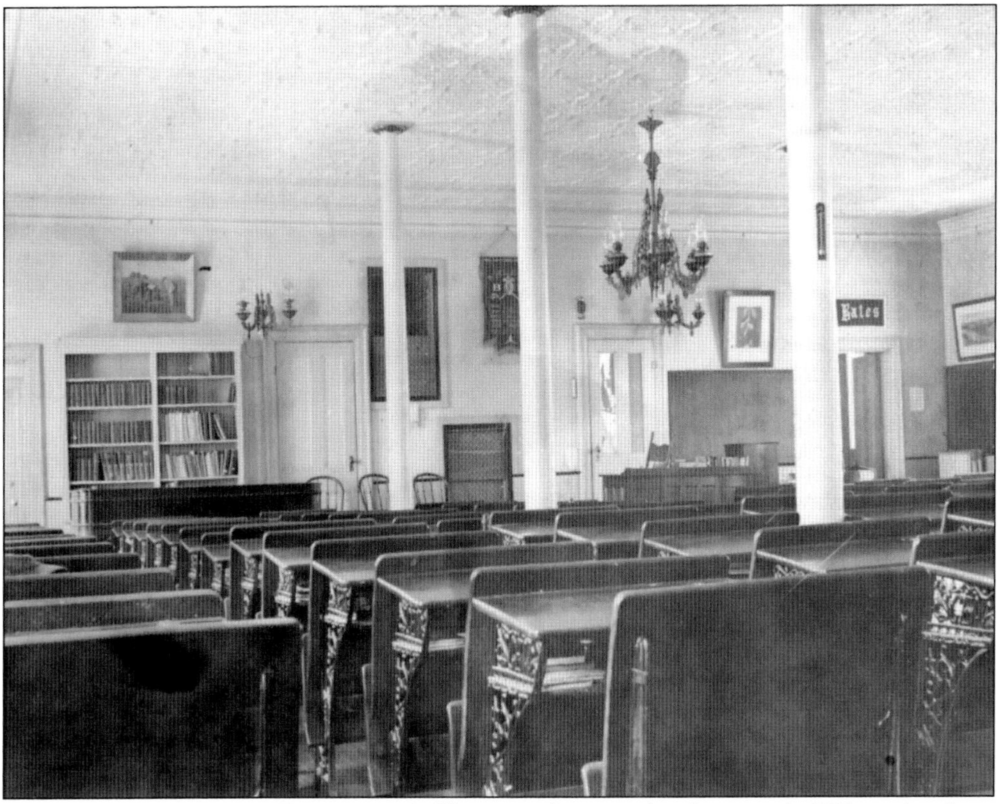

WILTON ACADEMY MAIN ROOM, 1915. This is a photograph taken inside Wilton Academy some time after the addition, which included two large and convenient recitation rooms, a large assembly room, a library and reading room, a hall for social occasions and graduation exercises, and some smaller rooms.

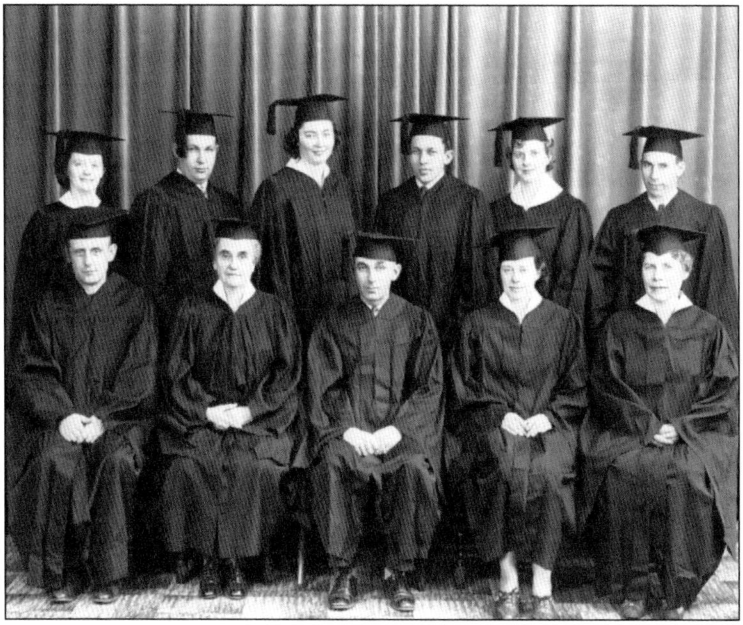

Wilton Academy Faculty, 1943. These Wilton Academy faculty members are, from left to right, (first row) Abner Toothaker, Susan Weston, Maurice Earle, Dorothy Dumais (Latin and French), and Leah Peterson; (second row) Mary York, Preston Whittaker, Eloise Macomber, Harold Karkos (English and sciences), Ruth Robbins Adamo, and P. Warren Legge.

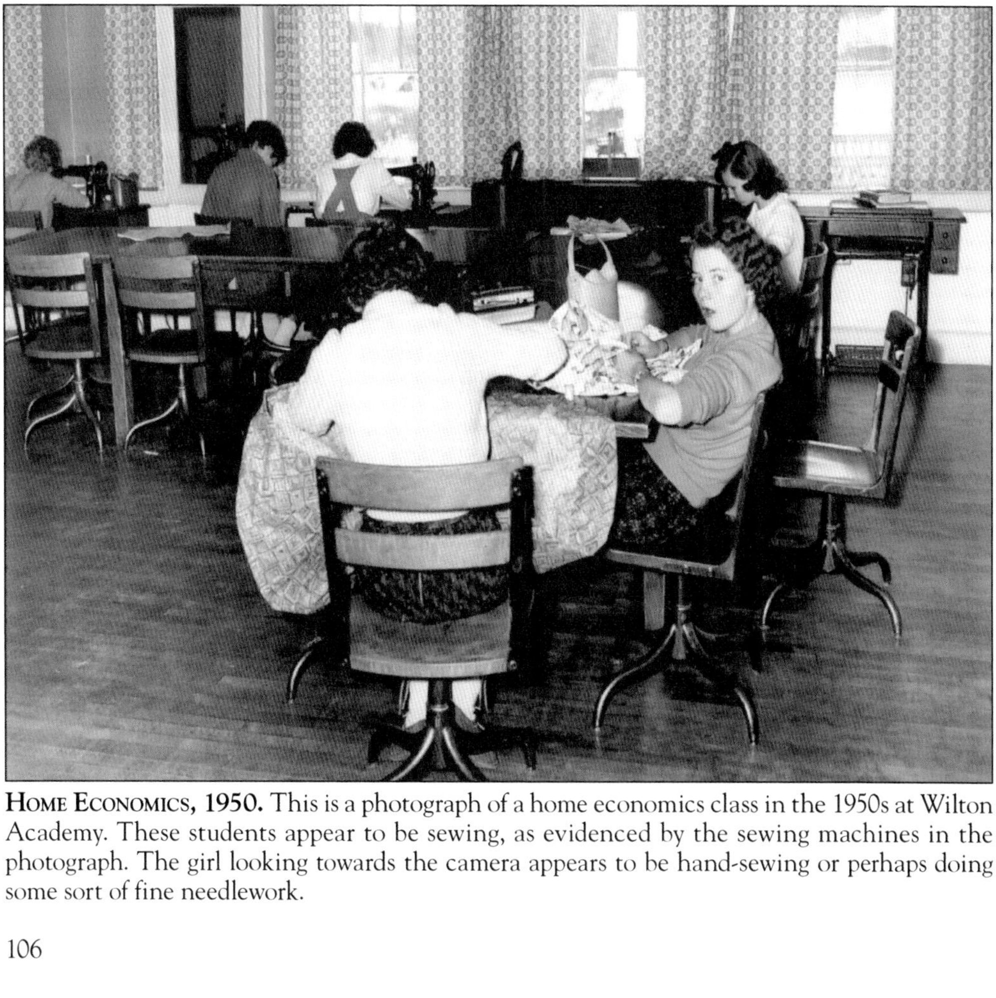

Home Economics, 1950. This is a photograph of a home economics class in the 1950s at Wilton Academy. These students appear to be sewing, as evidenced by the sewing machines in the photograph. The girl looking towards the camera appears to be hand-sewing or perhaps doing some sort of fine needlework.

WILTON ACADEMY OFFICE, 1959. This photograph was in the 1960 Wilton Academy yearbook, the *Eagle*, and shows Roberta Chaffee, who is referred to as the "Head Office Girl." At this time, students, all of them girls, helped in the office. They were referred to as "Office Girls." The yearbook wrote, "These girls get much practical experience in office work by answering telephones, copying attendance lists, and delivering messages."

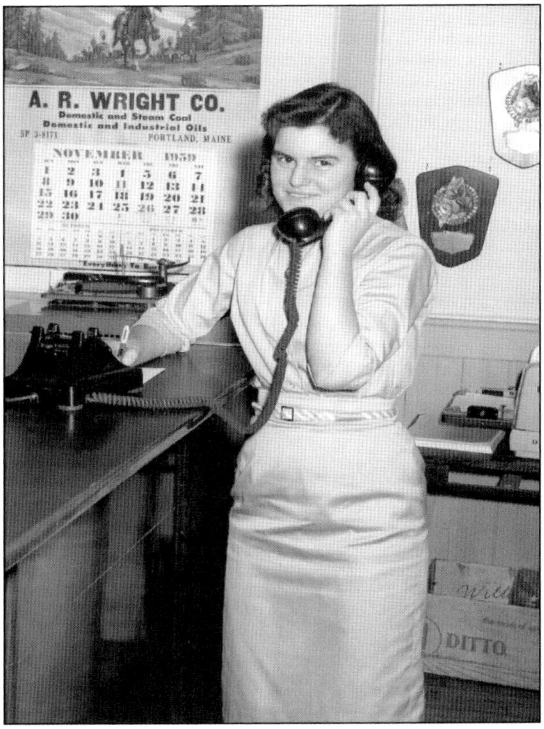

WILTON ACADEMY OFFICE, 1950S. This photograph is of some of Wilton Academy's "Office Girls." In this photograph, they are making copies. It appears to be an involved process involving a mimeograph duplicator.

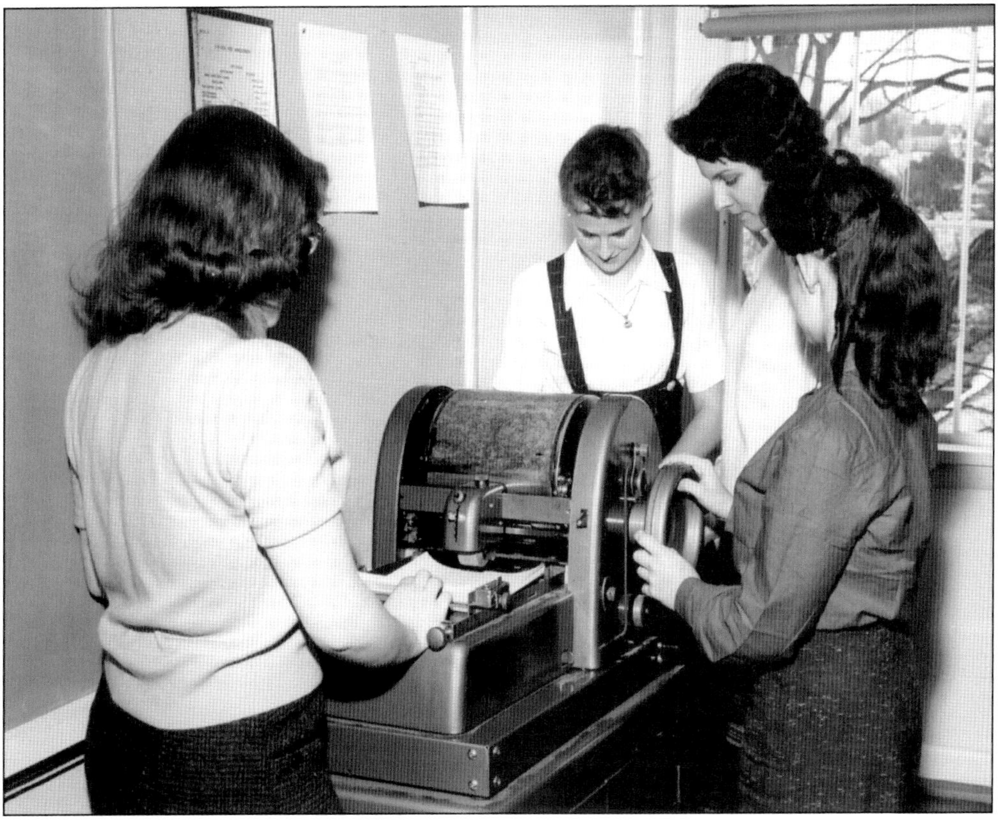

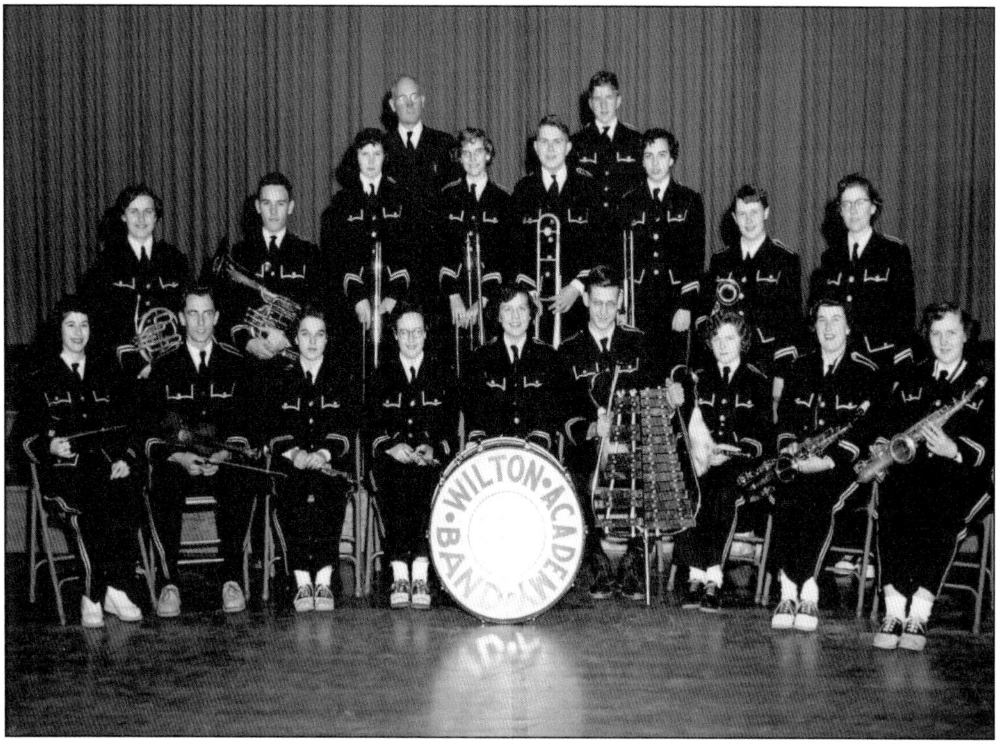

WILTON ACADEMY BAND, MID-1950s. In 1950, K.H. Foster built the Wilton Academy gymnasium. It was a gift of the Wilton Woolen Company. It had a seating capacity of about 850 people, a basketball court, and a stage. It served as the center for Wilton Academy events for the next 20 years. This is a photograph of the Wilton Academy band, taken in the gymnasium.

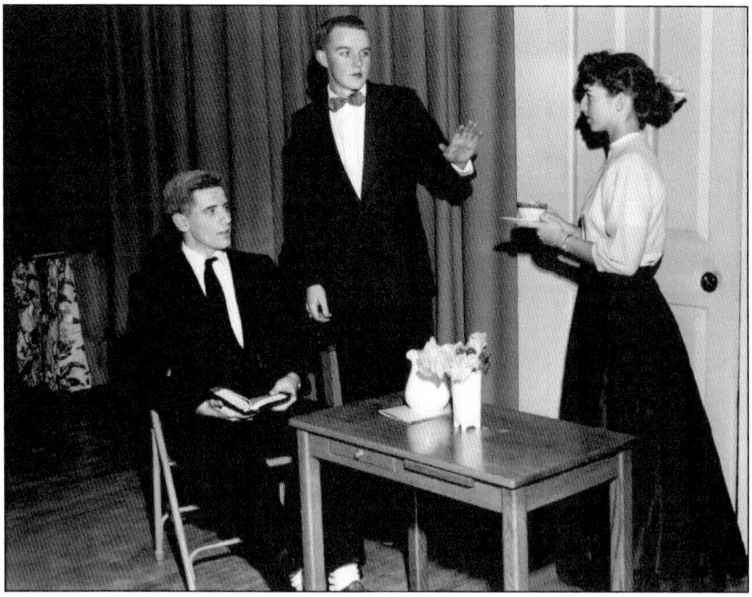

SENIOR PLAY, 1953. This is another photograph taken in the new gymnasium, on the stage. In this photograph are seniors (from left to right) Spencer Trask, Herbert Randell, and June Smith. The play was *Fog on the Valley.*

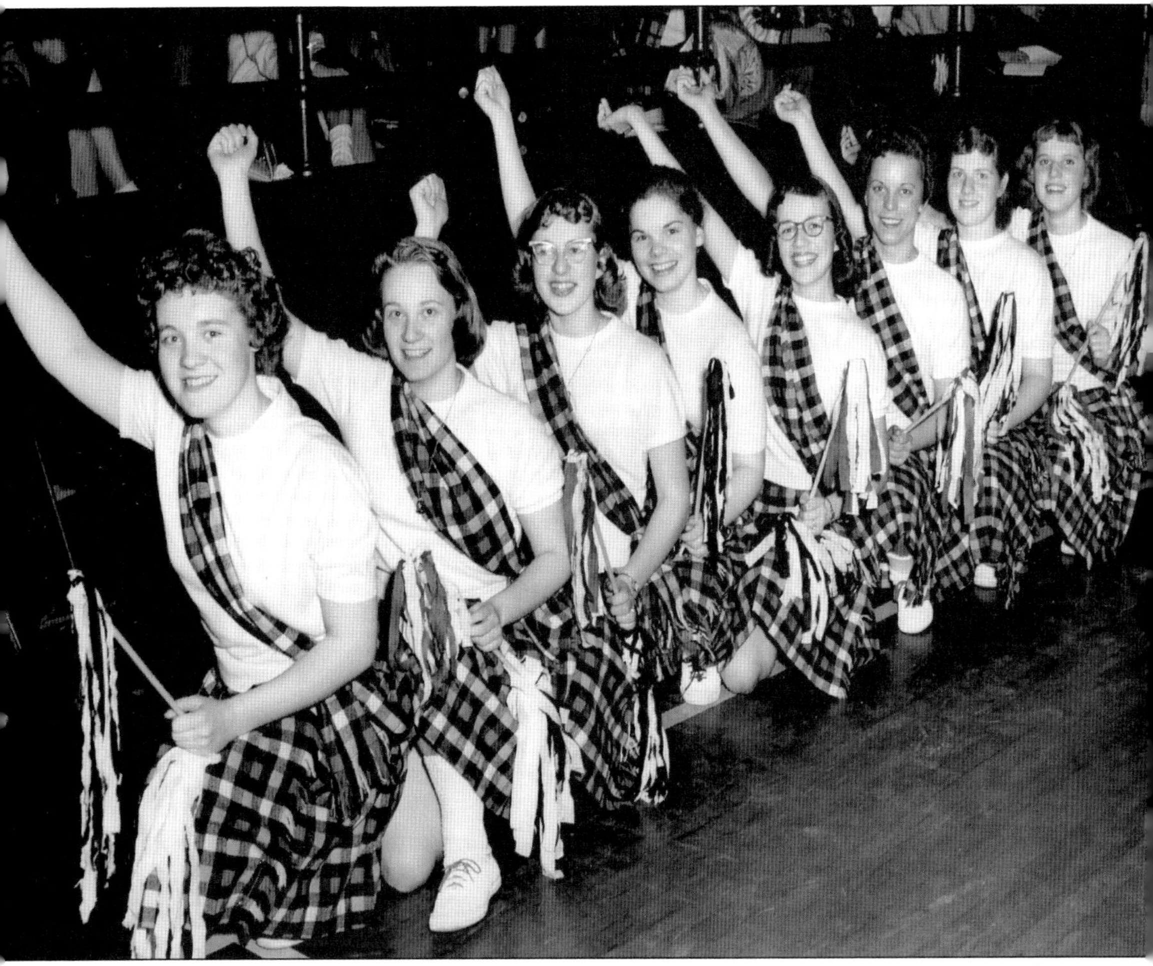

WILTON ACADEMY CHEERLEADERS, 1958. The Wilton Academy cheerleaders in this photograph are, from left to right, Irene Kenney, Janet Gillespie, Lorna Poulin, Deborah Hardy, Maurie Stinson, Joyce Johnson, Marie Kenney, and Eleanor Partridge.

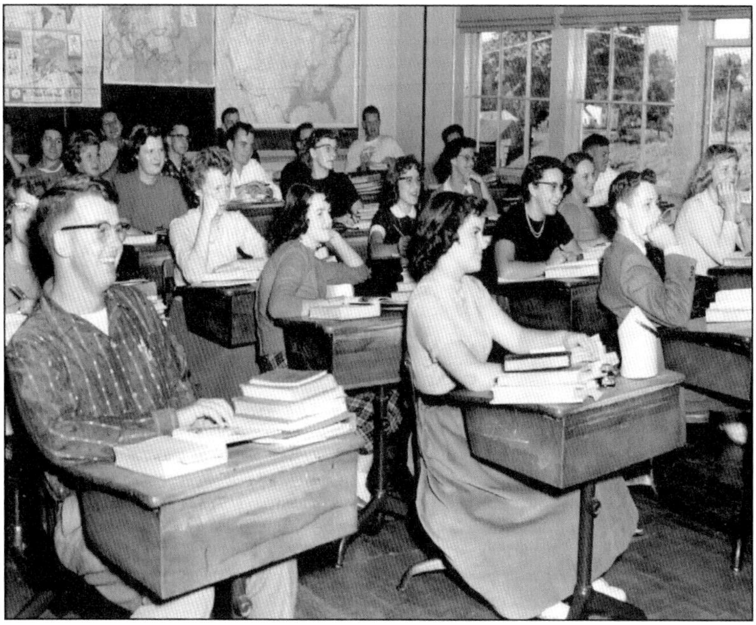

Wilton Academy Classroom, Late 1950s. This photograph appears to be of a geography, history, or civics class at Wilton Academy. The students seem to be enjoying their lesson and are at rapt attention.

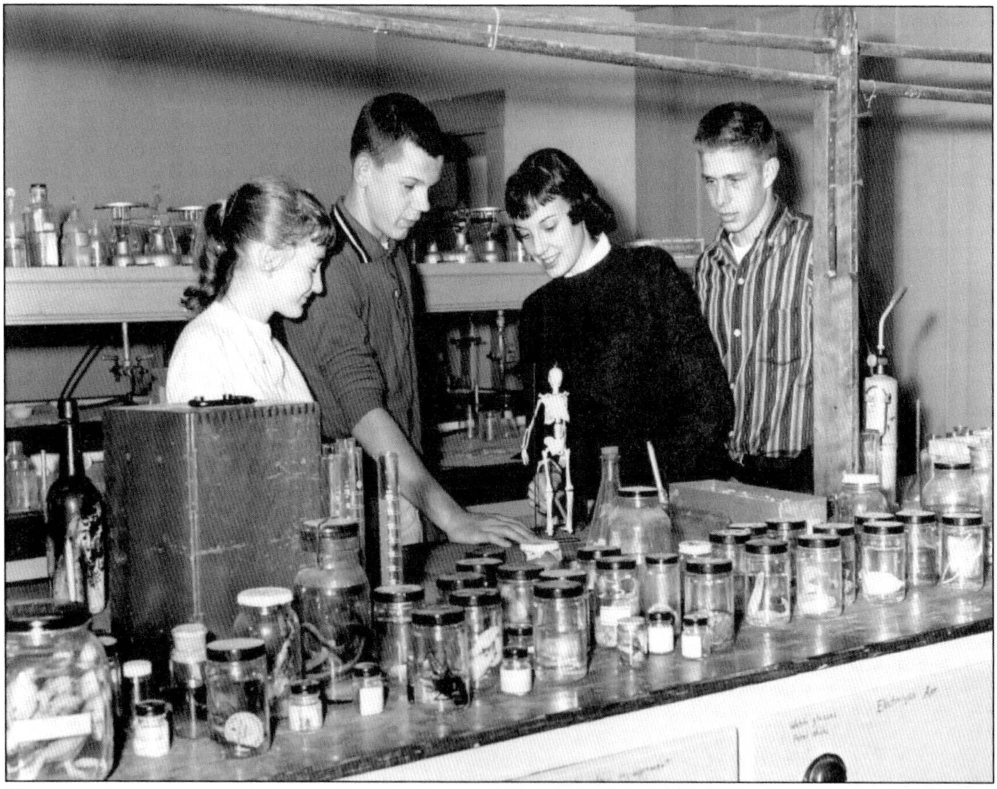

Wilton Academy Classroom, Early 1960s. This photograph is of a science laboratory in the early 1960s at Wilton Academy. There are a number of specimens in the jars, as well as assorted science equipment.

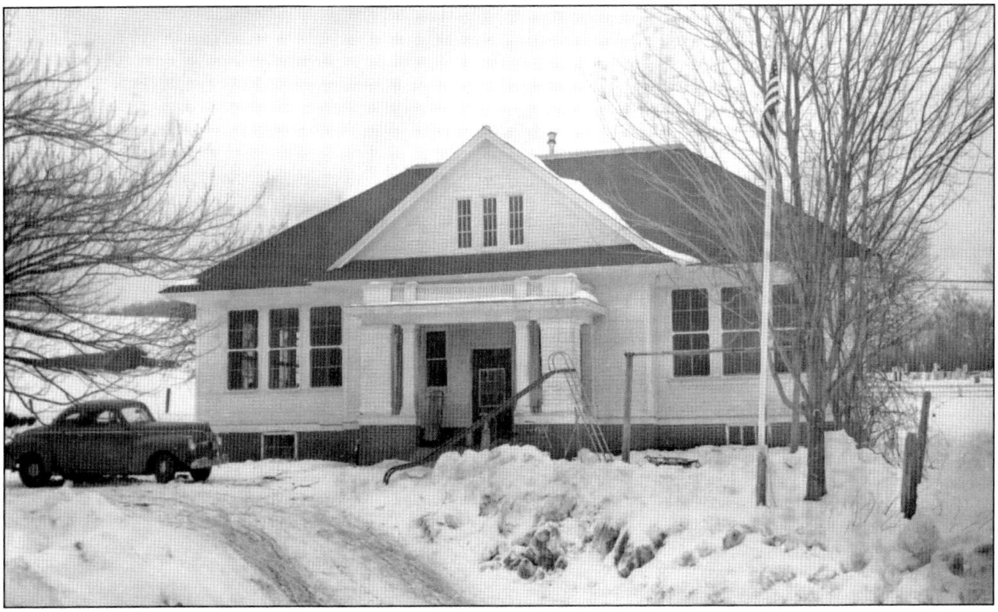

EAST WILTON SCHOOL, 1953. This school was built in 1923. In 1953, the principal was Walter Webber. Students in sub-primary through eighth grade were educated there by the four teachers on the faculty. This later became the Western Maine Community Action building.

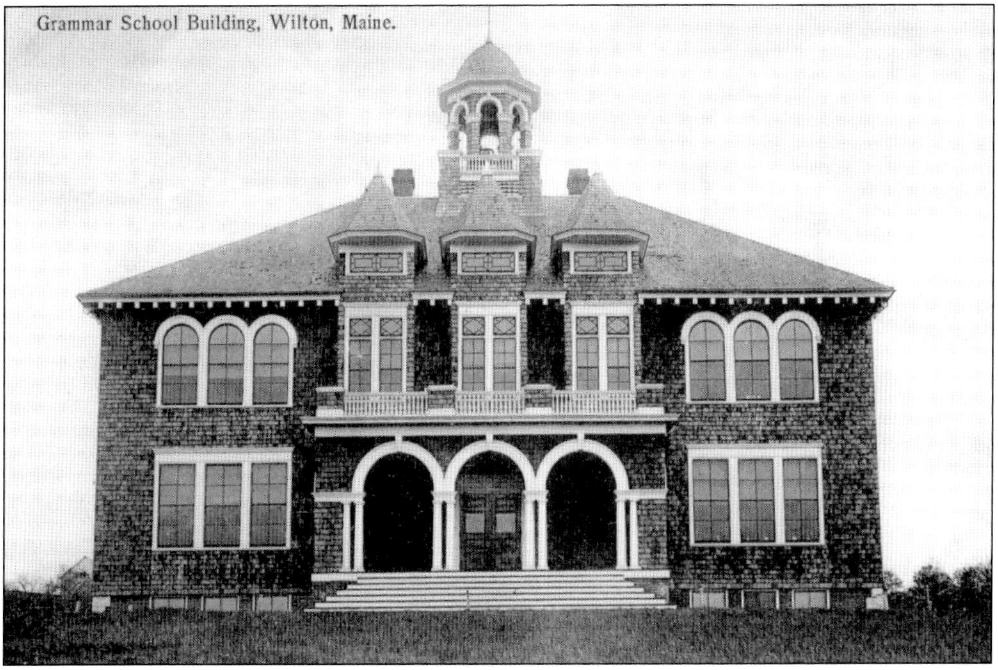

GRAMMAR SCHOOL BUILDING, 1911. The grammar school was also known as the Central School. It was built in 1903 in what was then known as district nine. It opened in the fall after Wilton's centennial celebration. This school replaced the Wilton Village School. In 1953, at the time of the sesquicentennial, this school was still in operation. Foster Sanborn was the principal, grades four through eight attended school here, and there were eight teachers. This photographic postcard was published by the H.R. Dascomb Store in Wilton.

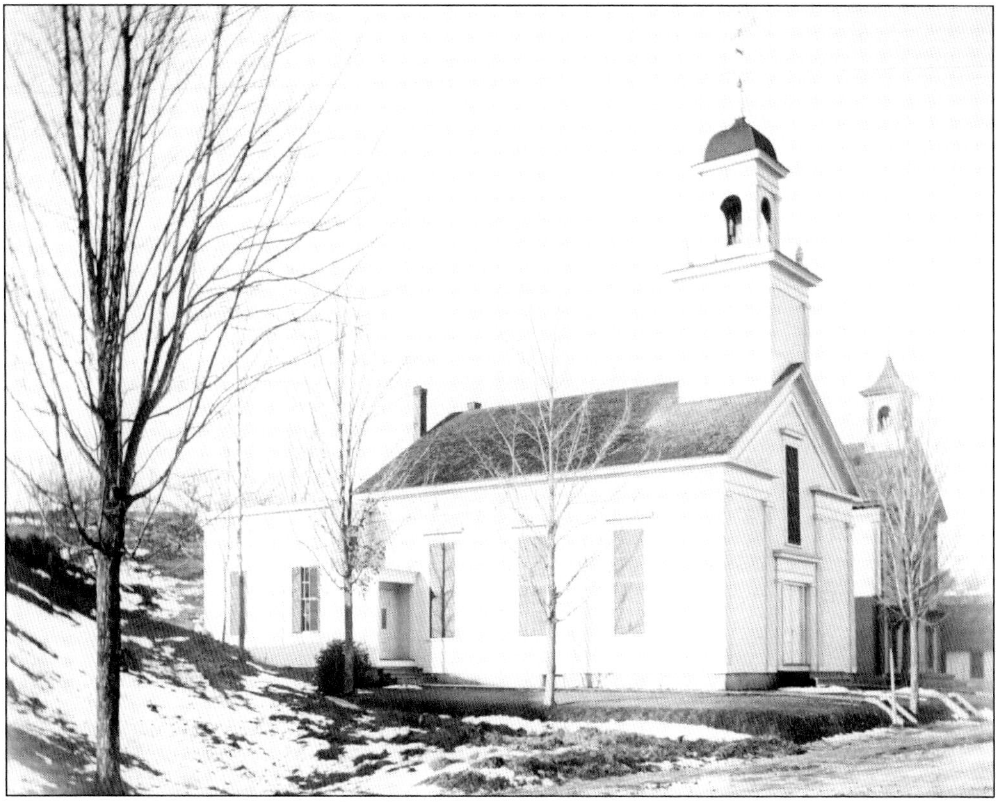

METHODIST CHURCH, C. 1900. This church was built in 1859. The first Methodist society in town is believed to have been formed in 1794 by Rev. Enoch Mudge. In 1820, the Wilton Methodists constructed a crudely finished building on Weld Road as their first house of worship. In December 1837, the Methodist society voted to build another church near the Wilton Upper Mills. This house of worship was finished in 1850 at the cost of $1,700. It, too, was on Weld Road, and it proved to be too far from the center of the village of Wilton. It was used until this new church was built in 1859 on Main Street at the cost of $2,500. This church would later get an addition.

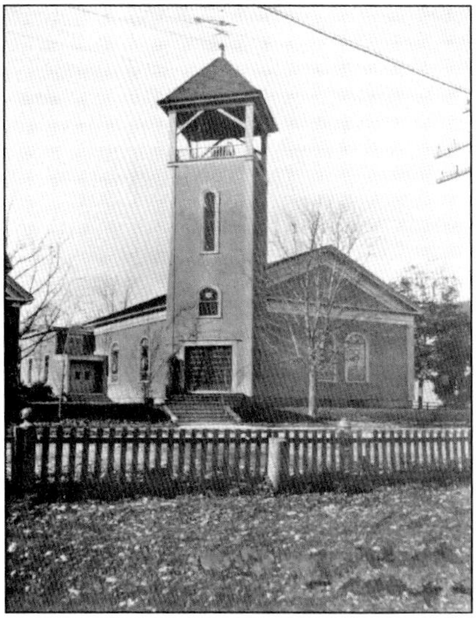

METHODIST CHURCH, AFTER 1905. This photograph was taken some time after 1905, when an addition was added to this church. This addition included a large tower and was set diagonally to the street. The interior of the church was also remodeled, and the stained-glass windows were added. Previously, the tower had been at the top of the church, as a belfry over the central doorway.

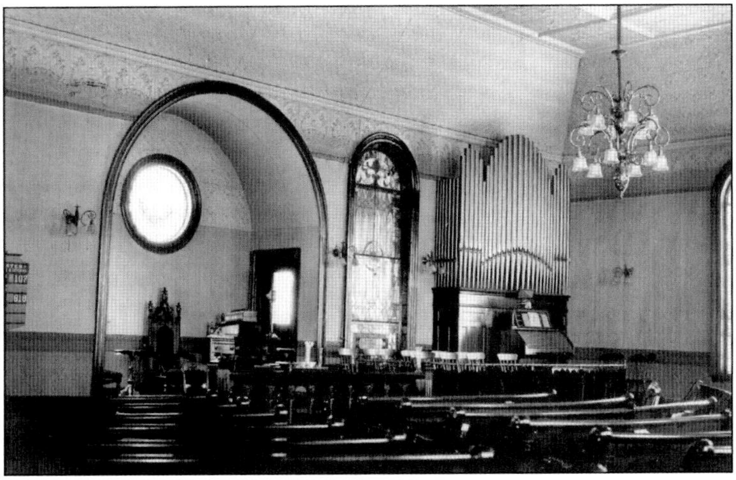

INSIDE THE METHODIST CHURCH, C. 1920. This photograph of the interior of the church shows the woodwork inside the sanctuary of the church, as well as the stained glass and the church organ. The chairs have been set up at the front of the church, near the organ, for the choir.

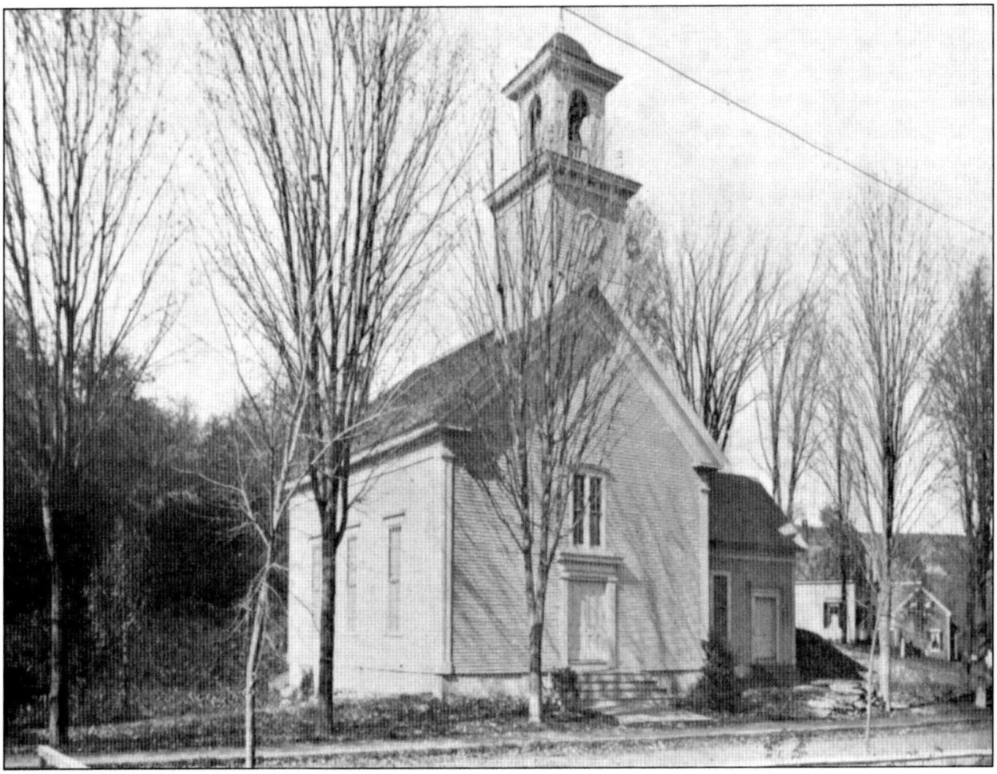

CONGREGATIONAL CHURCH, C. 1910. This is a photograph of the Congregational church. The Congregationalists had long hoped for a church of their own; however, for many years, they met either in members' homes or in the Old Meeting House (later Wilton Academy). By the 1850s, members were ready to have their own place of worship near the center of town. Members opted to use Walker's Hall as a place of worship until 1857, when the church was finally built by Philbrick Marston. The cost of the church was $2,000. Money was raised in part by selling pews to individual members. Unfortunately, heavy snows caused the roof and building to collapse in March 1869. Funds were then solicited to build a new church. The vestry was added in 1882 on the north side of the church. This increased the facilities for Sabbath school and social activities for the church.

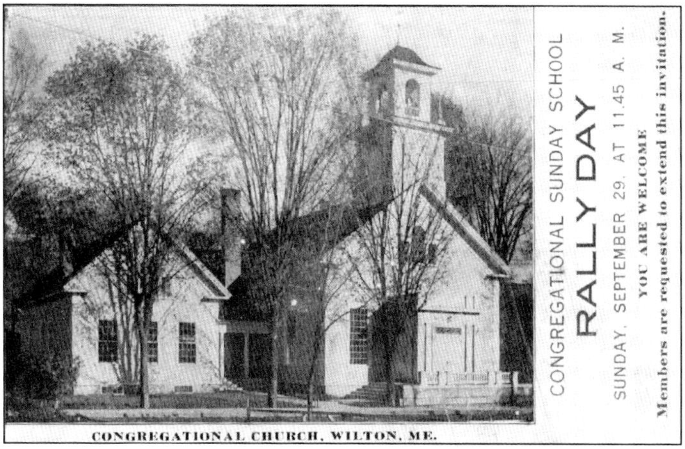

CONGREGATIONAL CHURCH, 1912. This photograph postcard is also an invitation, as the Congregationalists were trying to increase their membership. It was taken after an addition was added to the church.

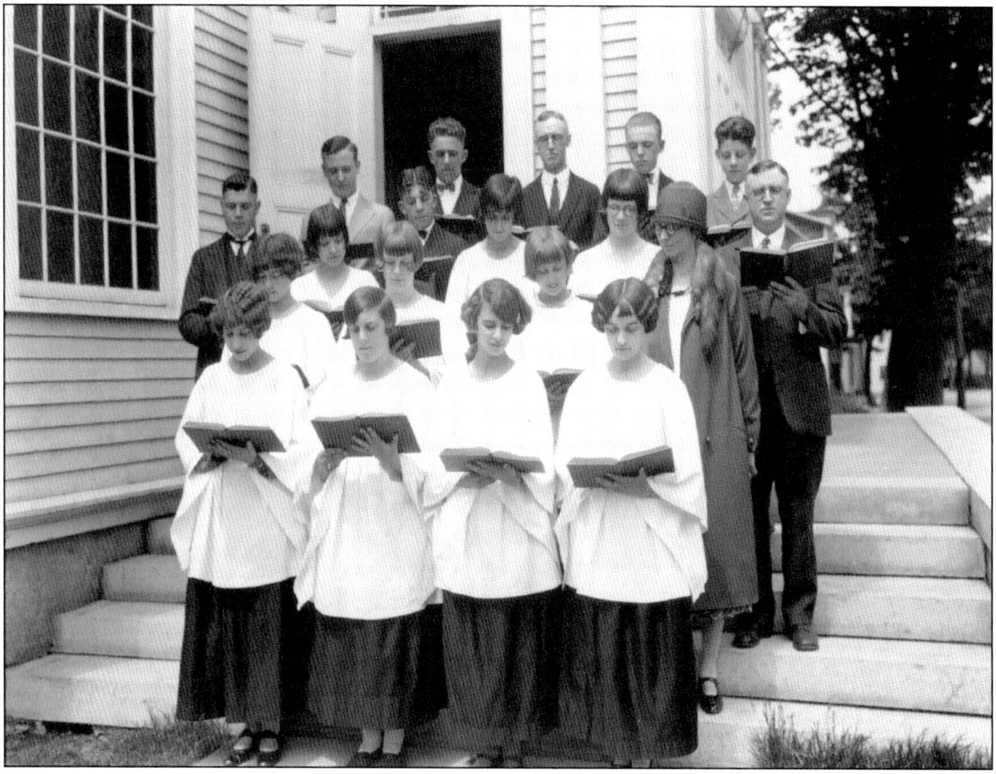

CONGREGATIONAL CHURCH CHOIR, 1920S. This photograph was taken of the Congregational church choir. They are, from left to right, (first row) Muriel Farnham, Marcia Colby, Myrtle Stinson, and Beulah Moar; (second row) Grayce Sands Benson, Doris Stevens, Marion Merrill, and Harriet Bass (organist); (third row) Rev. C. Donald Plomer, Kathleen Fletcher, unidentified, Alice Scribner, Hermine Larrabee, and Fred Cole (choir director); (fourth row) Carl Sewall, unidentified, Arthur Cole, Lester Eliot, and Foster Sanborn.

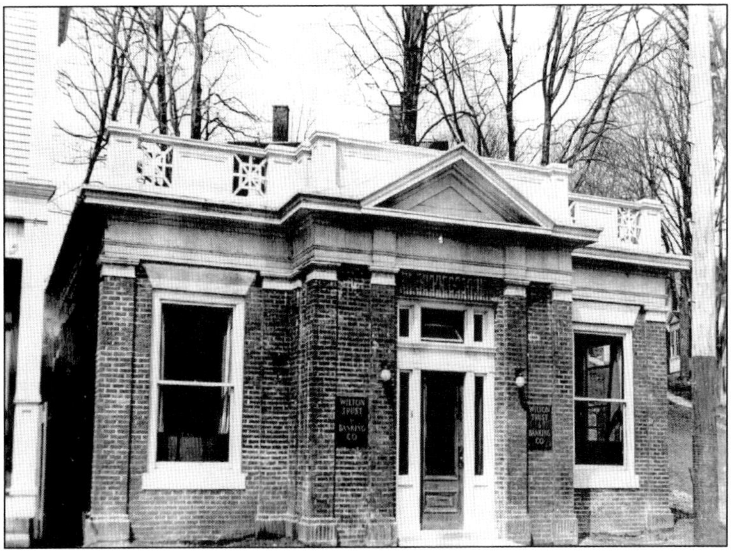

Wilton Trust and Banking Co., 1911. Wilton Trust and Banking Co. was first established in 1911. It had previously been a branch of Livermore Falls Trust. In 1923, the bank got its first enlargement, and, in 1929, the second floor was added.

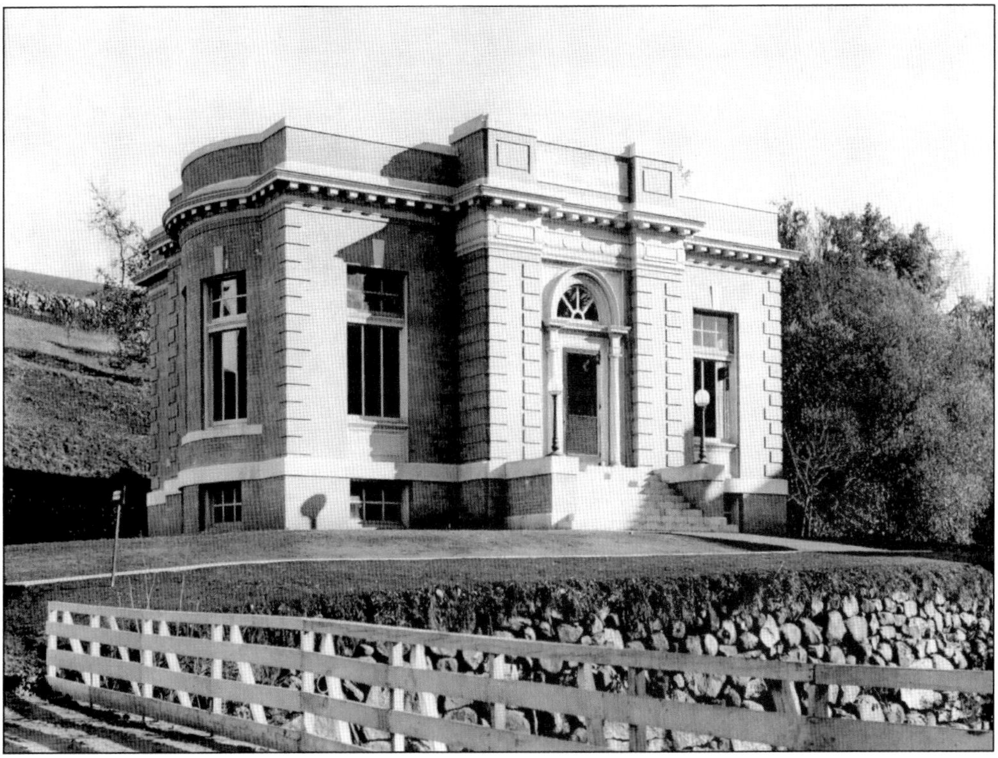

Goodspeed Memorial Library, c. 1915. Wilton acquired a town library in 1902. In 1901, Hamilton Potter sponsored two "entertainments" that provided enough money to purchase about 60 volumes. The Wilton Free Public Library Association was formed in June of that year, and it opened officially to the public in the Holmes Block on December 6, 1902. Mary E. Bass was the librarian. By 1903, the library contained 1,000 volumes. In later years, Frank and George Goodspeed of Wilton Woolen Company gave money for the present library, on the hillside on Main Street, in honor of their parents. It was named Goodspeed Memorial Library and was presented to the town on October 23, 1915.

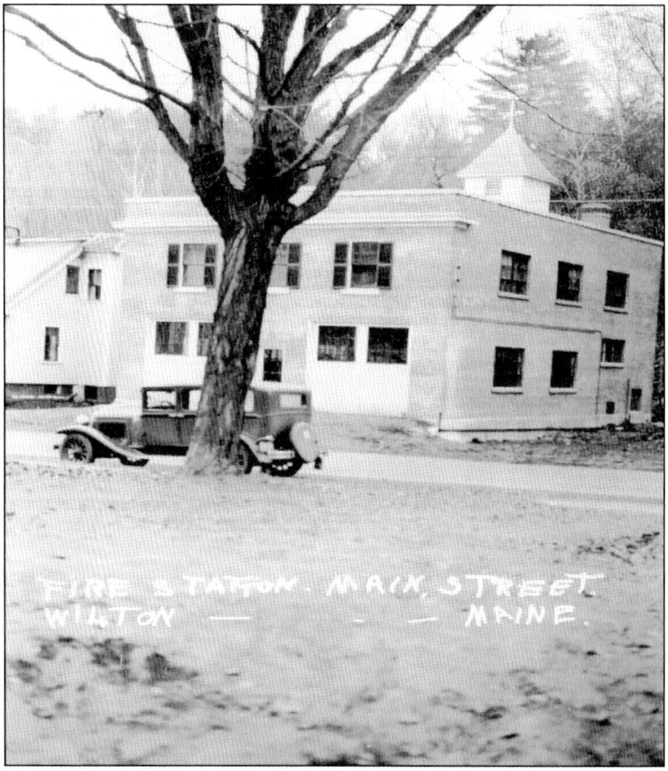

FIRE STATION, C. 1930. This fire station was on Main Street and was started in the 1920s. The first chief was W.G. Colby, the principal of Wilton Academy at that time. The department itself was organized in the early 1920s. In 1921, a sum of $2,500 was raised for motorized equipment.

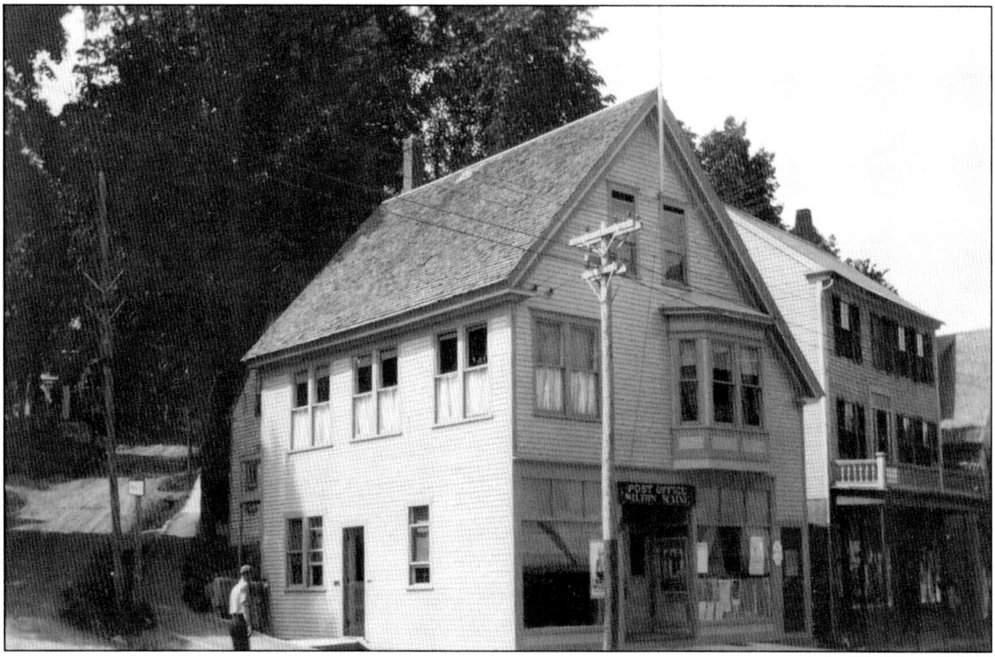

THE OLD POST OFFICE, 1920S. This photograph is of the post office that served the town for many years at the foot of High Street. In this photograph, one can see an "Uncle Sam" poster displayed in the front. A number of people held the position of postmaster in Wilton over the years, including Cyrus Fenderson, A.H. Jones, and Fred R. Young.

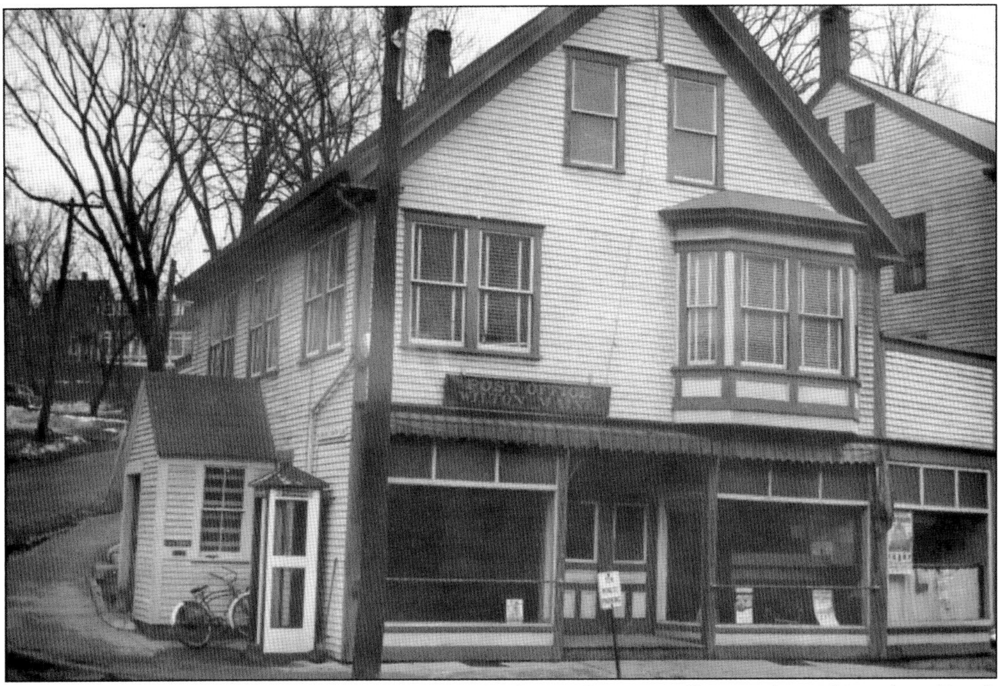

The Old Post Office, 1953. This photograph shows the post office in the 1950s, when Frank Scott was postmaster. The main differences from the previous photograph are that the side door now has a covered entrance, there is now a telephone booth, and there are now bicycle and parking signs.

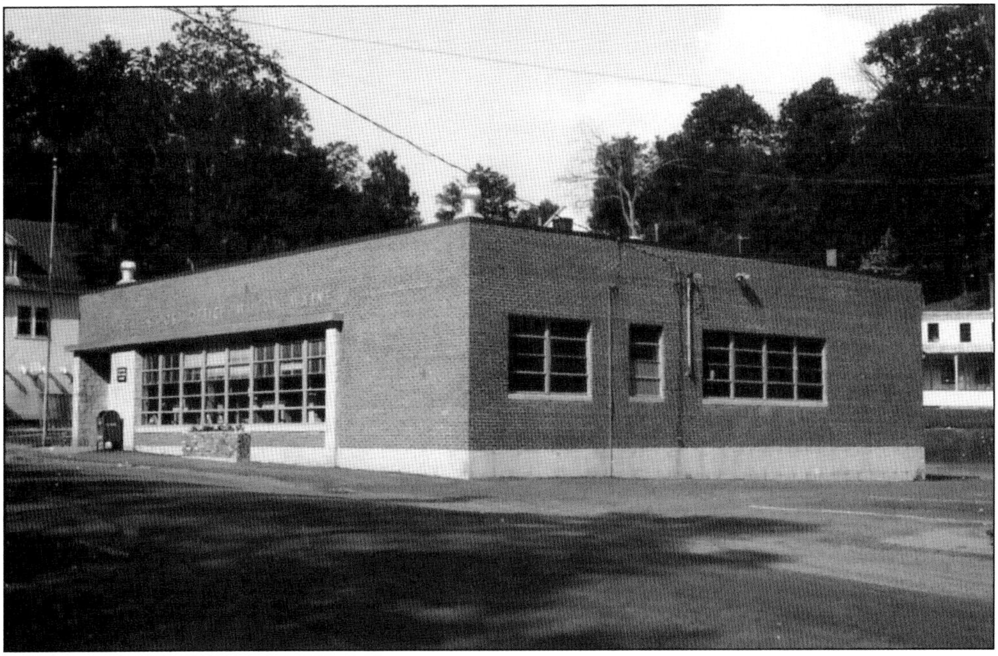

The New Post Office, 1960. This post office was built on Main Street in 1959. This photograph was taken on opening day, February 1, 1960, by Harold Karkos, when the construction was nearly complete.

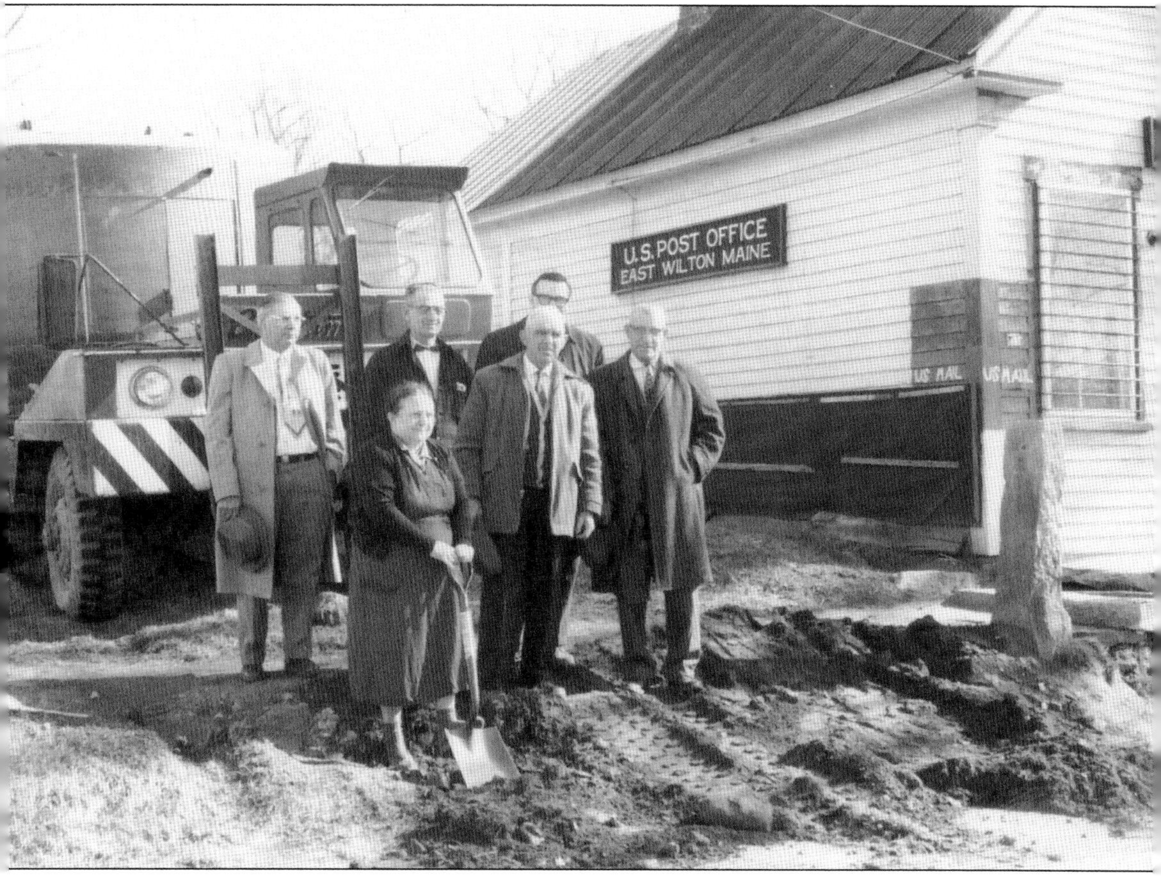

EAST WILTON POST OFFICE, 1950s. The woman in this photograph is Hilda Sawtelle, who served a postmaster for 48 years. She also sold magazine subscriptions and greeting cards. At one point, one could even send out customers' dry cleaning from this post office.

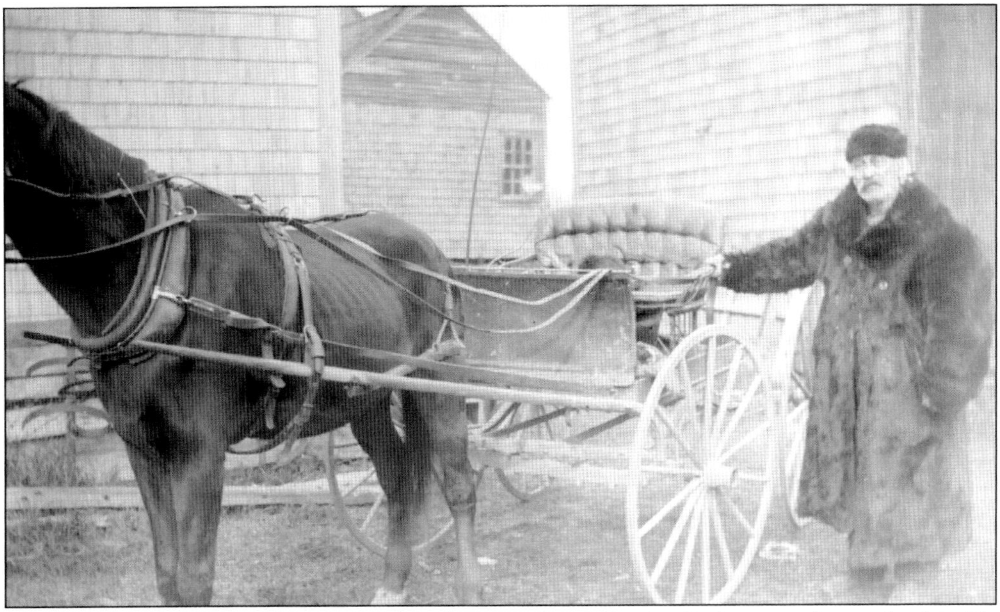

Luther B. Jennings, Late 1800s. This photograph is of Luther B. Jennings late in his life. He is wearing a fur hat and coat and is standing beside his horse and carriage. Jennings was a Civil War veteran.

East Wilton Band, c. 1900. This photograph was taken in front of the East Wilton gazebo. The information provided with the photograph included the band members' names, listed according to what instrument they played. They are as follows: clarinets: A.D. Brown, J. Slingsworth, and G.H. Webster; cornets: A.B. Widdors (leader), C.A. McCully, A.A. Hosmer, V. Delano, and E. Rackliffe; altos: J Widdors, E. Widdors, and C. Hardy; trombones: B. Farnum and F. Lamkin; cymbals: ? Widdors; basses: C. Brown, ? Wade, and V. Woodcock; drum major: G. Farnum; tenor: C. Woodcock; and baritone: F. Farnum.

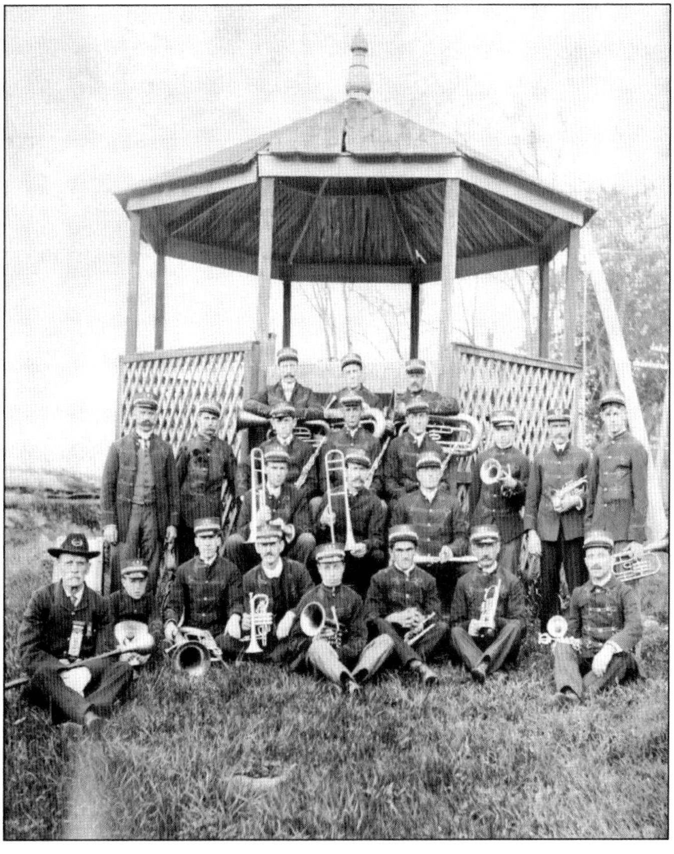

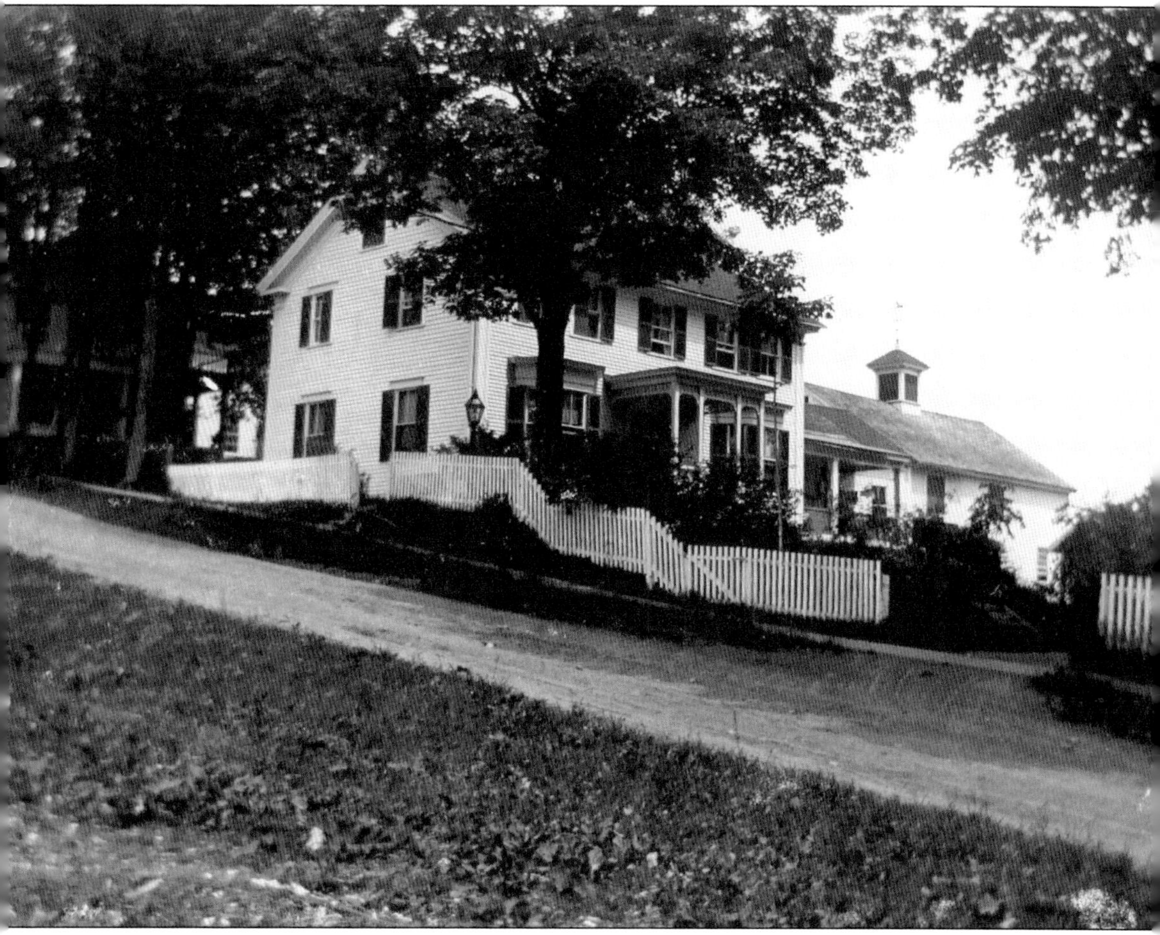

Dr. Adams, c. 1900. This is the home of Dr. Alonzo B. Adams, on High Street in the village of Wilton. He was a physician and surgeon.

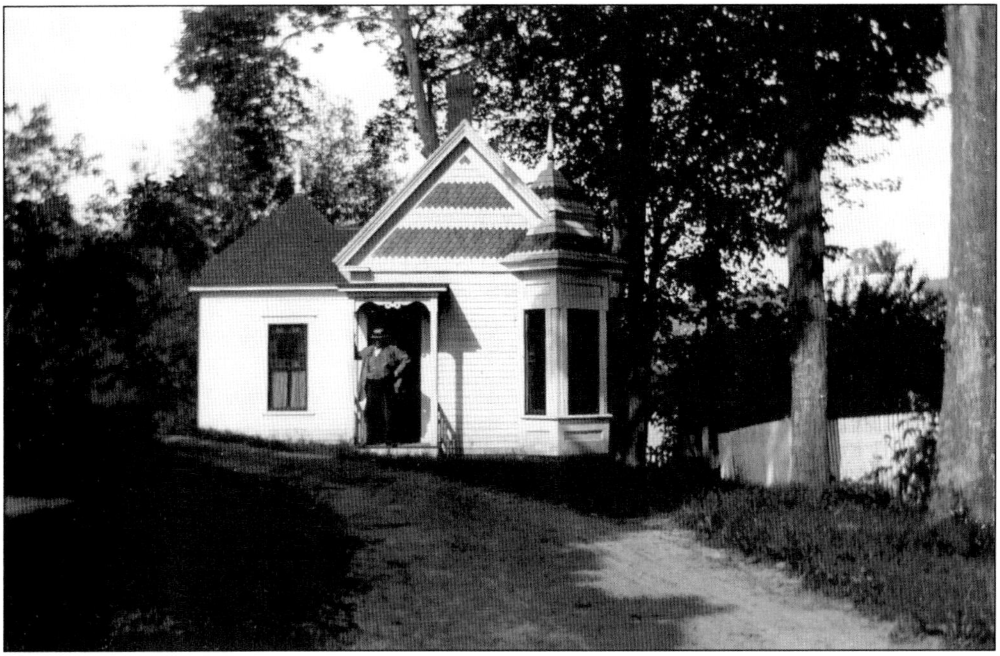

OFFICE OF DR. ADAMS, c. 1900. The photograph above shows the office of Dr. Alonzo B. Adams, with him standing outside his door. The photograph below once again shows him outside of his office, this time with his horse and buggy. Perhaps he is heading out on a house call, which was a common practice at this time.

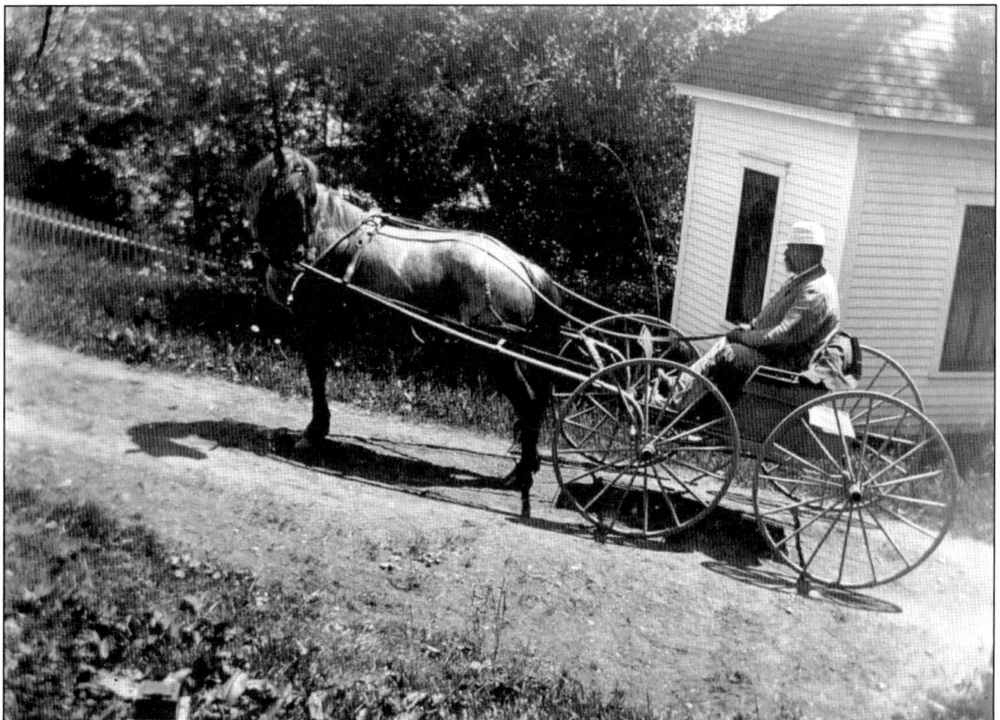

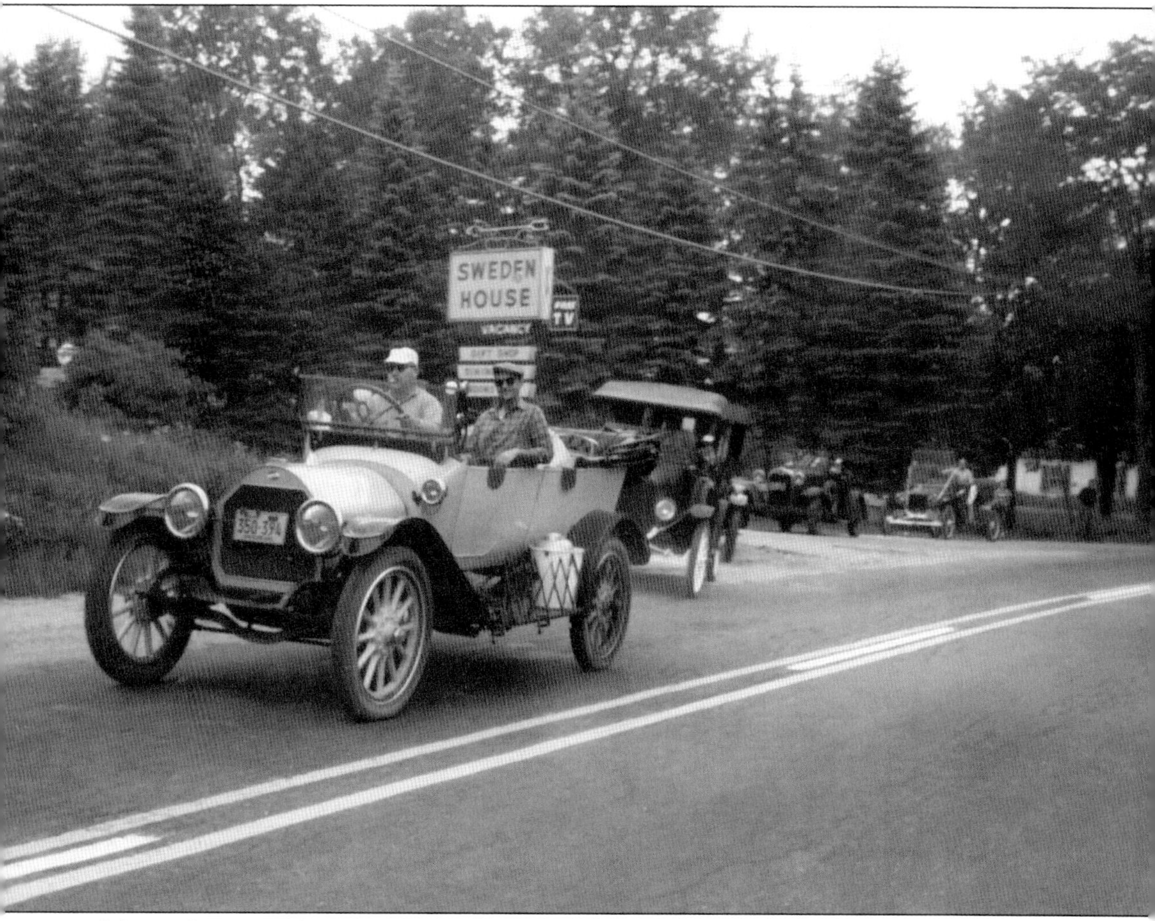

Maine Obsolete Auto League, c. 1960. This is a photograph taken in front of the Sweden House, an inn and gift shop with Swedish imports and gifts in East Wilton. At one time, this inn was called the Blue Spruce Lodge, and it also served as a residence for the Lockhead family at another time. This photograph is of the Maine Obsolete Auto League. They were parading cars from earlier days down Main Street in East Wilton.

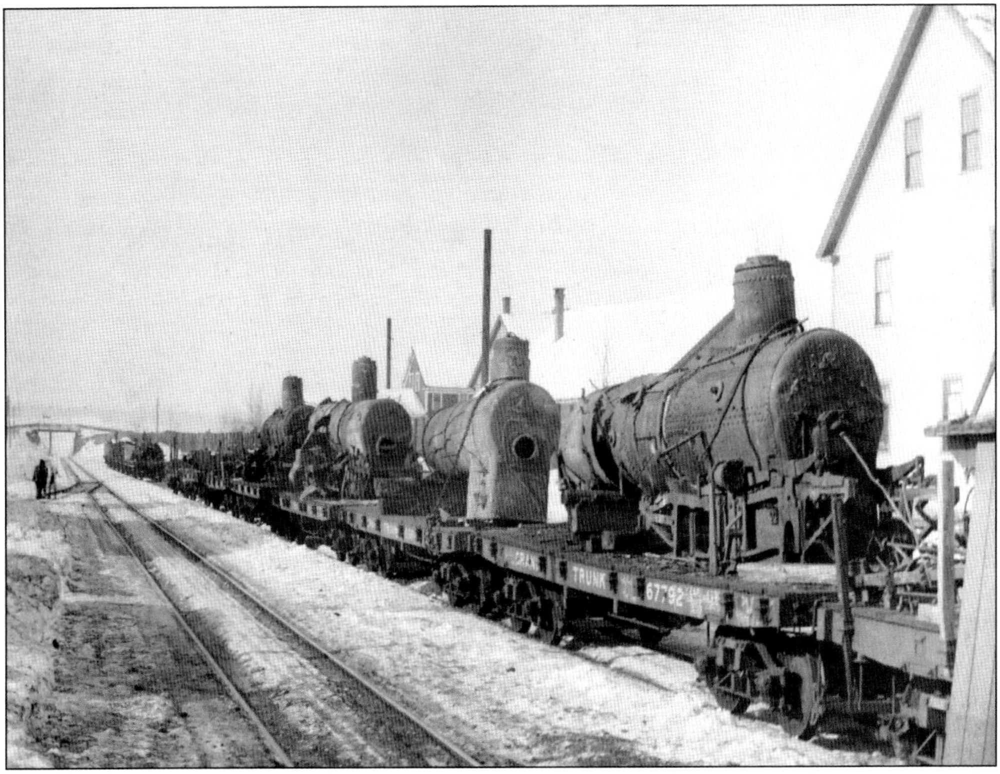

GRAND TRUNK NO. 67792, LATE 1800S. This is a Grand Trunk train that appears to be transporting assorted train parts. These photographs were taken behind the B.F. Stanley Store by Wilfred Bowler. They were taken after the rails were upgraded to standard gauge in 1862 to accommodate heavier freight. By the late 1800s, several trains stopped daily in Wilton.

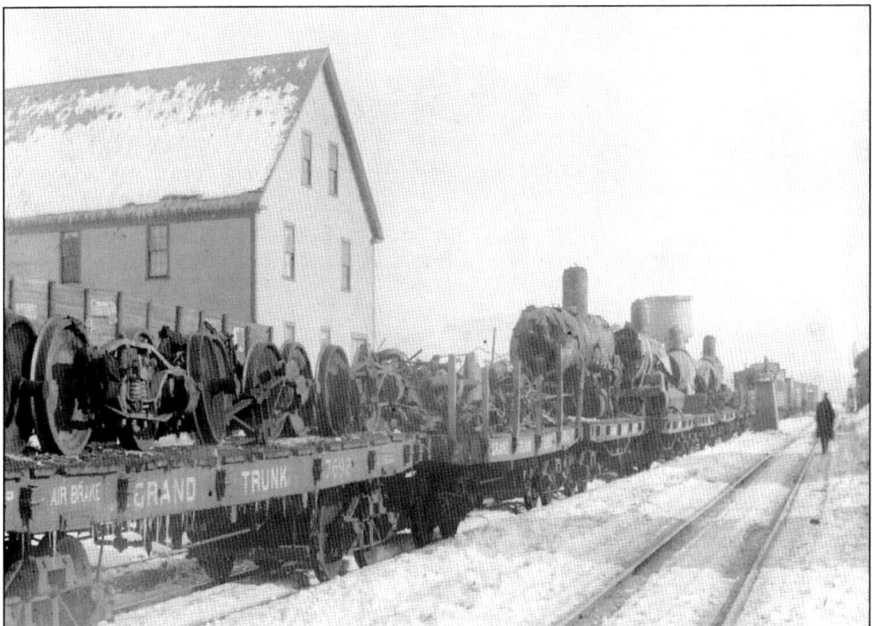

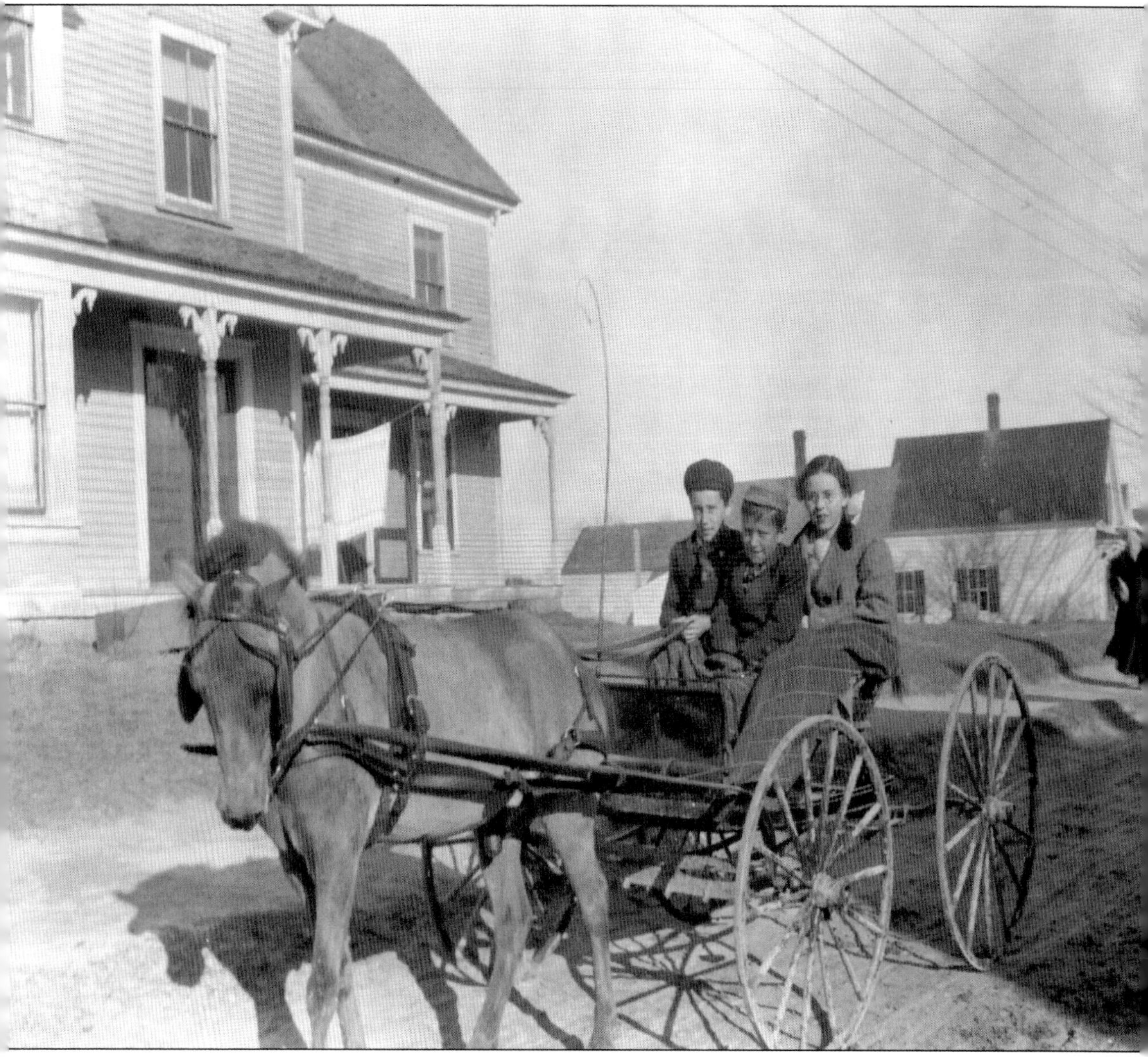

Depot Street, c. 1900. This is a photograph of three children, one of whom is at the reins of the horse-drawn buggy on Depot Street in Dryden. There is a woman walking a ways behind them who is perhaps their mother.

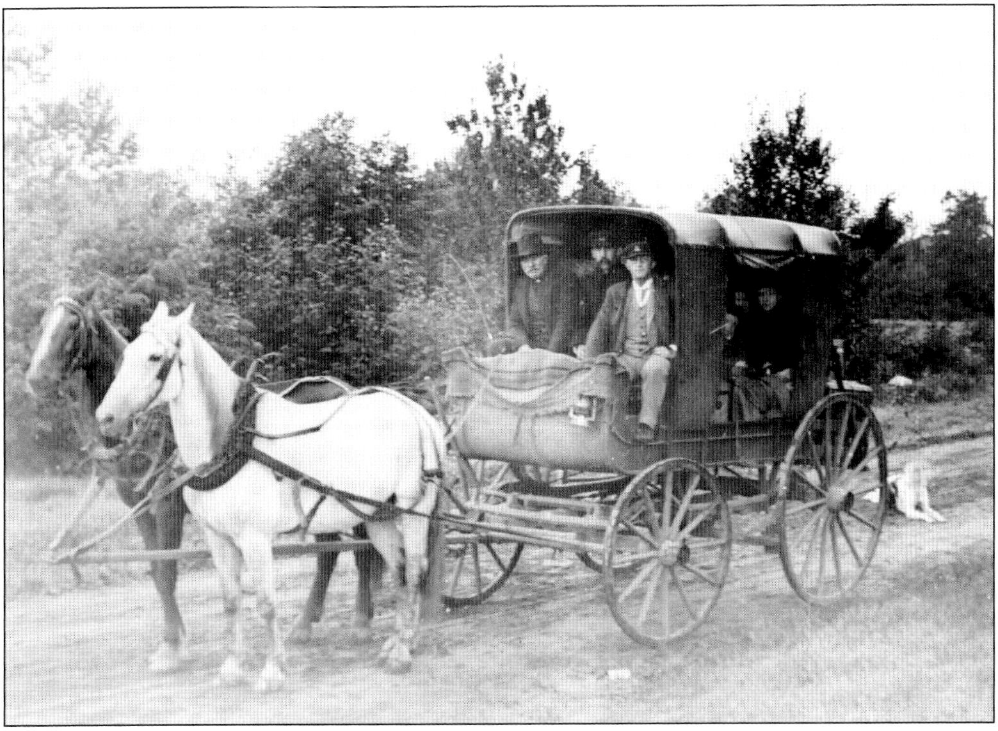

Stagecoach from Wilton to Weld, c. 1890s. This stagecoach was driven by "Uncle John Pickens." Stagecoaches typically included a covered wagon, had four wheels, and were drawn by two horses.

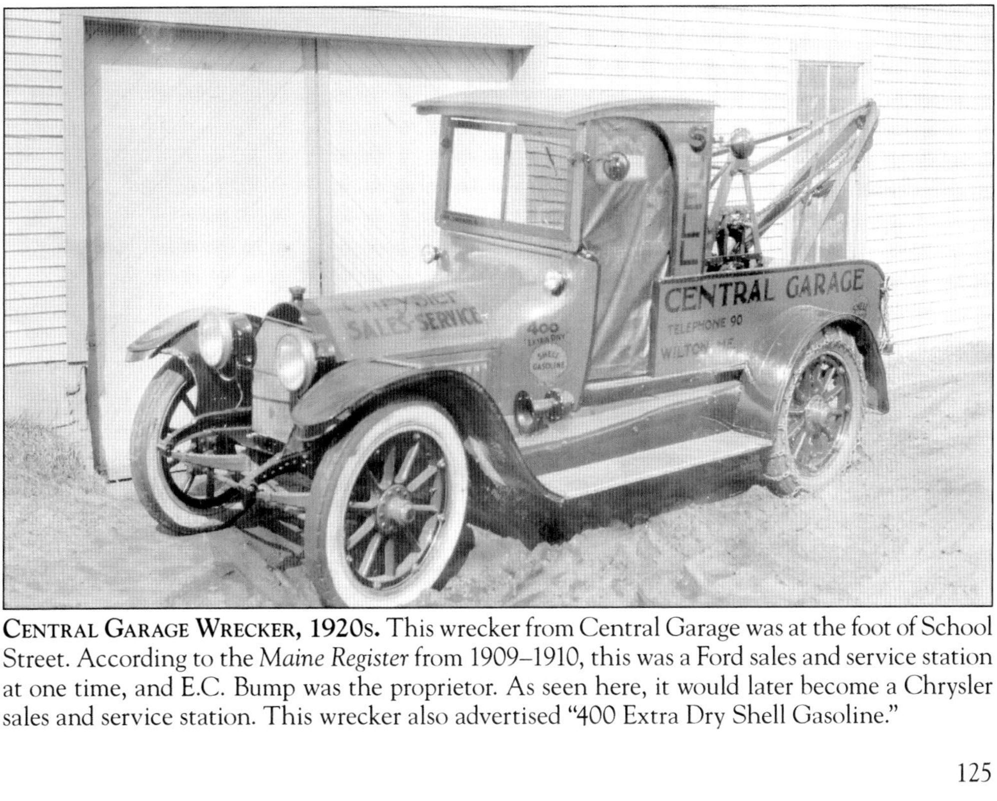

Central Garage Wrecker, 1920s. This wrecker from Central Garage was at the foot of School Street. According to the *Maine Register* from 1909–1910, this was a Ford sales and service station at one time, and E.C. Bump was the proprietor. As seen here, it would later become a Chrysler sales and service station. This wrecker also advertised "400 Extra Dry Shell Gasoline."

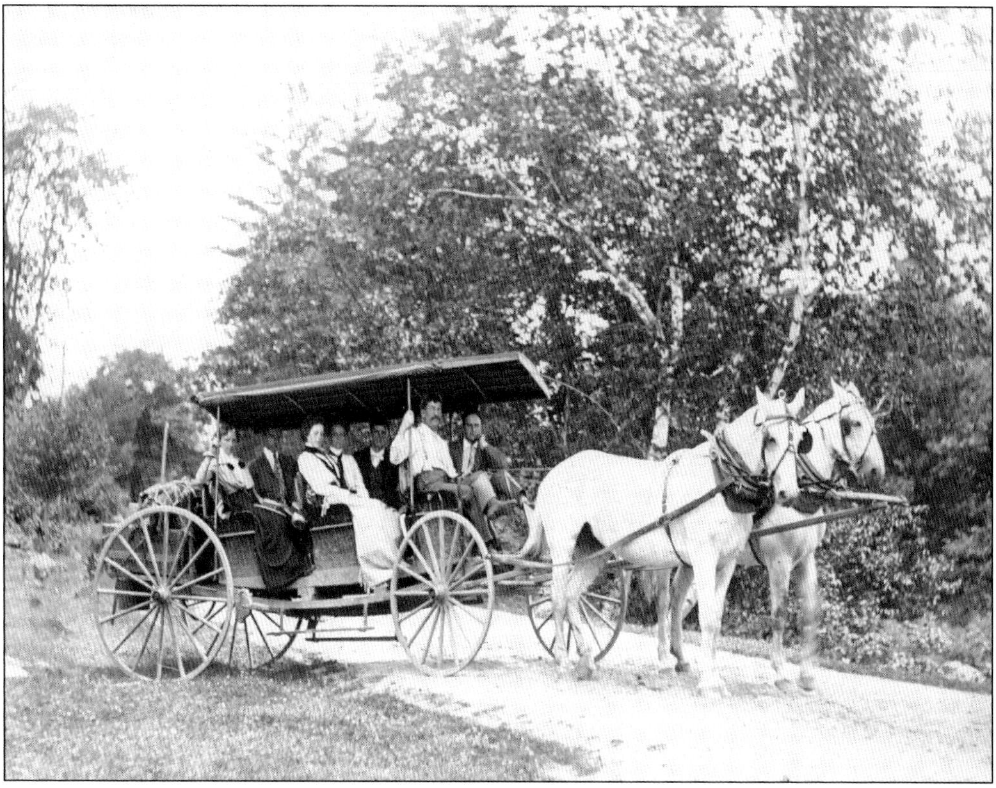

Stagecoach, Late 1800s. This four-wheeled vehicle is a stagecoach. It is being pulled along a dirt road in Wilton by two white horses. This stagecoach was likely either going to or from the railroad station.

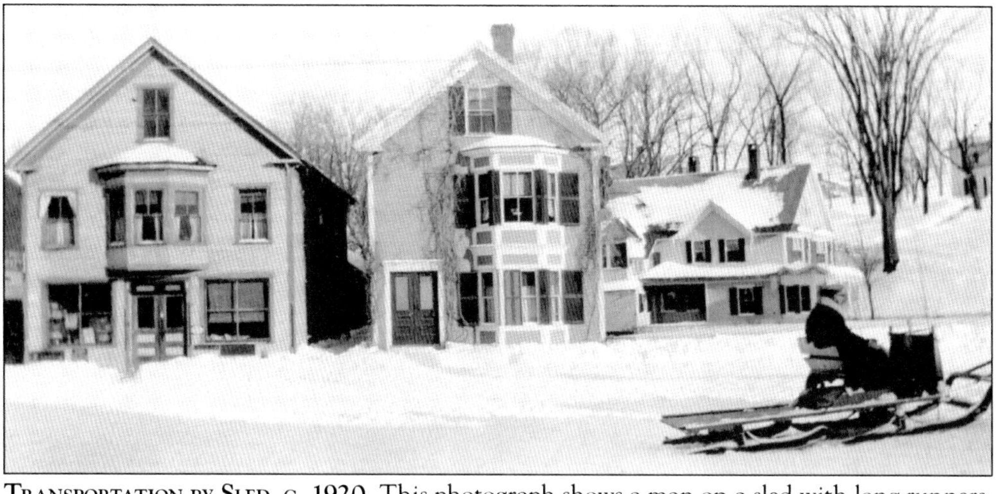

Transportation by Sled, c. 1920. This photograph shows a man on a sled with long runners. This was his mode of transportation to wherever he was going on Main Street.

Bibliography

Adamo, Ruth. *A History of the Town of Wilton*. Rumford, ME: Rumford Publishing Company, Inc., 1971.

Franklin County Business and Personal Directory. Farmington, ME: Strout Service, Inc., 1926.

Karkos, Harold and Elizabeth. *Wilton's 150 Years: 1803–1953*. Wilton, ME: Wilton Printing Service, 1953.

Maine Register, State Year-book and Legislative Manual 1901–1902. Portland, ME: Grenville M. Donham, 1901–1902.

Maine Register, State Year-book and Legislative Manual, No. 40, June 1909. Portland, ME: Grenville M. Donham, 1909.

Maine Register, State Year-book and Legislative Manual, No. 49, July 1918. Portland, ME: Albert G. Donham, 1918.

Maine Register, State Year-book and Legislative Manual No. 101. Portland, ME: Tower Publishing Company, 1969.

Mitchell, Harry E. and Rosco Hiram Remick. *The Wilton Register 1903–1904*. Kents Hill, ME: H.E. Mitchell Publishing Company, 1903.

Noyes, L.F. and Rollo E. Gould. *The District Schools of Wilton, Maine: 1803–1890*. Wilton, ME: Wilton Historical Society, 1976.

Sleeper, Frank, Maine Historic Preservation Commission. Images of America: *Farmington, Wilton, Kingfield, and Sugarloaf*. Portsmouth, NH: Arcadia Publishing, 1997.

The Town Register: Farmington, Wilton, Chesterville, New Sharon, 1910. Brunswick, ME: The Maine Map & Register Co., 1910.

Turner's Franklin County Directory of the Inhabitants, Institutions, Manufacturing Establishments, Business Firms, Societies, County Census, etc. Auburn, ME: A.R. Turner Publishing Company, 1898.